pages of this book: the problem of freedom and responsibility. It is to such basic questions—basic to the life of the individual and society—that the author has addressed himself courageously and consistently throughout his career as one of the nation's outstanding educators.

Harry D. Gideonse has had a distinguished career as an economist, educator, and interpreter of international affairs. After teaching at Rutgers, Chicago, and Columbia, he assumed, in 1939, the presidency of Brooklyn College, an office he held for twenty-seven years. An articulate and forceful speaker and writer, he has been a leader in numerous educational and civic causes and organizations; he served the State Department in India and Germany, and has been president of Freedom House for many years. Dr. Gideonse has received various honorary degrees and was decorated by the governments of France, Netherlands, and Sweden. At present, he is serving as chancellor of the New School for Social Research.

Alexander S. Preminger is assistant professor and chief, humanities division, Brooklyn College Library of the City University of New York. A fellow of the Bollingen Foundation, he is the editor of the *Encyclopedia of Poetry and Poetics* and a contributor to various literary and professional journals. Currently, Professor Preminger is also serving as a publisher's consultant.

Against the
Running Tide

Against the Running Tide

Selected Essays on Education and the Free Society

Harry D. Gideonse

edited by Alexander S. Preminger

TWAYNE PUBLISHERS, INC.

31 Union Square

New York 10003

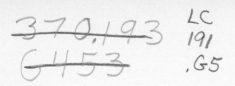

Contents

Foreword

IN A DAY WHEN INNOVATIONS HAVE BECOME IMPERATIVE IN THE educational program provided by an urban college, the strong pressures upon it to adapt all its operations to novel demands are apt to result in a strenuous battle. The leadership and educational statesmanship required to create and develop a program of higher education which includes standards of excellence in every phase of operation are qualities which are essential and invaluable in a college president. And they are relatively rare because the role of college president is one which has to be largely learned empirically, without formal prior training.

Harry David Gideonse, the president of Brooklyn College from 1939 to 1966, is the rare individual who has in a conspicuous way met the tests of leadership and educational statesmanship which his post imposed. The nature of the community in Brooklyn in 1939 required not only that a new demand for higher education be met but that it be augmented. The family backgrounds of the college-bound youth were all too often devoid of college or professional experience. Middle class homes with intellectual interests and background for student enrichment were not typical. Yet the opportunity for a free college education appealed strongly to more and more family groups with different ethnic traditions. Intuitively or otherwise, these students and their families viewed continued study as the road to the New Jerusalem in a recently adopted land. And this meant that the teaching and learning process in and out of the college classroom had to assure a meaningful personal motivation for the student, supply a richer cultural content, enhance a sense of intellectual relevance to contemporary life, and minister to aspirations and goals for which the students' sights were con-

stantly raised as personalities unfolded through a deeper awareness of their developing potential.

President Gideonse's background fortunately included a combination of wide international awareness and local concern, and
provided personal standards of scholarship which were at once
rigorous and broad, assuring a splendid kind of universalism
of intellectual commitment and moral enthusiasm.

A thumbnail biographical record helps one to understand
how all this could come about. He was born in Holland in
1901 and the family moved to Rochester, New York, in 1904.
After his elementary education there the family returned to
the Netherlands where he received his secondary education.
Upon return to this country, he attended and was graduated
from Columbia University in 1923, took his Master of Arts
degree in 1924 and lectured until 1926 in Economics at Columbia
University and Barnard College. During the next two years he
directed the Students' International Union in Geneva and, at
the same time, completed his graduate studies at the local
University which granted him the Diplôme des Hautes Études
Internationales. He returned to the United States to teach at
Rutgers University for two years, after which there were eight
years as professor of Economics at the University of Chicago.

While there, he engaged in an educational dialogue with
President Robert M. Hutchins, who published in 1936 a scathing
critique of American higher education entitled *The Higher
Learning in America*. In response to this view Dr. Gideonse
wrote in 1937 a scholarly and vigorous rejoinder published
under the title *The Higher Learning in a Democracy*. This
brought his personality and his ideas to a national audience.
He parted company with the University of Chicago in 1938 to
become professor of Economics at Columbia University and
Barnard College, from which he was called in 1939 by the
Board of Higher Education to the presidency of Brooklyn
College with an enrollment at that time of 13,000 and a newly
built campus in central Brooklyn.

The growth of Brooklyn College from 1939, the year of
President Gideonse's arrival on the campus, to his retirement
in 1966 was indeed impressive. From a total enrollment of
13,000 the figure has advanced to 30,000; from a faculty of approximately 400 in 1939, the College has acquired a faculty of

968 in 1966. More important than mere numbers, however, is the spirit of innovation and evaluation that Dr. Gideonse brought with him. This spirit has made itself felt in the achievements in curriculum revision; in the development of techniques to individualize the educational programs of large masses of students; in the establishment of student services programs; in the encouragement of co-curricular activities; in coping with the special problems imposed by two major wars; in recruiting a distinguished faculty; in promoting programs for young people with qualifications somewhat below those required for admission to the baccalaureate programs; in pioneering in programs for continuing education for adults; in initiating the means for the research interests of a growing faculty; in stimulating a variety of educational and cultural opportunities for the community at large; indeed, in numerous other instances as well.

More than casual mention, however, should be made of President Gideonse's interest in developing the means by which each student, despite the size of the institution, would have the opportunity to discuss with a faculty member his educational objectives, his nagging concerns, his need for financial or other assistance, the rationale for his choice of courses, along with a multitude of other student problems. Faculty counseling and guidance of students have been of a high order of sympathetic intensity: not only in course and career guidance but, for example, in aid and rehabilitation for the failing student before it is too late, in tutoring by superior upper class students, in improving the chances of entrance into professional schools such as the medical colleges. All this has sharpened the focus of concern and caring for the individual student, in order to offset the impersonal relations which can so readily prevail where enrollments are so high. Indeed, all of this emphasis antedated by many years the student protestations current in other large universities against faculty aloofness.

This same solicitude has prompted constant attention to restricting the size of class units and to keeping the teaching load within those reasonable bounds which would assure continuing awareness of individual students by every faculty member. Whatever may have been the pressures for a greater emphasis on research, this trend has been kept at a point where excellence of undergraduate teaching and student relations have always remained a primary concern.

All of this has implied and required the most careful attention to the recruiting of faculty, to the strengthening of the teacher-learner relation, and to the improvement of faculty salaries and promotions. Throughout his incumbency, President Gideonse has placed continuous, reiterative emphasis upon a budgetary adequacy which would implement a program of quality and excellence in every activity contributive to a productive climate of learning. Both in his relations with the appropriate city officials and with the Board of Higher Education, he has been a truly educational force in persuasively making known all the ways and means of improving the quality of his institution.

This has meant, for example, a stressing of the need for more classroom space, more faculty office space, improved library facilities, enlarged auditorium provisions, closer relations with the staffs of Brooklyn high schools in order to ease the transition to college and to minimize overlapping of course material.

The achievement of closer relationships with local agencies—religious, civic, social, educational—on the part of both faculty members and student groups was another emphasis pursued in so rewarding a way as to bring understanding community support of the College over the years to an impressively high level. This was not achieved without episodes of crisis in public relations, which through patient presidential guidance have become virtually a thing of the past. Anyone wishing to document this statement as to confronted crises will find it accurately elaborated in the excellent volume by Dean Thomas E. Coulton published in 1955 under the title *A City College in Action.* Indeed, that volume supplies a wealth of detail on many activities necessarily mentioned here in a most summary way.

When it was discovered that there were increasing numbers of students who could use to advantage the less elaborate curriculum of a two-year course (often taken in the afternoon or evening), the College introduced two new plans of study. One in the liberal arts became an Associate in Arts Program, and the other, specializing in business, an Associate in Applied Science Program. These pioneering efforts met such a real educational need that they helped to stimulate the growth and extension of the embryonic so-called community colleges, of which there are now six in the several boroughs of the city, conducted under the auspices of the Board of Higher Education.

Special mention should be made of the sensitive awareness developed in Brooklyn College concerning the problem of the "disadvantaged" high school student and his difficulties in qualifying for admission to the College with its relatively high entrance requirements. But these requirements are necessary to assure an intellectually qualified student body and to keep the undergraduate enrollment down to a point where there are adequate physical accommodations for those admitted.

With nation-wide attention being paid to the "culturally deprived background" of many Negro and Puerto Rican youth, a fact which makes college entrance for them highly improbable, it became apparent that special efforts must be made to upgrade their pre-college academic performance. And Dr. Gideonse was among those who early saw this as a challenging problem in the urban college life of New York City. His Biennial Report to the Board of Higher Education for the years 1963-1965* presents the splendid, creative attack on this problem made over the years by his own institution. This program becomes one more evidence of well-timed innovative ingenuity and creativity.

Mention should also be made of the elaboration of the adult education programs, as well as of the continuing faculty committee work on long-term curriculum development and evaluation. These were both novel features at a time when other colleges tended to be slow or even unmindful of such sensitive areas of urgent need.

Other outstanding innovations in the curriculum included the College Honors Program and the Scholars' Program. Both offer opportunities for individual study and both—the Scholars' Program in particular—challenge the special talents of exceptional students. The growth of the Area Studies Program was another significant development, designed to break down the parochialism of a Western-oriented education and to extend the

---

* Issued in part also by President Gideonse as a separate pamphlet entitled *Brooklyn College and the "Disadvantaged."* It is appropriate to add here that the President's Biennial Reports to the Board have constituted a comprehensive and rewarding record of many accomplishments only summarily referred to here. They truly add up to a splendid, searching, inside history of educational growth over thirty years.

student's understanding to the growing and dynamic cultures of Africa, Asia, and Latin America. All these programs have a proud record of distinguished student achievement.

In the area of student co-curricular activities, the Junior Freshman Committee developed into the Student Orientation Committee, with its functions significantly enlarged. Its members —a selected group of upper class students—write to freshmen before their arrival on campus and assume responsibility for them in the trying period before and during registration. Members of the Committee also serve on all programs sponsored by the College to acquaint prospective students and members of the community with the facilities and opportunities offered at Brooklyn College. This voluntary service as well as the Student Adviser Leadership Program were widely noted and imitated on other campuses. A unique educational plan, the Student Adviser Leadership Program enables carefully chosen students to receive theoretical and practical leadership training, preparing them for service as advisers to student groups. Student advisers are now working with approximately 150 groups and are successfully performing functions which are normally assumed by junior faculty members.

It seems pointless to elaborate on the factors of controversy and struggle which were characteristic of the earlier years of his incumbency. Dr. Gideonse is not one who, as the phrase goes, suffers fools gladly. His standards of intellectual excellence, his awareness of the changing complexion of our culture, economically, scientifically, and morally—both at home and internationally—these were controlling influences in the innovations already referred to. And it was only to be expected that the pace of change should not have been precipitous, but rather solidly and wisely conceived, grounded, and nurtured.

Sacred educational cows were necessarily assailed again and again, and affronts to personal status, convictions, and prestige, both in faculty and student groups, were inescapable in the earlier years.

Gradually, however, the collaboration of the president with both faculty and student bodies, with the resulting impressive gains, has brought a fuller understanding and sympathetic acceptance by all involved of the aims and purposes he set forth.

It can truthfully be affirmed that Dr. Gideonse departs from Brooklyn College with the sincere admiration and regrets of his associates. Forthrightness, clarity of vision, vigor in pressing for carefully defined goals—these have gradually won the day. And it is generally recognized that a truly great and creative college statesman is stepping out.

I have deliberately omitted any formalized restatement of what we may call the president's educational philosophy for the good reason that on this score he speaks fully and cogently for himself in many of the papers which comprise this book. Beginning with his inaugural address, and repeatedly thereafter, there has thus been offered for all to examine a body of higher educational doctrine keyed to the urban setting. The quality, balance, and growth of these utterances in intellectual, esthetic, and moral values interpreted in every college activity have gained the allegiance of urban youth and enlisted their commitment to a personal and public life at a high level of responsible achievement and of continuing personal growth.

Dr. Gideonse's public life beyond the campus has been deeply interwoven with his tenure at Brooklyn College. On assuming the presidency in 1939, he set out, deliberately and imaginatively, to achieve local and then national recognition for the College. Perhaps most helpful in focusing the name of Brooklyn College before a national audience has been his association with Freedom House, first as its board chairman and since 1958 as its president. To him the problem of freedom has never been an abstraction, but rather a living, central concern; and he has been instrumental in formulating new and concrete programs for action, invariably insisting on a realistic and logical approach. As one of his colleagues at Freedom House described him: "He is intolerably intelligent, a pillar of strength when he agrees with you, a withering opponent when he disagrees. He has a mind like a razor blade. He is impatient of error, and it would be impossible to work with him were it not for the admiration he wins by his high standards, his insistence on clarity, consistency, demonstrable accuracy, and verbal precision. He is the intellectual rampant."** These were the qualities, combined with

** Quoted in Aaron Levenstein and William Agar, *Freedom's Advocate: A Twenty-Five Year Chronicle* (New York: Viking Press, 1965), p. 55.

integrity and the courage to act, which won the day when he firmly and unequivocally defended his faculty during the witch-hunt of the McCarthy era.

I would fail to do justice to the rounded portrait of this innately warm and loving man if I omitted this brief word of recognition of the staunch and devoted support over the years of his wife and helpmeet, a woman of charm, intellectual vigor, and breadth of human sympathies, whom he married in 1926. She has stood stalwartly beside him through troubles, tensions, and criticisms, making his home, one must believe, a haven of comfort through a courageous career of public strife and struggle.

"If you would see my monuments, look about you"—could be repeated here as a truly apposite sentiment to summarize the educational leadership of this retiring president. If, however, he were to voice it himself he would not be in character, for there is also here the saving grace of modesty and humility.

Thus, in 1966 an assignment assumed by Harry D. Gideonse in 1939 comes to a close at Brooklyn College. When, at the first commencement, he addressed the students from the balcony in Boylan Hall, he looked at his huge audience, and his eyes fell on the flag of the City of New York. He reminded the students of the fact that the colors of that flag were the colors of the old Dutch republic of the seven provinces, the colors of William of Orange, William the Silent. The motto that goes with that flag is one of the great mottoes in the history of freedom. The original —as he has reminded every graduating class of Brooklyn College since that time—was *Je maintiendrai*. Dr. Gideonse has maintained.

The measure of the man does not reach its fullness in the written word alone as it is recorded in this book. Missing are the components of physical presence, style, voice, élan which cannot easily be evoked from the printed page except by those who can recall the oral delivery of many of the ideas presented in this volume. The imposing figure of Harry D. Gideonse, the sonority of his voice, the phrasing of words, the texture of his thoughts, the conviction and sincerity of his being—these qualities one had to see. Having seen them, the viewer acquired an indelible image.

President Gideonse's greatest passion was the molding and fashioning of young people, intellectually, socially, and—paradoxical as it may seem for the head of a secular, public college —spiritually. It should be remembered that his Dutch heritage had a strong Old Testament cast. He exemplified this zest for the development of young people in a remark reported by a colleague who accompanied the president in the subway to a meeting at the Board of Higher Education. Sitting opposite the president with an open book before them were two young Brooklyn College men engaged in a vigorous discussion of a mathematics problem. Their attire was far from elegant, revealing the indifference they felt for conventional standards of grooming; their hair was disheveled and their faces unshaven. The president listened to the discussion of the two young men, who seemingly had blotted out everything about them but the problem in the book before them, and he summed up the present and the future of these boys, along with his own hopes, in the words: "Diamonds in the rough." In a sense, of course, Harry D. Gideonse has been a diamond cutter working not in stone but in the vastly more difficult substances of mind and heart and spirit.

Scholar, writer, administrator, economist, orator, Harry D. Gideonse is all of these. But in his professional life he is in the first instance a teacher. All of his other activities are merely the means through which he does his teaching. His effectiveness as a teacher comes through in the classroom, on the public platform, in a small social group, in an article, in a memorandum, in a dinner conversation—indeed, one can properly ask, when is he not stimulating? Henry Adams must have had just such a teacher in mind when he said: "A teacher affects eternity; he can never tell where his influence stops." With this reassurance of the pervasive and enduring influence of the teacher, the colleagues and students at Brooklyn College can take comfort in the thought that despite Harry Gideonse's departure "to fresh woods and pastures new" his influence and style will still be with them.

ORDWAY TEAD

Chairman Emeritus, Board of Higher Education
Chairman, 1938-1953

Preface

THIS VOLUME PRESENTS A SELECTION OF THE ADDRESSES AND PAPERS of Harry D. Gideonse from the year 1937, two years before he became President of Brooklyn College, to the present. During the twenty-seven years of his presidency he also served in various capacities in Freedom House and in several educational associations, as well as fulfilling assignments at home and abroad for important agencies of the Federal Government. His was no ivory tower presidency.

A major—if not the governing—concern in these years was his concept of freedom and responsibility in both personal and social life, in academic and civic endeavors. That there are pervading values in these facets of human activity is his inescapable conclusion. That man must recognize the need of an inner moral governor is a corollary conclusion.

Like Al Smith, President Gideonse is a believer in "the record." That term embraces his reiterative use, as points of reference, of such diverse basic documents—to cite only a few—as the Bible, the works of Shakespeare, Dante, and other poets; Dostoyevsky and Tolstoy, the papers of Woodrow Wilson and John F. Kennedy, the encyclical "Pacem in Terris," the Constitution, and the Declaration of Independence.

His professional interests as an economist and an educational administrator are evidenced in his vigorous service on significant committees of national, state, and local import. Their reports and recommendations quite frequently embrace his thinking and proposals.

To mark the occasion of his departure from Brooklyn College in order to engage in other educational endeavors, this volume is issued as a permanent record of President Gideonse's lively concern for the abiding values which form the substructure of his thought and conduct.

Dr. Ordway Tead's words, which comprise the Foreword of this book, come from a long-time colleague who, as a member and chairman of the Board of Higher Education of the City of New York, worked closely with President Gideonse in endeavors related both to the College and the community.

Professor Alexander S. Preminger, of the College library staff, editor of *The Encyclopedia of Poetry and Poetics,* contributed his professional skill and services in the assembling and editing of the contents of this volume.

The preparation of this book, which in the main follows carefully the text of the originals, has been a labor of affection and respect. While the number of hands and minds that were directly involved in the selection and compilation of the papers included in the volume were necessarily limited, the presentation of this work represents a vastly wider body of admirers of the President. It is hoped that the signatories of this Preface will serve the broader constituency in conveying its esteem of and gratitude to Harry D. Gideonse.

ABRAHAM S. GOODHARTZ   WALTER H. MAIS

FRANCIS P. KILCOYNE   HERBERT STROUP

October, 1966

Acknowledgments

THANKS ARE DUE TO THE INSTITUTIONS, PUBLISHERS, AND EDITORS who have so courteously granted permission to reprint, in slightly adapted form, the addresses, articles, and essays which comprise this volume.

The American Academy of Political and Social Science for "Academic Freedom: A Decade of Challenge and Clarification" in its *Annals,* September 1955. Copyright 1955 by the American Academy of Political and Social Science.

The American Council on Education for "Free Science and the Security of an Open Society," in *Education for the Preservation of Democracy,* a Report of the Thirteenth Educational Conference, copyright 1949; "Political Education," in *Education in a Period of National Preparedness,* a Report of the Sixteenth Educational Conference, copyright 1952; "On Rethinking Liberal Education," in *Strengthening Education at All Levels,* a Report of the Eighteenth Educational Conference, copyright 1954; "The Literature of Freedom and Liberal Education," in *Measurement and Research in Today's Schools,* a Report of the Twenty-fifth Educational Conference, copyright 1961; "The Purpose of Higher Education: A Reexamination," in *The College and the Student,* edited by Lawrence E. Dennis and Joseph F. Kauffman, copyright 1966 by the American Council on Education.

The American Association of Collegiate Registrars and Admission Officers for "Economic Growth and Educational Development," in *College and University,* Summer 1963.

The Association Press for "Is Citizenship Enough?" in *Do We Still Need Religion? Three Addresses and Discussions by Charles P. Taft, Harry D. Gideonse, Kirtley F. Mather.* Copy-

Acknowledgments

right 1942 by the International Committee of the Young Men's Christian Associations.

Freedom House for *The Challenge of Soviet Education* (A Freedom House Report, September 30, 1958).

Harper & Row, Publishers, Inc. for two passages from *The Waist-High Culture* by Thomas Griffith. Copyright 1959 by Thomas Griffith. Reprinted by permission of Harper & Row, Publishers, Inc.

Holt, Rinehart and Winston, Inc. for *The Higher Learning in a Democracy*. Copyright 1937, c. 1965 by Harry D. Gideonse. Reprinted by permission of Holt, Rinehart and Winston, Inc.

The National Association for Mental Health, Inc. for "The Golden Opportunity for Public Education," in *Mental Hygiene*, January 1947. Copyright 1947 by the National Committee for Mental Hygiene, Inc.

Rutgers University Press for "Colonial Experience and the Social Context of Economic Development Programs," in *Economics and the Public Interest*, Robert A. Solo, Editor. Copyright 1955 by the Trustees of Rutgers College in New Jersey.

Syracuse University for *Plato and Eisenhower's America*.

The Unitarian Universalist Association for "The Discipline of Freedom," in *Christian Register* (now *Unitarian Universalist Register-Leader*), September 1941. Copyright 1941 by the American Unitarian Association.

The Woodrow Wilson Foundation for *On the Educational Statesmanship of a Free Society*.

1

The Higher Learning in a Democracy*

INTRODUCTION

IN THE DESTRUCTION OF POLITICAL, ECONOMIC AND INTELLECTUAL freedom in the totalitarian countries of Europe, the universities were early victims of the forces that contrasted the "confusion" and the "chaos" of freedom with the "order" of the dictatorships. Similarly, in the defense of a free society in America, education has become a battleground for those who think of the school as an instrument of public policy and for those who regard it as an institution for the development of the potentialities of our youth and for the unfettered pursuit of knowledge.

Vested interests of diverse descriptions have sought to impose upon our educational institutions their own particular pedagogic nostrums. Some professional educators have deserted the traditional search for objectivity in which they claim to see a mask for the perpetuation of the *status quo*. They have quite deliberately sought harmony and order by the choice either of a collectivist frame of reference or of a set of metaphysical principles within which experience would be systematically ordered. Upsetting questions about the postulates, implied in the choice of the framework, have been conveniently overlooked by both groups.[1]

To this controversy Abraham Flexner and Robert M. Hutchins have contributed a special note by their emphasis on the university and its functions. Mr. Flexner's book, published in 1930, can be summarized in one of its sentences: "No sound or consistent philosophy, thesis, or principle lies beneath the American university of today."[2]

---

* A Reply to President Hutchins' Critique of the American University (New York, Toronto: Farrar & Rinehart [©1937]).

Mr. Hutchins' more recent volumes—*No Friendly Voice* (1936) and *The Higher Learning in America* (1936)—have an essentially similar thesis. While Mr. Flexner's familiarity with scientific research gave his volume a significantly different orientation in many respects, both authors express essentially the same criticism of the dilution of course material, the exaggeration of athletics, the surrender to current pressures and vocational fads, and the conception of the college as a place where a student may advance himself socially. We even find the same witty remarks about educational research concerning the functions of janitors in school buildings and—more disconcertingly—we find the same reluctance to give a clear picture of the principles of philosophy (Flexner) or metaphysics (Hutchins) which will serve us in bringing order to "the chaos that we mistake for liberty."[3]

American education is, for a fact, critically in need of a searching scrutiny of its ends as well as its means. No one should resent informed and constructive criticism of institutions that have developed with amazing speed in a hit-or-miss fashion to meet a large variety of needs and pressures. Unfortunately, however, these recent criticisms have tended to confuse rather than to clarify the essential issues.

It is possible to agree with a great many of the specific criticisms of Flexner and Hutchins and still be thoroughly dissatisfied with their proposed solutions. They failed to recognize the forces that led to present conditions, and to supply specific evidence of the direction in which reorientation should take place. In the writings of both these critics the question that presses is the question that is begged: How find a metaphysics, if there be one, which will remedy rather than intensify prevailing "confusion"? It may be true that no consistent philosophy or metaphysics "lies beneath the American university of today." It would be more significant to inquire how much more consistency a country's educational institutions can have than the society in which they exist. It would be an even greater contribution to suggest—if only for discussion—the specific character of the metaphysical principles which would bring "rational order" out of our free "chaos." The plea that the entire structure of higher education should be recast to accord with some set of metaphysical principles turns upon the nature and acceptability of those principles. To write volumes in support of the thesis that there should be a unifying philosophy, without specific indication of the type of unity or of philosophy, is to miss the essential problem underlying the modern dilemma.

If the higher learning is to be unified, is the unity to be voluntary or mandatory? If the unity is to be voluntary, must it not be developed within the community of scholars and based upon the multiplicity of contemporary data and methods of attaining insight? If the unity is to spring from *agreement,* will it be the fruit of "the single-minded pursuit of the intellectual virtues"[4] or will it be derived from a new stress on human values? And if the unity is to be mandatory, rather than voluntary, who will choose the philosophy that is to be imposed from above? Is there not acute danger that the "clarity" of the unifying metaphysical principles will be achieved by sacrificing a multitude of contemporary methods of acquiring knowledge and insight?

American scholars and scientists are not unaware of these intellectual problems. Our best educational institutions are today experimenting with a wide variety of departures from traditional objectives and procedures. There is little or no mention of this vigorous self-criticism in *The Higher Learning in America.* Mr. Hutchins' own criticism of the confusion that has arisen as a result of the freedom of selection, which President Eliot's generation used as the most effective weapon against the rigidity of the traditional college curriculum, is a college administrator's reflection of a broad movement that has been visible in our leading colleges since the war. With the abandonment of the classical kernel of the academic curriculum, we have witnessed a variety of efforts to devise a curriculum based upon a defensible discipline. The new plan in the college at the University of Chicago is one such attempt to substitute a twentieth-century *cosmos* for the *chaos* that has arisen as the unplanned result of our rebellion against the traditional curriculum.

Mr. Hutchins' administrative office at the University of Chicago might easily lead—and has led—to a confusion of his personal views on this subject with the actual program now pursued at the University of Chicago. To correct such misapprehensions, this contribution to the discussion of the issue particularly stresses the comparison of the current program at the University of Chicago with the proposals its president has submitted for discussion in his two volumes. The following pages will deal first with the general intellectual orientation of Mr. Hutchins' criticism, then with the college and general education on the one hand and the university, research, and professional training on the other hand, while a concluding section will once again return to the fundamental principles involved in the entire discussion.

THE INTELLECTUAL BASIS OF MR. HUTCHINS' CRITICISM

The heart of Mr. Hutchins' indictment of the higher learning in America lies in the charge of "confusion," "chaos," or "disorder." The essence of his proposal for change is a plea for a return to a rationally ordered unity to be achieved by restoring the primacy of "metaphysics" in the curriculum.

No doubt is permissible as to the negative side of the proposed curriculum. With the exception of mathematics (as taught by Euclid) and of a few classics such as Aristotle's *Physics* and Newton's *Principia,* science is conspicuously absent in the college and subordinated to metaphysics in the university. In the university program the natural sciences, the social sciences, and even the professions are to get their first principles from metaphysics, recent "observations" being introduced to "illustrate, exemplify, or to confirm these principles" (HL, 108).[5] Education is to be called back to the Great Tradition, to the "fundamental principles of rational thought." It is explicitly held that "the false starts, the backing and filling, the wildness, the hysteria, the confusion of modern thought and the modern world result from the loss of what has been thought and done by earlier ages" (HL, 79). The sores of modern education, and through it the sores of the modern world, are to be healed by contact with the science of first principles, metaphysics.

But what metaphysics? Here again only the negative side of Mr. Hutchins' argument is clear. He explicitly repudiates the Cartesian tradition. He completely neglects modern logic and modern philosophy. His only suggestion of a positive answer is in the form of constant reference to the writings of Plato, Aristotle, and Aquinas. It is true that he often refers favorably to Euclid, Galen, Galileo, and Newton, but in general he approves of the sciences only in so far as they carry on an ancient heritage: "Contemporary physical and biological research inherited the analytical procedures which, combined with observation, constitute a science; and to a great extent the heritage has been fruitful." By a process of elimination many readers and most reviewers have come to the conclusion that the heritage in question is the Platonic-Aristotelian-Thomistic tradition. This is precisely the tradition from which modern science progressively freed itself. Is this the metaphysics which is to be used as the core of the higher education and the norm for the contemporary world?

It may be that Mr. Hutchins' objectives are compatible with a variety of methods, but it is highly questionable whether for the modern world a reversion to the older metaphysics is either feasible, desirable, or necessary. In the course of the last few centuries the scientific approach has been gaining acceptance as the guiding principle for the intellectual activities of Western man. While it may be argued on various grounds that science is not an unmixed blessing, it can hardly be blamed for all our ills, and we cannot repudiate science without repudiating in the same breath our confidence in knowledge and in human reason. Nor is science without its own techniques of rational analysis; indeed, it had to develop its own techniques precisely because of the inadequacies of the inherited metaphysics. Science stresses generalization, logical analysis, and systematization, but it insists that every analysis, every generalization, every systematization be held subject to revision whenever new data seem to warrant it. Thus scientific principles are necessarily formed in the presence of empirical data and, however much they are developed by logical analysis, they are never removed from the control of new data. The Great Tradition in metaphysics, to which Mr. Hutchins seeks to recall the modern university, seemed to hold that after confrontation with a certain amount of data it could reach first principles which were absolute and subject to no further modification. And so, under the emotional seduction of having achieved absolute truth, an early and in itself noble stage of thought came to be considered the final stage of thought.

The claim to have isolated immutable ideas and indubitable first principles has not fared well in the history of thought. Absolutism—as Santayana said in the concluding sentence of *The Genteel Tradition at Bay*—"Smells of fustiness as well as faggots."

The endless disputes between metaphysicians and the vagueness of the terms "metaphysics" and "first principles" do not produce confidence in such claims. Scientists have tried to rescue the eager and flexible mind of Aristotle from the dogmatic immobilization of that mind by the Aristotelians. Galileo's words are notable in this connection:

> Do you question whether Aristotle, had he but seen the new discoveries in heaven, would not have changed his opinions, amended his books, and embraced the more sensible doctrine, rejecting those silly gulls who go about so timidly to defend whatever he has said? Do those defenders consider that, if Aristotle were such a one as they fancy him to themselves, he would be a man of an untractable wit, an obstinate mind, a barbarous soul, a stubborn will, who, accounting all other men as silly sheep, would have his oracles preferred before the senses, before experience, and before Nature herself? It is the sectators of Aristotle that have given him this authority and not he who has usurped or taken it upon himself.[6]

Newton's words in the *Optics* came to represent the judgment of science upon the traditional metaphysics of form and matter:

> [Substantial forms and] . . . occult qualities put a stop to the improvement of natural philosophy, and therefore of late years have been rejected. To tell us that every species of things is endowed with an occult specific quality by which it acts and produces manifest effects, is to tell us nothing.[7]

The traditional logic, which became intertwined with metaphysical first principles, proved to be inadequate to the demands of science for a logic of relations; it was found to harbor contradictions fatal to the development of mathematics; the whole logic of probability and induction which science needed had to be erected—and in its development it was found that scientific method did not even have to assume the uniformity of nature which the metaphysician had laid down as a first principle. At present the traditional logic has become only a special case of a much vaster domain of logic. An increasing demand for rigor showed the logical gaps in Euclid, and the development of the non-Euclidean geometries finally removed all justification for the claim that Euclidean geometry had any privileged relation to existence. By the time of Newton, in fact, mathematics was no longer regarded as a special method of obtaining knowledge of nature; instead of being a rival to the method of obtaining knowledge by generalization from observations it had passed to the status of being an instrument used by science in knowing the observed world.

Parallel to these developments, the principles of Aristotelian physics had in the hands of Galileo proved to be inadequate, the Ptolemaic astronomy had as the result of the work of Copernicus outlived its usefulness, the anatomy and physiology of Galen had been vanquished by Vesalius and Harvey, alchemy and astrology had gone with the Aristotelian cosmology upon which they had been based, the four-elements and four-humour theories of the Greeks had been discarded as bases for chemistry and medicine, and the advance of biology had shown the development and mutability of the very species which had led the metaphysicians to extol the immutability of forms and ideas. Thus modern science, on the basis of new data and new tools of intelligence, has replaced the old doctrines by new systems of greater generality—and so the process continues. In modern science confidence in *methods* has taken the place of confidence in the *results* obtained at any particular time by the use of any particular methods. The same Whitehead who formulated the scientific temper in the motto "Seek simplicity—but distrust it" has also warned us that the ultimate anti-intellectualism is the enthronement as final of any particular stage of rational inquiry.

In the light of this intellectual history Mr. Hutchins seems to many persons to have selected out of man's rich intellectual heritage one metaphysical tradition as the standard, and to have designed his program for higher education so as to inculcate this system of metaphysics. Those who do not accept this simplification of intellectual history may feel that all the major defects of Mr. Hutchins' proposals stem from his apparent selection of certain stages of human thinking as final, for the general description of his proposed college and university curriculum is determined by this selection.

We shall return to this fundamental question of the orientation of Mr. Hutchins' criticism in a general fashion in the concluding part of this discussion, but this brief introductory treatment seemed desirable because the orientation of the program is alien to the dominant tradition of American educational philosophy, and because most of the concepts involved in the specific criticism and proposals derive their meaning from the philosophical framework in which they are set. Mr. Hutchins may disavow any intent to propound such a philosophic framework, but it is difficult to see how so many readers and reviewers have so uniformly misinterpreted his terse and pointed style. Mr. Hutchins has in fact in recent articles[8] denied that his proposal imposes an absolutistic system of metaphysics, and that his emphasis neglects science. He has not, however, stated how far he regards himself as misunderstood, nor developed explicitly the change of emphasis which these denials seem to involve. Certainly he cannot then believe that the reading of a few classical scientific books is adequate college training in science. Nor can he continue to stress the importance of past results to the neglect of present-day methods as well as results. For the intelligent action which he envisages demands the best knowledge available, and contributions to human culture demand the ability to use the best tools at hand—and in these respects even general education cannot be the same at all times and all places. Nor if these qualifications and repudiations are seriously meant can he oppose in substance the position which is taken in this essay.

The dominant emphasis, the detailed criticisms, and the educational suggestions which Mr. Hutchins' books present originate from and make sense only within the framework of the traditional metaphysics of rational absolutism. It may well be that their author is changing his emphasis and perhaps to some degree his philosophical position. But until this is explicitly stated and the implications for specific problems are drawn, discussion must center around the larger published presentations of his views. No one would be more delighted than its author if Mr. Hutchins, recognizing in this essay the substance of his views, allays the apprehensions which his own pages have raised. But the fact remains that the misapprehensions—if misapprehensions they be —are responsible for the idea that the higher education in America is to forsake the path of science and humanistic concern for a democratic society and to return to the Ivory Tower of absolutistic metaphysics. There are even rumors—incredible as it may appear—that the faculty of the University of Chicago, nourished by Scholasticism, is to take the lead in charting this new course for the higher learning. This essay is contributed to the discussion with the purpose of correcting these misapprehensions and rumors.

THE COLLEGE AND GENERAL EDUCATION

In Mr. Hutchins' proposals the function assigned to the college is to provide "general education," which—as he informs us without further argument—"should be given between the junior year in high school and the end of the sophomore year in college" (HL, 9).[9]

We have as Mr. Hutchins' specific indication of the general education to be provided during these four years "a course of study consisting of the greatest books of the western world and the arts of reading, writing, thinking and speaking [elsewhere described as 'grammar,' 'rhetoric,' and 'logic'] together with mathematics." It is stated that "all the needs of general education in America seem to be satisfied by this curriculum" (HL, 85) which specifically *excludes* "body building and character building" (HL, 77) as well as modern science and foreign languages (HL, 82).

It is possible to share Mr. Hutchins' criticisms of athleticism, and still to cherish the classical maxim *mens sana in corpore sano*. It is possible to agree with Mr. Hutchins in his distrust of the loose talk current in some circles as to character building, and still to feel that it is not the objective that has been at fault but rather the means chosen to attain the end. It is also possible to deprecate with Mr. Hutchins the enormous waste involved in our current methods of language training, and yet to feel that the command of at least one language beside the native tongue is essential to a liberal education. Finally it is possible to share Mr. Hutchins' enthusiasm for the classics, and still to feel it pertinent to remark that modern readers who have never closely examined any of the "excellent translations" (HL, 82) of which Mr. Hutchins speaks so hopefully, might easily fail to realize the difficulty of preserving the fine intellectual edge in translation.

These are matters of varying importance. But the main issue lies elsewhere. The underlying principle of Mr. Hutchins' proposed curriculum is the rationally ordered unity without which all is "confusion," and with which all achieves clarity through pure intellectuality. Perhaps the significance of Mr. Hutchins' proposal is best illustrated by a comparison with the point of view of the College Faculty at the University of Chicago as reflected in some essential paragraphs from a resolution on *The Educational Objectives of the College in the University of Chicago*, adopted on April 21, 1934, after the present reorganization of the curriculum had been in effect for almost three years.

It will be noted that this program stresses the education of the "whole person," and that it eschews the isolated and exclusive cultivation of the intellect as such. It stresses the understanding and enrichment of "twentieth century life in all its phases," including therefore proper emphasis upon the sciences and their dramatic significance to our culture.

The University of Chicago has been characterized by its devotion to research and its sense of responsibility to the community. It has remained far enough from the community to maintain perspective, but near enough to have a sense of the moral and social significance of its work. Its attitude has been at once scientific and humanistic.

The result has been that the University, and especially that part of it which constitutes the College, has sought to deal educationally with the whole person—with men and women as knowers and doers and appreciators. This concern with the true, the good, and the beautiful points to the University's basic objective: to produce well-rounded men and women, equipped with accurate knowledge and sound methods of investigation and reflection, appreciative of the best that has been produced in the various fields of human endeavor, and concerned with the understanding and enrichment of twentieth century human life in all its phases. This threefold expansion of a single aim, to be accomplished by whatever educational means may prove effective, clearly must encourage the initiative, the resourcefulness, and the responsibility of students.

In our judgment devotion to ideas is incompatible with the cult of Ideas. As Whitehead has written, "A self-satisfied rationalism is in effect a form of anti-rationalism. It means an arbitrary halt at a particular set of abstractions." The ideal of a community of scholars and students recognizable as the University of Chicago is not compatible with that intolerance of liberal, scientific, and democratic attitudes which is characteristic of the anti-intellectual atmosphere of rationalistic absolutism.

For over forty years the University has led a distinguished existence without being officially committed to any single system of metaphysics, psychology, logic, religion, politics, economics, art or scientific method. To follow the reactionary course of accepting one particular system of ancient or medieval metaphysics and dialectic, and to force our whole educational program to conform thereto, would spell disaster. We cannot commit ourselves to such a course.

We are proceeding in the confident belief that a sound general education, consisting in part of intensive training, will in itself be an excellent preparation for more specialized work. To this end, the four General Courses (in the physical sciences, the biological sciences, the social sciences and the humanities) are designed to introduce the student to the main fields of knowledge. In a summary and perspective fashion they indicate the types of material, the problems and the methods of approach involved in the study of the physical universe, of the world of living organisms, including man, of human society, and of ideas and ideals and their expression in literature and the arts. To all of this the course in English Composition relates itself closely. A large part of the more intensive training which we regard as an essential part of a general education is provided by the several departmental or divisional sequences available to College students. The College Faculty believes that the program should be continued along its present general lines at least until the results of the program can be evaluated.

A project for the further development of the present program has recently been approved by the faculty. Its most interesting innovation provides for an experimental philosophy course to be staffed by faculty members drawn from the four general fields as well as from the philosophy department. Such an enterprise should grow out of the four general courses, and it will use the concepts and materials that are there presented to the students. Instead of imposing a set of metaphysical principles upon the subject matter, the materials of such a course should grow out of the basic courses and would ultimately react to the advantage of the general courses in so far as any significant synthesis of methods and values emerged from the joint enterprise.

If the general education in the college is to acquaint the individual with the best that men have thought in the various realms of knowledge and to give him an appreciation and understanding of the good, the true, and the beautiful as envisaged by man in all times including our own, it can obviously do so only by selecting from the total store of knowledge certain representative items which of necessity must include much of the thought of our own times. No one could possibly, even in several times four years, assimilate more than a fraction of the history, the art, the science, and the other products of human civilization. Nor could such a general education mean very much to those exposed to it if it confined itself exclusively to the most general ideas. As Kant put it, perception without conception is blind, but conception without perception is empty. The emptiness of the most general ideas and the bewildering accumulation of specific factual knowledge are equally incompatible with a general education. The four years to be spent in general education in the college must therefore aim at the mediation of these two extremes. Other things being equal, the test for deciding the inclusion or exclusion of a given subject matter in the curriculum must be its significance for living the life of our society. Nothing, however, should be included in such a curriculum merely because it has the prestige that comes with antiquity or because it is called a classic.

Apart from esthetic values—which are clearly not the main value to Mr. Hutchins—it is hard to see any justification for the central position assigned to the classics in his scheme. In the present College program the student is given an opportunity through two full years to acquaint himself with a large number of literary, scientific, and philosophical masterpieces. In general, the material chosen must be based upon the fullest and most fruitful collection of data. In the natural and social sciences this must—in the very nature of the case—generally be material resulting from modern work. Hence there are obvious limitations that govern the use of the classics in college instruction.

The test to be applied to what Mr. Hutchins proposes as general education is therefore not merely the test of the universality and permanent validity of the ideas to be taught but of their significance and relevance. If there is any meaning, as he seems to think, in the statement that the good and the true and the beautiful are the same in all places and in all times, it is still evident that the aspects significant for education vary in time and place.

The present program in the college at the University of Chicago was chosen for comparison simply because of this author's familiarity with its content and its history. It is certainly not perfect and its experimental traits could be matched in other institutions. It is in constant revision in the light of accumulating experience, and the devotion of its faculty to the task guarantees a continued self-criticism. This program is based upon a rejection of the same excesses of elective freedom which Mr. Hutchins criticizes so sharply. In other words, the existence of such critical efforts at reconstruction illustrates the inadequacy of Mr. Hutchins' picture of the higher learning in America because it entirely overlooks such major efforts within the American system to overcome the difficulties that have arisen. We believe that Mr. Hutchins is under obligation to deal with such programs and to deal with them in specific detail.[10] This he has not done thus far in his writings, at least with reference to the specific content of the curriculum now offered, except to state that the reading and discussion of a number of books mostly consisting of the so-called classics is a method of acquiring a general education superior to the reading and analysis of modern work. Assuming that average students could profitably read the writings Mr. Hutchins suggests, assuming furthermore that they could acquire enough knowledge about the times and circumstances under which these writings were produced to comprehend their meaning, it is still his obligation to show that these materials have a prior claim on the students' time in comparison with other subject matter. He must still demonstrate that more time should be spent upon them than is now being spent in the present college program. Examination of the content of the courses in the college will reveal how widely inclusive of significant contributions to man's thought the present materials are.

Our modern conception of education is not separate and distinct from knowledge of any particulars. General knowledge is valid only in so far as we have valid particular knowledge upon which to base it, and vice versa. General ideas are con-

stantly being changed by the discovery of particular notions, in
the light of which they have to be modified, and while there are
certain rules for discovering and testing truths which have a
broad or even universal validity, reasoning calls for assessment
of ideas in the face of data and experience, and its conclusions
must constantly be tested in the light of results.

THE UNIVERSITY, RESEARCH, AND THE PROFESSIONS

While the "college," according to President Hutchins' proposal, has the function of serving a general education, the "university" is concerned with the higher learning. Since the higher
learning is contrasted with general education, it might be assumed that it is to be concerned with special education. This,
however, appears not to be the case. The higher learning in
the university, corresponding chronologically to what are now
called the junior and senior years and the first year of graduate
study, would, in Mr. Hutchins' plan, consist exclusively of the
following studies (HL, 108):

1. "Metaphysics, the study of first principles" and "also all that
follows from it, about the principles of change in the physical
world, which is the philosophy of nature, and about the analysis
of man and his productions in the fine arts including literature"
(HL, 107).
2. "The social sciences, which are practical sciences, dealing
with the relations of man and man" (HL, 106). These "embrace
the practical sciences of ethics, politics, and economics, together
with such historical and empirical materials as may be needed to
supplement them for the guidance of human action. The theoretical principles of ethics, politics, and economics are, of course,
principles of speculative philosophy. The principles of ethics,
theoretically considered, are to be found in metaphysics. In ethics
itself the same knowledge is viewed in the practical order. To
speak of ethics, politics, and economics as practical philosophy
is to indicate that they are philosophical knowledge organized
for the sake of action. In the law we have a practical application
of this body of practical principles" (HL, 107-8).
3. "Natural science, which is the science of man and nature"
(HL, 106). "The natural sciences derive their principles from the
philosophy of nature, which in turn depends on metaphysics.

In the study of them such recent observations as serve to illustrate, exemplify, or confirm these principles must be included. Medicine and engineering are applications of this whole body of knowledge" (HL, 108).

The university—in other words—is also to be concerned with general education. In Mr. Hutchins' plan "special education" begins "only at the end of the three-year 'university.'" Translated into particulars, this means that students would begin the preparation for a professional or practical career at the age of twenty-two or twenty-three, with the exception of those who are preparing themselves to pass on the Great Tradition in education. It must also be observed that in Mr. Hutchins' proposal no place is provided for the mastery of the elementary disciplines which underlie the professions, unless it be mathematics (as taught by Euclid) and medicine (as taught by Galen) in the period of general education. The foreign languages are specifically eliminated, and since at the university level all studies are to be pursued as aspects of metaphysics, the mastery of the basic techniques of the particular natural and social sciences cannot be an essential part of intellectual training. In other words, the prospective chemist would come to the period of special training with a knowledge of the general principles involved in the physical sciences but with no detailed knowledge of chemistry. At the age of twenty-two he would begin the elementary laboratory work. Mr. Hutchins is apparently not aware of the amount of time required to master the special techniques in each of the fields of knowledge. He would, perhaps, deplore it if he were aware of it. But the fact remains that under present conditions the period of specialization is a long one, long because of the constantly increasing complexity of each field of learning and because of the growing multiplicity of interrelations of the various disciplines with one another.

As science advances, it invariably becomes more specialized, and it is, of course, inevitable that no person can have all the knowledge of all the specialties. It is recognized that, as Mr. Hutchins says, "neither the world nor knowledge of it is arbitrarily divided up as universities are" (HL 59). Whereas in earlier periods of human history a single mind could comprehend all that was known, precisely because the stock of knowledge was less extensive, in our day one of the measures of scientific maturity is that "we have become increasingly and painfully aware of our abysmal ignorance. No scientist, fifty years ago, could have realized that he was as ignorant as all first-rate scientists now know themselves to be."[11] The abysmal ignorance to which Mr. Flexner refers is, of course, an inevitable concomitant of the expanding horizon of science.

The unprecedented scope and differentiation of modern scholarship and science have created a number of pressing problems not merely in general and higher education but in research on the frontier of knowledge. Among these the problem of means of communication between scholars in different fields is outstanding. Scholars and scientists operating in highly specialized fields, and working with complex and highly diversified techniques which presuppose differentiated training and mastery of a large technical literature, recognize the need for a common universe of discourse. Otherwise they would fail to make their maximum potential contributions because they would neglect the ramifications and implications of their own work. Moreover, unless they had a breadth of knowledge extending into realms other than their own, they would not be able to impart to their students and the younger workers whom they have undertaken to train the perspective and meaning of their tasks. The present college program at the University of Chicago with its core in the four general courses and in the proposed philosophical course based on their concepts and materials, as well as on the study of human values, represents an experimental effort to provide this perspective in college education.

The university must seek to train men who will use learning in the service of the society about them. For such a goal the first requirement is the habit of deriving conclusions from the analysis of relevant data, and this habit is best achieved, perhaps uniquely achieved, by work on concrete problems. The danger that Mr. Hutchins professes to see in scientific specialization is well answered by Mr. Flexner: "It is fashionable to rail at specialization; but the truth is that specialization has brought us to the point we have reached, and more highly specialized intelligence will alone carry us further."[12]

Mr. Flexner proceeds to emphasize the generalizing intelligence as inevitably interwoven with the specialized pursuit of new

truth, of new materials, of new data. Mr. Hutchins appears frequently to hold the position that the gathering of new data is
carried on without reference to generalization. Above the level
in the university which is concerned with the "higher learning,"
three distinct activities are defined with great precision. These
are:

1. "Research in the sense of gathering data for the sake of
gathering them." This has "no place in a university" (HL, 90)
but is nevertheless "of great importance" and "must be carried
on somewhere. It is useful and economical, perhaps even essential,
to have it carried on in part under the auspices and protection of
universities and in connection with them" (HL, 109). Persons
engaged in collecting information in the social or natural sciences
"should, though they have no place in the university proper,
find a haven in connection with it" (to wit, in "research institutes") "in which all the current and historical facts now collected
by professors, and more, can be assembled. The members of these
institutes would not be members of the university faculties, unless
they were also working on fundamental problems in metaphysics,
social science, and natural science. Men working on such problems, and only these, would have a voice in matters affecting the
conduct of the university and the content of its work" (HL, 110).
Research institutes "will train people to carry on research of the
type that they carry on themselves" (HL, 111), but will have no
other educational function.

2. "Research in the sense of the development, elaboration, and
refinement of principles together with the collection and use of
empirical materials to aid in these processes." This "is one of the
highest activities of a university and one in which all its professors
should be engaged" (HL, 90), but "the collection of data" should
be "put in its proper place," and "that place is, in any intelligible
scheme of higher education, a subordinate one" (also HL, 90).

3. Training for specified learned professions such as law, medicine, and theology. "If the learned professions cannot be trusted
to communicate the practices of the professions to the young,
it may be desirable in certain cases . . . to attach to the university
. . . technical institutes in which the student may become familiar
with these routines" (HL, 110-11). The relationship of these
technical institutes to the university would be like that of the
research institutes. "Students should in no case be admitted to
technical or research institutes until they have completed their
general and higher education" (HL, 116).

It is important to stress again that Mr. Hutchins nowhere specifies or illustrates the so-called "first principles" that are to be taught in the university. It is therefore impossible to discuss either their existence or their relevance to the higher learning. But it is possible to challenge some of his assertions and their implications.

Outstanding in his book and underlying his not always consistent pronouncements is the deprecation of facts as such. He regards "research in the sense of gathering data for the sake of gathering them" as having "no place in a university" (HL, 90). The obvious implication is that a great deal of activity of this sort is actually going on in universities. Since he does not state what he means by "facts," "data," and "information," and gives no examples, it is impossible to examine the validity of his criticisms. At any given moment there will always be a certain amount of misdirected research, but it may well be doubted whether even on the lowest level there is any appreciable amount of "gathering data *for the sake* of gathering them." The question might be raised whether in general it is possible to collect facts without having at least implicit hypotheses or generalizations in mind.

The same separation between facts and ideas, between particulars and generalizations implicit in Mr. Hutchins' critique of the universities leads him to draw a line between the university and the research institute, and between the university and the professional school. To him research appears to be altogether too often the mere piling up of data rather than the advancement of knowledge, and professional training too often a lapsing on the part of the university into gross vocationalism.[13]

Mr. Hutchins' praise for recent developments in medical education draws attention to the instructive experience of American universities—and particularly of the University of Chicago—in this field. The science and practice of medicine in our country were in a sad state until taken over, nourished, and administered by the universities. By so doing the universities not only rendered a great service to science and to society, but they rendered the university a richer training ground for young men and women. And specifically in the recent developments at the University of Chicago all parties concerned were agreed that medical science and training could best be served by the closest integration (physical and educational) with the university. The present medical unit at the University is the concrete realization of this view. The new buildings were deliberately erected on the north side, rather than on the south side of the Midway, in order to facilitate the integration with the university as a whole. The "medical school" exists on paper only. The work is organized as departments in the Biological Division, the staff members are bona fide members of the divisional faculty, and of the Senate. These so-called medical departments carry on research similar to that in other departments of the Division, and offer work toward the Ph.D. degree. Apparently Mr. Hutchins does not consider this development an error which should be speedily corrected. But if it is not an error should it not suggest some qualifications in the statements about the complete separation of general and vocational training in other fields? Should not Mr. Hutchins' approval of this trend in medical education lead to the conclusion that such an integration of vocational training with the university is a healthy development well worth encouragement elsewhere?

Mr. Hutchins' views on the separation of general and vocational education seem to be related to the admiration for the medieval university which he frequently expresses. These medieval institutions were often, however, largely vocational institutions. Some of the most learned students of medieval education leave little room for doubt as to the possible consequences of the pursuit of "first principles apart from the facts." One of these scholars, Hastings Rashdall, writes:

For the fairly competent student the main defects of a medieval education may be summed up by saying that it was at once too dogmatic and too disputatious. Of the superstitious adherence to Aristotle or other prescribed authority sufficient illustrations have already been given. It is of course a direct outcome of the intellectual vice of the age—a vice of which the human mind was by no means cured by the Renaissance or the Reformation. It lasted longest where it was most out of place. In the middle of the seventeenth century a doctor of medicine was compelled by the English College of Physicians to retract a proposition which he had advanced in opposition to the authority of Aristotle under threat of imprisonment. It may seem a contradiction to allege that this education by authority was at the same time too controversial. Yet the readiness with which the student was encouraged to dispute the thesis of a prescribed opponent, and the readiness with which he would swear to teach only the system of a prescribed authority, were but opposite sides of the same fundamental defect—the same fatal indifference to facts, the facts of external nature, the facts of history, and the facts of life. Books were put in the place of things. This is the defect which was certainly not removed by the mere substitution of classics for philosophy. If in medieval times words were often allowed to usurp the place of things, they were not allowed to usurp the place of thought. For a moment no doubt the human mind was brought into real and living contact with a new world of thought and action, of imagination and art, of literature and history, by the "New Learning"; but ere long classical education in turn became almost as arid and scholastic—as remote from fruitful contact with realities—as the education of the Middle Ages. The history of education is indeed a somewhat melancholy record of misdirected energy, stupid routine, and narrow one-sidedness. It seems to be only at rare moments in the history of the human mind that an enthusiasm for knowledge and a many-sided interest in the things of the intellect stir the dull waters of educational commonplace. What was a revelation to one generation becomes an unintelligent routine to the next. . . . [14]

"Books were put in the place of things"—this is not only the thesis of this essay but it is an historical evaluation that is perhaps the final comment upon an educational proposal to substitute the classics of the Western world for scientific training in our modern society. To have it come from the University of Chicago—which has stressed the method of science since its birth —adds to the confusion in the higher learning in America.

The University enjoys an enviable reputation as an institution not afraid to try the new. But this involves the correlative need to preserve such gains as have been made and not to give up known and tested practices until a reasonable chance exists that a superior practice is at hand to be tried. In education, as in everything else involving a change in social policy, the burden of proof is upon the innovator. It is he who must show that what now is, is defective, and that what might and can be contains a reasonable probability of advance.

Of the two functions of a university—the transmission of knowledge and its advancement—perhaps the most important is the latter, for unless knowledge is constantly broadened and refined it tends to become static and authoritarian and fails to keep pace with changing reality and emerging problems. From this standpoint a separation of the university in personnel and in administration from research and the professional schools contains a double danger: a segregated intellectual life on the one hand and an exaggerated vocationalism on the other.

The cross-fertilization of theory and practice is the very life of each. It can be achieved only by constant preoccupation with both the universal and the particular—and to isolate these functions in the formal organization of institutions of higher learning is to destroy our principal reliance for new knowledge and insight.

CONCLUSION

"Confusion" and "disorder"—which to Mr. Hutchins are the outstanding characteristics of our present activity—are a negative view of a condition that also has positive qualities. The unfettered competition of truths—which is "confusing" and "disorderly"—is at the same time the very essence of a democratic society. Democracy is a plant that must be cultivated; only a continuous tolerance of and vigilant care for variety will preserve and extend our heritage. To crystallize truths into Truth and to substitute metaphysics for science is to arrest a process of intellectual growth that is the basis of the democratic process.

There can indeed be no acute interest, as Alfred N. Whitehead has told us, "which puts aside all hope of the harmony of truth. To acquiesce in discrepancy would be destructive of candour and of moral cleanliness."[15] To seek harmony is one thing, however; to impose Truth by eliminating or by subordinating the very process of arriving at new truth or of testing old truth is quite another.

It was a commonplace to classical philosophy that each main type of political organization must have its corresponding type of education, and that every educational plan would create or reinforce its proper social scheme. Thus Plato and Aristotle. Mr. Hutchins writes that the "intellectual virtues remain the same in a democracy, an aristocracy, an oligarchy, or a monarchy" (NFV, 66-7), or, again, that the heart of education is "the same at any time, under any political, social, or economic conditions" (HL, 66). The higher learning, in other words, is neutral to the social order in which it exists. Educational ground neutral to democracy is likely to be educational ground precarious if not hostile to democracy.

Liberal education has always aimed at both theory and practice with the dominant concern of making the theory available for practice, and of correcting and fertilizing the theory by the practice. It is now proposed to truncate this process and to restrict the content of the higher learning to pure theory and a few facts chosen to illustrate it. At the college level the content proposed is directed away from laboratory concreteness, field work, and in general from exposure to "raw" experience. "Facts" appear to be foolish when ageless ideas are in the offing. Education is to Mr. Hutchins, in a word, sensitization to the abstract, to the universal, to the "intellectual," and the preference appears to rest upon the presumption that a person thus exposed to generality is more proficient in practice than others, once he turns his hands to industrial work or his mind to professional cares.

Fundamentally, the entire proposal is based upon an unproved assumption about the transfer of learning. It is taken for granted that participation in practice requires no special training; a brief apprenticeship under technicians will suffice to make a superior practitioner of the theoretical product of the higher learning. This easy faith arises out of a prejudgment as to the inferiority of the practical to the intellectual. Such a view involves a fallacy as to the transfer of training, indeed a most difficult transfer— that from theory to action. It is precisely the mutual cross-fertilization of theory and action that is the hardest task of all. If education does not achieve this, it fires wild, and it will more nearly achieve it if the aim is quite deliberately set.

Experience does not suggest that the accommodation of general ideas to specific facts and concrete action can be safely trusted to an educational afterthought. This is precisely the most common source of present failure. To know *in general* is as easy as Aristotle indicated; but to know the *when,* the *where,* the *wherefore,* the *whereunto,* and the *how much*—this, as Aristotle concluded, is the final test of a wise man. An education which does not recognize this, and specifically provide for it, makes not wise men, but educated fools. It might hide the shame engendered of its weakness by perpetuating a division of labor that will exempt its graduates from the test of life and action, assigning to them the task of passing on the "metaphysics" in education—and in so doing it might also contribute to the strength of the forces that are now undermining freedom of thought as the most effective attack upon freedom in general.

We must meet the present on its own terms. If there is confusion in our present situation, there is also unparalleled promise. In place of the metaphysical orientation of the classical academy, the theological orientation of the medieval university, and the literary orientation of the Renaissance university, modern higher education must put its main emphasis on the method of science. This does not mean that the activities of former systems of higher education are not to be included in the present system; it means that the intellectually distinctive characteristics of the modern world—scientific methods and results, and a philosophy cooperating with scientific and humanistic interests—should be the dominant quality of modern higher education. We can do full justice to the richness of man's intellectual and cultural heritage, and yet give science a high place in meeting the demands of active living in the modern world. This is a modern alternative to exclusively theological, metaphysical, or literary orientations. Science can be at once its own reward, and the highest award of living thought to the life of action.[16]

Science is obviously not worthy of such praise if it does not resist its own tendencies to dogmatism and its occasional disdain for humanistic interests. It must not neglect its own rich historical past; it must acknowledge responsibility for exhibiting its own unity and for developing an organized curriculum on the basis of that unity; it must help make explicit its methods; it must be interested in the humanistic implications of the scientific habit of mind; it must, in short, be willing to round itself out logically and philosophically. It is in aiding science to develop into a logically analyzed and synthetically integrated whole, and in assessing the cultural implications of scientific methods and results that modern philosophy may make a momentous contribution to the history of ideas and to the demands for synthesis within the contemporary world. Linked in a common task, science and philosophy may claim to be the modern form of the Great Tradition. Here, clearly, is the basis of a sense for "the

grand scheme of the intellect and the unity of thought" which
rightly stirs Mr. Hutchins' imagination. Here, and not in the
ranks of the dogmatists and pseudo rationalists, are the lineal
descendants of Plato, Aristotle, Galileo, Leibnitz, Newton, and
Darwin.

Let there be no doubt as to the crucial characteristic of this
alternative orientation. Instead of stressing the Truth enshrined
in Books—and overlooking the fact that the selection of these
books is made by those who are already confident that they
possess the Truth—it stresses the methods by which new truth is
established and ancient truths are corrected. Instead of presenting as final a set of results attained by thinking men, it
stresses the significance of the procedures by which results are
achieved. Instead of embalming a set of First Principles, it
exhibits principles in relation to the subject matters out of
which they arise and the methods by which they must be
corrected. Instead of merely contemplating Knowledge and the
Good, it displays the techniques by which Knowledge and the
Good may be made more secure. In this stress of method the
conflict between Ideas and Facts drops away, as it has long since
dropped away in science itself and in discussions of scientific
method, for the scientific method, as the observational-hypotheti-
cal-deductive-observational procedure, unites in one process the
most abstract tools of analysis and the most refined observational
controls. Neither is the systematic side of science sacrificed to
the observational side, nor the observational to the systematic.
To acquire the scientific habit of mind the student must himself
participate in all stages of the method. Thus alone can he come
to see both the power and the limitations of generalization. If
to be philosophical means to be concerned with conceptual
analysis, with method, with the pursuit of the unified system
of knowledge and reliable methods, then the whole of higher
education can be philosophical without running foul of the
charges which we have raised against the projected metaphysical
orientation.

Such an orientation as is here proposed does not oppose science
to the humanities. This false and tragic divorce may be the
primary cause of our current "confusion." The student must
not merely "cultivate" his "intellect," but he should have direct
contact with great religious, scientific, philosophical, and artistic

products. He must not only know about the arts, but must be given opportunities to enrich esthetically his own experience. Without being subjected to any form of propaganda, he should be expected to acquire an interest in the application of intelligence to mankind's quest for the good. To stress first principles without the constant challenge of experience is to produce intellectual conceit and reactionary attitudes. Plato—to whom Mr. Hutchins refers so often—drew back from such extremes. The students in the Platonic Academy were carefully grounded in the arts and sciences. Only at the age of twenty were the connections between their previous studies to become conscious objects of attention, and then only for the chosen few. From the ages of thirty to thirty-five, the survivors of this precarious preoccupation were to be students of metaphysics or dialectics:

There is a danger lest they should taste the dear delight too early; for youngsters as you may have observed, when they first get the taste in their mouths, argue for amusement, and are always contradicting and refuting others in imitation of those who refute them; like puppy-dogs, they rejoice in pulling and tearing at all who come near them.[17]

Unlike his puppy-dogs, Plato's educated men could not remain spectators on the heights, but must descend to the cave of common life to take their places in the company of men and women.

The historical parallel with the Greece of Plato and Aristotle is in some respects rather striking. Theirs, too, was a time of question and scrutiny. Old beliefs in all ranges of human experience had become increasingly inacceptable. The story of Socrates testifies to the yearning for security of the Athenian community. The critical spirit of the philosophers seemed to endanger all that was sacred and orderly. If we are to do for our time what they did for theirs, we should certainly not repeat the very practice of a nostalgic return to some past security which these philosophers encountered as their chief obstacle. It is true that a clear and systematic indoctrination in some set of dogmatic first principles might be more comfortable to the young, the weary, and the frightened, but an educational institution not yet committed to outright indoctrination in some secular or formal religion will insist that broken rays of true light are preferable to the glamour of a spurious metaphysical clarity that has no relation to experience. Occasionally the result might be confusing, but a clear and rationally intelligible picture would under the assumed circumstances be indefensible from the standpoint of elementary intellectual candor.

The clamor for a rational order, for a comprehensive set of first principles with due subordination of historical and current empirical material selected with an eye to illustration or confirmation of the metaphysics, is essentially a claim to intellectual dictatorship. Reason, however, is not necessarily a principle of order. It is analytical; it discriminates and distinguishes. Order historically is the fruit either of authority or of shared values. The clamor for rational order, therefore, boils down to a demand for submission to the particular metaphysical dogma that is advocated.

If philosophers are to contribute their share in the mastery of the ensuing perplexity as to what the knowledge means and what its potentialities might be, they will have to drop medieval claims to match the position of theology as the queen of the sciences. Essentially the integrative quality of medieval theology did not lie in its intellectual superstructure but in the common *faith* of those who elaborated the theology. Mr. Hutchins seems to hesitate here on the brink of a vital distinction. He stresses the role of theology in the medieval university but thinks it is not possible for our generation, which is "faithless" and takes "no stock in revelation." To our modern mind, however, metaphysical first principles require as much revelation as the medieval theology requires.

The integration of medieval society—such as it was—was essentially that of faith in common *values*. The disintegration of modern culture is not primarily the fruit of intellectual error but rather the inevitable result of an outlook that regards values as the concern of individuals, and, if anything, as an obstacle to academic achievement. Our basic problem is not that of improved *means* to unimproved *ends,* but rather that *means* are ever more available to *ends* ever more muddled and evanescent. Philosophy's most tempting opportunity lies in the clarification and statement of the values by which we live, and such a clarification of values will spring from a detailed and synthetic knowledge of the conditioning *means* rather than from sterile parroting of a discarded metaphysics.[18]

Such a view—in John Dewey's words—"renounces the traditional notion that action is inherently inferior to knowledge and preference for the fixed over the changing; it involves the conviction that security attained by active control is to be more prized than certainty in theory."[19]

The multiplicity of modern paths to significant insight can be reduced to order by the regrouping of available knowledge and capacities for action that would result from the clarification of values and ends. If religion seems to have degenerated from the living embodiment of the shared values of the group to a part-time embellishment of our leisure, that is one of the penalties attached to identifying spiritual matters with the *status quo* in scientific and social evolution. If philosophy is to avoid a similar fate, it must direct itself to the task of revitalizing our values by restoring their relevance to the life of reason. Thus it might recover its position as the basic moral and social science by ceasing to be a device to deal with the problems of philosophers and becoming, in John Dewey's words, a method, utilized by philosophers, for dealing with the problems of men.

Integration thus conceived might save us from the imposed social cohesion with appended "made to order" *Weltanschauung* that is the sad reality in the totalitarian states. To select a collectivist frame of reference is to beat the enemy by joining him. To withdraw to metaphysical first principles, with due subordination of the historical and current facts, is to run away from the battle altogether. If we are to succeed in avoiding an imposed social cohesion, the substitution of an integrative striving for coherence will demand a new approach to values.

For several generations the idea has prevailed that there was something peculiarly strong-minded and scientific in discarding ethical considerations in the pursuit of knowledge; and the quality of traditional preachment helps to explain the tendency. In imitation of the physical sciences, mechanical theories prevailed even in the study of society, but in an increasingly plastic environment the old mechanical theories, which had their roots in the assumption of a fixed environment, lost their interests even in the explanation of the physical universe. In social matters, new habits of thought intimately involved in the new experience of continuous remodeling of man's environment once again focused attention upon the *ends* which the new *means* sought to implement. If reason is to serve us in our present confusion, it will be through the clarification of our *ends* in relation to ever more diversified and powerful *means*. If those who are at the frontiers of advancing knowledge have cavalierly disregarded their responsibilities in these matters, able and aggressive leadership faces a new responsibility.

To repeat, it is possible to agree with much of Mr. Hutchins' criticism of the American university of today and yet to reject his proposals for reconstruction. Unity imposed by authority is only another term for uniformity. While chaos and disorder have their disadvantages, they at least maintain a field that is wide open to new truth and new methods of gaining insight. The true scholar recognizes the need for integrating his own work with the body of knowledge pertaining to other fields and with the values of his society. He does not look for a verbal nostrum nor for a superimposed authority to introduce meaning, significance, and unity into his work.

Truth to finite man is never single, complete, and static. It is rather multiple, fractional, and evolving. The true scholar finds his unifying principles in the humanistic spirit and in the methods of science. It is not so much the tentative truths that he discovers, as the developing methods for discovering and analyzing truths, that unite him with his associates into a community of scholars and of scientists.

Mr. Hutchins is convinced that the objections to his proposals "cannot be educational objections" (HL, 86). He sees the main obstacle in the faculty's "lack of acquaintance with the books," its resistance to change of its habits, its desire to produce a crop like unto itself, or in "love of money," "false notions of democracy," a "distorted idea of utility," and "anti-intellectualism."

Educational objections of the first magnitude have been stated in this essay. Educational considerations apart, however, the proposed reorientation is open to question because it is conceived and born in authoritarianism and absolutism, twin enemies of a free and democratic society. Acceptance of the curricular primacy of a set of first metaphysical principles would reduce science to dogma and education to indoctrination. The temper of the modern mind is well expressed in the motto of the University of Chicago

> Let knowledge grow from more to more, and thus be
> human life enriched.

If these are times of confusion and disorder, the results and the methods of science also make them times of unparalleled promise. Now—as never before—educational leadership calls for a persistent and critical emphasis upon the significance of present achievement and its promise for the future.

To describe the higher learning in America as if it were almost entirely vocational and provincial in the chronological sense is to overlook some of the highest achievement and some of the most seminal inquiry ever pursued under academic auspices. Critical scrutiny of abuses of academic privilege is essential to continued vitality—and even the best of our American institutions afford abundant opportunity—but to avoid the abuse by the advocacy of a monastic withdrawal to a community of scholars primarily concerned with the elaboration of a discarded metaphysics is to abandon the very essence of modern achievement. The contemporary scene is full of societies in which the logical development of first metaphysical principles with "due subordination" of observed facts is diligently pursued. It is sad to reflect that a commendable concern for moral and intellectual integrity should be deflected by distortion of focus into a weapon against the very forces it seeks to strengthen.

2

*Inaugural Address**

EDUCATION HAS BEEN SUPPORTED WITH UNPARALLELED PUBLIC sacrifice because equality of opportunity is a basic and traditional value of American life. Since our activities are for obvious reasons not exposed to the continuous challenge of competitive economic enterprise, we have sometimes been tempted to regard "security" and "tenure" as ends in themselves rather than as essential means to professional effectiveness. Professional effectiveness obviously depends upon the things we as a profession are asked to effect. It requires, therefore, continuous self-criticism, particularly in a time in which the functions of education are shifting very rapidly.

It is a commonplace that our high schools and colleges are ill-suited to a large percentage of the youth in attendance. Within a single generation the composition of the student body has undergone almost revolutionary change. Throughout the country an academic curriculum, designed for a relatively small group with well-understood social and intellectual "backgrounds," has been put through a shift in personnel that threatens to make it a complete misfit for the great majority of students now in the colleges. We have more of our people in secondary schools and colleges than all the rest of the world put together. Can we honestly say that we have responded to the public challenge with the professional resilience which such a shift in responsibility implies? Can we earn anything but ultimate contempt with the plea that our present drift is really design, or with the pathetic proposal to return to an educational pattern that was designed

---

* From Brooklyn College. *Inauguration of Harry D. Gideonse as the Second President.* The Quadrangle, Brooklyn College, October 19, 1939 (Brooklyn, 1939), pp. 13-26.

for the social and economic conditions of an earlier age and for a radically different selection of the human material then available?

I have discussed these problems in a number of recent papers and, since I have had no recent occasion to revise my judgment, I shall inevitably cover some of the same ground.[1] We have thought of the school as concerned with the training of the mind. In a sense the depth of this tradition is perhaps illustrated by our complete inability to understand (note that I do not say: accept) the famous dictum of the German Nazis when they propose "to think with their blood." We usually dispose of this strange utterance with the categorical statement that we know of other parts of our anatomy more efficiently designed for the purpose. If we should search our minds sympathetically for the kernel of truth in the characteristic exaggeration of *Sport-Palast* oratory, we might find ourselves on the track of a crucial weakness of Western culture.

Western civilization has for more than two thousand years sought to establish a rigid separation between reason and emotion, between "objectivity" and "values." The material fruitfulness of the separation in the past is the chief reason for its uncritical acceptance in the present. The intellect, however, is not simply an aspect of human life—and a superior aspect in typical Aristotelian tradition—but it arises out of the emotional and ethical life, is deeply rooted in it, and draws its strength and stamina from it. The moral and emotional bleakness of typical intellectual communities, and many of the characteristic problems of the American college and university, can only be understood in the light of the persistence of this tradition. When we discuss our "problems of teaching" and set large staffs at work on the problems of "youth" and "teacher's training," we are simply tracing some of the symptoms of a malady that is rooted in this distinction of reason and emotion that underlies most of our thought about the entire educational process.

The usual discussion of the problem of teaching is a good example. It is typically a survey of methods of improving the quality of teaching, the selection and training of teachers, and so on. Solemnly the customary banalities about "the teacher vs. the research man" are repronounced and reevaluated, and

equally solemnly the conventional conclusions are rediscovered
about the inevitable togetherness of good teaching and good
research.

I am not inclined to deny that different methods of motivating,
selecting, or training the teaching personnel have promise if
we are interested in improvement of the job that is at present
done. The entire discussion, however, tends to be concerned with
methods of teaching, *methods* of teachers, yes, even *methods* of
improving the *methods*. The *end* that is to be sought by these
means is taken for granted or is discussed in only an incidental
fashion.

Obviously mathematics, French, or economics can be taught
with more or less competence, and, all other things being equal,
we all share the preference for the greater competence. The point
about the modern problem of teaching is, however, precisely
that, even with a very high level of competence in the teaching
of the various "subjects," the gnawing doubt about the "purpose"
of it all remains, as certainly in the sensitive teacher as it does in
the minds of a growing number of his students.

The entire tradition is analytical. All the professional motivation and the conventional premiums are on the side of division
of labor, specialization, and dissection. From the beginning of
the freshman year we proceed to analyze, to dissect, and to take
the bones apart until we have so many bones piled so high that no
one can put them together again—and then we hastily graduate
the class, and start all over again with a new group of freshmen.
These things are true of teaching—the transmission of learning
—and they are equally true of creative scholarship. Anyone
familiar with our great centers of creative scholarship knows the
peculiar atmosphere generated by the mechanization of the
process of thought itself. Men and women with great human
potentialities have lapsed into that state of resentful coma known
as research, while a battle-front bleakness hangs over the intellectual landscape.

Occasionally, a teacher in the humanities or the social sciences
will venture the statement that the "relations" of subjects or the
"meaning" of the learning is the heart of good teaching, but
beyond that point few will risk themselves lest they be accused of
"preaching." So, in the language of the Sermon on the Mount,
while the young clamor for bread, we continue to offer them

stones, and if the discontent of the young provokes critical discussion, it is limited to the quality of the stones and to methods of improving methods of manufacturing more excellent stones.

The reason for our studied avoidance of "ends" is historically obvious. With the emergence of a secular education, "values" were jealously reserved as the prerogatives of the church, the family, and other intermediate social groups. Historically secular education could not have touched this side of education if it had desired to do so. And, for a variety of reasons, it did not desire to do so. It made a virtue of "objectivity"—meaning detachment from value judgments. It built up a professional taboo against consideration of values, even if it is, of course, sheer objectivity to observe that all learning and all activity derive their meaning from human values. Education, i.e., the limited formal procedures that are usually described by this broad term, could do this with impunity, even if social cohesion without values is inconceivable, because the church, the family, and other social institutions maintained a sufficiently close grip upon the young to give meaning to the instruments and facts that the school had chosen as its limited field of interest and activity.

With the progressive development of our industrial civilization, the role of the family and the church declined, while social mobility and impersonal exchange relations continued to play an ever-increasing role. Educators, however, discussed the sphere of formal education as if nothing had changed in the social setting in which the school operated, although a good deal of rather opportunist experimentation developed in a more or less bootleg fashion via the academically less respectable channels of electives and extracurricular activities.

Perhaps the deep-seated character of the cultural lag in our ideas about the content of education is best illustrated by the fact that, in a decade in which totalitarian philosophies are spreading like a prairie fire, prominent discussion should be devoted to a proposal to discard all the "fads and frills," and to return to a strictly intellectualist program for the schools—justified with the explicit statement that the other-than-intellectual matters are a concern of the family and the church. While such a program might have a certain validity for a limited upper fringe of the educational structure, it obviously advocates a remedy that overlooks the chief cause of contemporary difficulties in general

education. It assumes that the position of the school with respect
to the whole of society is still identical with that same position
in an earlier period. We are, however, concerned with the fruits
of our modern teaching *precisely because that assumption is no
longer valid.*

Other contemporary proposals advocate the deliberate indoctrination of some *ism* of either a conventional character such as
"the American way" or of a more venturesome nature such as
one of the fifty-seven varieties of collectivism. Here again the
basic cause of contemporary difficulty is overlooked. Merely
baking ourselves back into some new cake of custom will not
remove the distress caused by the cracks in the comfortable crust
of convention that covered our routine in the past. For the new
cake of custom will give way before the same forces that sub-
verted the old, and neither the intellectualists nor the social
indoctrinators propose to do anything about these forces that
are inevitably interwoven with the drift of social policy throughout the world today.

What are these forces? Essentially they all spring from our
predominant modern preoccupation with increased material
standards of living, with our constant drive toward increased
productivity. All our twentieth-century political faiths agree
upon this objective and it is frequently envisaged as an end
in itself. In the United States, New Deal Democrats as well
as their more conservative brethren in and out of their own party
agree upon this objective. Disagreements are a matter of means
to achieve this end. Similarly Fascists and Communists are lyrical
in their description of the "waste" of laissez faire democracy,
and here, too, basic agreement upon ends exists, although it
comes in sidewise in fascism because of the emphasis on a war
economy. Now increasing productivity—generally accepted as an
end—precludes the choice of certain *means* and inevitably leads
to the selection of others. The social byproducts of these means
constitute our problem.

Productivity as a social *end* means specialization and division
of labor as means. It means heavy stress upon the rational and
impersonal and it means continuous undermining of the traditional, the social, and the other-than-intellectual. In a sense,
specialization has eaten the heart out of our social cohesion. To
be sure, the more specialization, the greater the need for careful

coordination of the specialists. The specializing, i.e., the differen-
tiating, aspects of our activity are, however, constantly stressed
in our day-by-day effort of earning a living, while the coordinat-
ing, the fitting into a common framework, is impersonal and
takes place through abstract devices like a price system or the
technique of an administrative bureaucracy.

In recreation—the very recognition of "recreation" as a separate
activity is characteristic of the system—we tend to passivity. We
listen, look, and thrill at the activities of specialists, and a general
"spectatoritis" develops in these fields. The sense and value of
participation have disappeared, and more and more people use
only one small part of their potential human equipment. Abstract
and impersonal relations predominate, and the general decline
of intermediate social groups, of the family, and church is obvious
to any observer. The community youth surveys of the American
Youth Commission tell a tragic tale in this respect.

In such a community, "specialists" will arise to cater to new
"wants" of a psychological and emotional sort. Commercialized
recreation like the movies and dance halls and pathic politics of
the totalitarian type illustrate the thesis. Life has to increasing
multitudes a quality that might be called absence of wholeness,
or perhaps emotional starvation. Segmental thought and organization become characteristic in economic and political life as
another typical expression of specialized endeavor.

If the real achievements of specialization are not to be more
than offset by these costs of the impersonal and abstract—de-
socializing aspects of the process—a social program will have to
be devised to make specialization safe for society, meaning safe
for that which makes for social cohesion.

Education in the broadest possible sense of the term—from
the nursery through the adult stages—will be a significant part of
such a program, and this will be true under any form of social
organization. Industrial development in the U.S.S.R. produces
exactly the same social consequences in this respect as the so-
called "capitalist" system. Part of the explanation for the lack
of understanding among radical critics of capitalism, of the
emotional and psychological factors that help to explain their
own radicalism, probably lies in the esthetic and spiritual poverty
of Marxism, which professes to see all these factors as dependent
upon the mode of production in its *ownership* aspect.

The legal technicalities of ownership, however, have little to do with the psychological impact of a given technique of production. Ownership by a cooperative, a capitalist corporation, or the federal government is likely to make little difference in the psychological impact of a conveyor-belt factory upon the workers involved in such production, unless suitable supplementary organization is provided, and the latter is as likely to occur under one form of ownership as under another. Clearly, if we are to avoid an obvious threat to most of the values of Western civilization, we must once again ask basic questions about the *content* of education as a whole. In other words, what should be the shift in direction and in content of curriculum, in view of the change in the social setting of which formal education is merely a part?

It is suggestive to examine briefly two examples of education in a pattern that avoided some of these modern tendencies. The first is historical, the second contemporary.

Medieval education could with impunity stress the purely intellectual or strictly vocational—often, again, the *same* thing. It operated in a society in which every member belonged to a single, strongly entrenched church and in which that church maintained a strong family system that was sacred in every sense of the term. Art in general, group expression in religious ritual and procession, production and consumption, and government itself, all derived their meaning from the same religion. In such a society, unified by a common faith, the problem of other-than-formal education could not even arise. All specialized activity derived its meaning from the common religious core of civilized life.

The Scandinavian countries supply us with a good contemporary example. Too frequently the relatively stable conditions in these countries are discussed in terms of social and economic policy and accompanying organization. The factor of cultural homogeneity is frequently overlooked and the deliberately *created* —as contrasted with historically grown—aspects of this homogeneity are seldom observed. The striking results of the movement for supplementary adult education in Denmark and Sweden are first of all attached to an other-than-intellectual emphasis in the program. In its origin, the movement might even be described as anti-intellectualist in the strict sense of the term. Heavy stress was placed by Grundtvig as early as 1844 on the social and cooperative aspects of education, on folk song and folk dance, on the role of tradition, myth, and religious observance, and on the peculiar educational fruits of working and living together.

To stress the significance of the contribution this movement has made is not necessarily to demand exact duplication of its program or procedures. Obviously, in a different social and historical setting another adjustment of content and techniques would be demanded, and this would be in strict accordance with the essential ideas involved in the movement.

The lessons of the historical and the contemporary example are therefore identical. To maintain social cohesion, something beyond the usual academic—intellectual—program is required. In the normal course of events this will be supplied by institutions like the family and the church. With rapid social change involving the position of these fundamental educational influences, the content of formal education must be reexamined and evaluated in terms of the social setting in which the institutions that supply formal education operate. When the institutions that are supposed to cater to other-than-intellectual needs of the human personality are rapidly shifting in their range of influence, basic questions are in order as to a corresponding shift in the direction and content of formal education. These questions should be asked with an eye to making up the deficiencies now revealed in the activity of the other institutions that play so important a part in the social, i.e., total, education of the young. The deepest challenge to formal education in a democratic society is to find emotional equivalents in their program for the type of thing that is likely to make the totalitarian appeal irresistible if it is not recognized at a sufficiently early date in the process.

At bottom, this is the meaning of the appeal for *integration* or *meaningfulness* that is so common in American education today. The solution, however, does not primarily lie in improved methods of organizing the subject matter or in better teaching, but in a radical reorientation in our thought about the content of formal education that will once again restore values to a central place in our program.

Frequently a plea to restore values in our formal education is met with the query: *Which* values? The question is itself a measure of the acuteness of the malady. We live in a free and democratic society. Are the values of freedom and the democratic way of life explicitly taught or even examined? We live in a culture which, even in its most secular activities, bears the marks of Christian and Jewish religion. To how many of our young people do these terms have a meaning? Nothing is more characteristic of our culture and our education than the emphasis upon science. How frequently do we spend any time at all on the basic values of truth and free inquiry that motivated the scientific movement? Are esthetic values to be left entirely to the appeal of tabloids, the movies, and competitive advertising? If it is replied that these things should take care of themselves, the obvious answer is that the facts indicate that they do no such thing.

In a sentence, this means that formal education should begin to think of other-than-intellectual aspects as a major part of its responsibility.

To be sure, much is now done along these lines. Throughout society, spontaneous effort has arisen in a wide variety of movements in response to these needs. It is the essence of a free society's method to encourage such diverse self-generated responses rather than to let matters drift until a regimented public program centered on the totalitarian state seems the only alternative to dissolution. Thus we find the arts—and particularly music and song—creeping into curricula all over the land. Physical education is already well established and although it often degenerates into team worship and nonparticipation of the mass of students, it certainly offers great and immediate opportunities for coordination with a general program.

Extracurricular activities with their almost unlimited opportunities for social education have notoriously flourished in spite of constant denunciation by academic pundits unable to cross the boundaries set for education in a different historical period. While this is a garden that calls for careful weeding, the multiplicity of its offerings is precisely its most encouraging feature. The progress of a sprawling movement for personal and vocational guidance is evidence of a similar trend. And, in a broader social field, the enormous development of such activities as the scout movement, the boys' clubs, the summer camps, the remarkable initiatives of a man like Bishop Sheil in the Catholic community throughout the Chicago industrial district, and the Civilian Conservation Corps camps, all point to deep-seated needs in diverse fields.

Leisure time agencies are still too much concerned with the spectator rather than with the participant. They are cast as entertainment rather than as creative self-expression and self-discovery. Such activities should channel a flow of energy and they should integrate a personality towards an aim. Here are wide areas of education which have remained without trained and professional cultivation because of a narrow "intellectualist" tradition that is now breeding forces that are inimical to the core of the doctrine itself.

The first need is therefore a complete shift of focus. What has partly developed as an unplanned byproduct must now be seen as clearly within the general responsibility of the educator. Talent and funds formerly restricted to academic purposes in the narrow sense of the term must now be shifted from sheer cultivation of intellectual virtues to education for the *whole* man, for men "as knowers and doers and appreciators." Thus far such statements describe significant objectives rather than actual achievement. Out of such a reorientation new insights, new techniques, and new personnel will develop, and a significant repercussion upon the established program can confidently be expected to follow.

Wherever in our contemporary educational world really significant teaching is being done by individuals or by institutions, it will be revealed that concessions to the *whole-man* theory have been made in fact, if perhaps not in explicit formulation. At the very minimum, this will result from the imponderable factor of a well-integrated teaching personality that has an impact that quite escapes the careful analysis of the actual text or of the spoken word—and frequently, of course, the successful teacher goes beyond the limits of the academic mores and does not hesitate to relate his subject matter to significant value judgments.

It is my thesis that we should make the really valuable parts of our current achievement explicit in terms both of ends and of means. It is time to consider the full and systematic development of the so-called "fads and frills" as an essential part of an educational program for the preservation of a free and democratic society.

No amount of discussion or even of achievement in the direction of improved methods of teaching will correct the errors made in the definition of the content of education. If we do not reorient ourselves in this direction—if we reach out for some collectivist philosophy or some road back to a pattern not designed to meet the needs of our generation—we may have to resign ourselves to a satisfaction of the esthetic, emotional, and physical needs of the young by the man on horseback. If it is not the man on horseback, it will be the irresponsible demagogue who will in some way manage to give expression to the emotionally starved, even if the result is certain destruction of all the values of a free society.

If we in the schools do not live up to our other-than-intellectual responsibility, if we do not reach into moral and emotional fields in a manner that is justifiable from the standpoint of the values of a free society, *someone else will.* For the need exists, and the trend is toward intensification of the pressures that have brought it about. Thus, in a real sense, the survival of a free society may be determined by the flexibility with which we think of the limits of formal education in a changing world.[2]

All these considerations are peculiarly relevant in the city colleges. If ours were the campus of a typical "football" college with the rah-rah spirit that goes with such country club education, mine would have been a different theme. Our emphasis has, however, been more exclusively intellectual than most American college education.

Academically our entrance requirements are so high that we can match those of the best colleges in the country. The quality of the intellectual work done after admission to the college can stand comparison with any other institution of college level in the city. But if man cannot live by bread alone, neither can a college live by training mind alone. The community holds us responsible—and rightly so—for the preparation of the best of its youth for significant and challenging citizenship. We are not just interested in training minds, but in the development of effective men and women. The responsibility for that part of the college program has not yet been adequately faced. It means a grave responsibility for the students and for the administrative officials in the college.

I might properly conclude with a remark which I also addressed to the student body of this college at our first meeting this fall: Brooklyn College has some 13,000 students working for the regular bachelor's degree. Some other institutions in the city have a larger total enrollment; none of them has a larger arts and sciences enrollment. It is difficult to visualize 13,000 students. If we could add up the total student body of Barnard College, Columbia College, Williams College, Amherst College, Colgate University, Smith College, Vassar College, Mount Holyoke College, and all of Princeton University, we would still be several hundred short of Brooklyn College's thirteen thousand. The administrative officials of these other nine institutions would number nine college presidents and some thirty deans. We have one president and the equivalent of four deans to match that army of administrative talent, and I think almost anyone would agree that the students in a big city college are far more urgently in need of administrative guidance than the students in most of the colleges enumerated. My final plea: If we go slow—and if we seem somewhat impersonal—keep the arithmetic in mind.

3

*The Discipline of Freedom**

To the modern democratic mind the word "discipline" suggests the big stick and regimentation, while the word "freedom" is regarded as peculiarly democratic and suggests individualist self-determination. It is conveniently overlooked that some of the worst forms of modern tyranny are democratically imposed, while on the other hand the common root of the words "discipline" and "disciple" suggests that the social restraint of the individual may be achieved by the democratic agency of shared values—that is to say, by moral like-mindedness, as well as by the authoritarian technique of imposition by central government.

The moral penumbra of freedom has been a central problem to me as a student, a teacher, and an administrator, and, most of all perhaps, as a citizen. I remember coming back from a long stay in Europe in 1919, as a student, passionately interested in politics and proud of the things with which Woodrow Wilson had managed to identify American democracy. I recall getting off the steamer in Hoboken, New Jersey, with the zeal of a pilgrim who reaches his chosen destination. I did not know that I was coming back to a city that was in the midst of a dock strike. As I walked along in youthful exaltation at the rediscovery of things once familiar to smell and touch, I arrived at a telegraph office. When I reached the door a big husky took me by the shoulders, and threw me down the steps. I understood later that he was a picket, on the alert for people who had been served by "scabs," and the labels on my bag had told the story. Amazed at such treatment, I asked a bystander for the explanation. His reply was, "It's a free country, isn't it?"

That same day the papers told of a huge dinner given to celebrate the visit of Lord Northcliffe. Everyone in New York seemed to be on the speakers' list, and Northcliffe did not get the

---

* The Ware Lecture, 1941. Published in the *Christian Register*, CXX (September 1941), 275-77, 297.

floor until after midnight. He raised a glass of water to the huge American flag that covered the ceiling of the hall and said he would toast "to the land of the free and the home of the brave, where you do as you please, and if you don't, they make you."

Everything that can be said about "freedom" lies between those two statements: "It's a free country, isn't it?" and "the land of the free and the home of the brave, where you do as you please, and if you don't, they make you." Perhaps the best way of drawing the thing into focus is to discuss the claims recently put forward by two spokesmen for the generation that was young in 1917, Professor Pitirim A. Sorokin of Harvard University [1] and Walter Lippmann.[2]

Professor Sorokin believes that the United States is now in a period comparable to that of the decline of the Roman Empire, because our youth is "fat and lazy" and "morally and physically softened." He proposes revolutionary entrance examinations for an ideal educational system whereby the young men would be tempted by a flock of Hollywood beauties reclining on luxurious lounges beside tables piled high with rich foods. If a student could pass up these temptations for three days, he would be regarded as "incorruptible" and his higher education would begin. Professor Sorokin obviously thinks that the main sources of corruption in modern youth are the sins which the Old Testament designates as "lust" and "gluttony."

Professor Sorokin's diagnosis and prescription probably throw more light on his own generation than on the twenty-year-olds now in college. Twenty years' experience among students leads me to say that if there are sins of which the present college generation is *NOT* guilty, they are the sins of which Dr. Sorokin is thinking. This complaint of the "soft" living of our youth is the characteristic smokescreen behind which adults hide their own responsibility. To those among us who have seen the gallant struggles which young people have made in the past decade to overcome unparalleled economic and social handicaps, such preachment will sound like verbal hogwash. Sorokin apparently said nothing about the sin which is abundantly more responsible for the corruption of Western democratic leadership: the drive to sacrifice all other values to "getting by," the prevalent "career-ism," of which one of the more vulgar academic forms presents itself in the temptation to tell the world what it wants to hear rather than what your conscience tells you it needs to be told.

Walter Lippmann's indictment of modern education is not so easily dismissed. He builds up a contrast between the confusion of modern politics and the statesmanship of the men who wrote the American Constitution and the Bill of Rights, and then proceeds to blame the difference on modern education which "is destined to destroy Western civilization" by refusing to transmit from generation to generation "the religious and classical culture of the Western World." Offhand, of course, we may first of all question whether part of his difficulty does not lie in the false perspective which so easily distorts such historical comparisons. How much truth is there in a picture of religious culture which includes men like Thomas Jefferson, Benjamin Franklin, and Tom Paine? Is it justifiable to speak of religious *and* classical culture as if they formed a homogeneous entity when the record clearly shows that these were two aspects of a cultural tradition which were frequently in conflict? Lippmann has come a long way since *The Preface to Morals,* and like many another modern he swings from religious relativism clear back to Thomas Aquinas and Étienne Gilson. Tempting as it is to follow these secondary issues, how much truth is there in the main thesis that the changes in character and in ability of our public men are due to the differences in the curriculum of formal education?

If we assume for a moment that the evaluation of the change in public men and in formal education is correct, it remains clear that the whole argument rests on the assumption that formal education plays essentially the same role in the total education of the young in 1940 as it did in 1750. This assumption is the fatal flaw in the argument. The significant change in "total" education is precisely the shift in the contribution made by the family, the church, the neighborhood, the region, and a variety of primary groups *relative* to the role of formal education in school and college. If formal education should follow Mr. Lippmann's advice and return to the classic pattern, it would simply bring out more clearly the deficiencies in "total" education that are due to the lessened "grip" of the other-than-formal educational agencies.

It is true that the schools are doing a number of things today which they formerly did not do, and did not have to do. It is not true, however, that we should return to the educational results of 1750 if the school should return to its 1750 program. For the stubborn social fact of the present is simply this: formal education is not supplemented by the educational influence of the community, the family, and the church at present as it was supplemented in 1750, and if the schools did not extend their program beyond the strictly academic program, *no one else would*.

An earlier pattern of formal education was quite content to reduce formal education to strictly intellectual, or academic, limits because the other-than-intellectual aspects of education were developed elsewhere. Modern insight and experience have thrown doubt on the validity of the "intellectual" discipline afforded by the classical pattern even in its narrow cultural confines, but the basic fact calling for a redefinition of the function of formal education is the speed of social change, the declining role of a number of social institutions that were formerly the very marrow of our culture, and the heavy reliance on impersonal social relations which inevitably accompany an economic system based upon refined division of labor and aimed at high material productivity.

A glance at the actual problems that face a school administrator in a typical American urban community is worth a volume of nostalgic generalizations. Church statistics show an appalling decline in the enrollment of the young—and for those still in its fold the church has become an anemic copy of the institution that preceded it. The family lives in an apartment house, the mother may be employed, the social functions of the family are in decline, and its limited size makes it imperative to supplement certain socializing functions in nursery school, which were formerly automatically discharged by brothers and sisters. The family is likely to have a social and religious background of rural stability, which has been changed within the past generation for the hectic pace of urban instability that characterizes industrial America. The twenty-year-olds are likely to be the first American-born generation, and partly because of our interest in "Americanization," their values and moral yardsticks are utterly distinct from those of their parents. Chronologically, the difference between parents and children is one generation; culturally, the gap in modern urban America is three or four generations if measured by the standards of colonial America.

In such a setting the shift in the educational effectiveness of community, church, and family has been so impressive that it would be criminal neglect of professional responsibility to ignore its impact when the role of formal education is under consideration. Nostalgic prescription of a program of classical studies, which may have served adequately in the past, is about as effective therapy under the circumstances as the traditional appeal to "tried and tested ideas of the past" in any case where the ideas involved were tried and tested under totally different circumstances. Under such circumstances the facts call for deliberate and purposeful reconstruction in the light of the total situation as it confronts creative professional insight, and the repetition of time-worn clichés is likely to be as effective as the best civil war strategy in modern total war.

The disintegration of social cohesion in our culture is apparent. We are losing faith in the shibboleths of the pre-1929 days which were based upon the assumption that all our problems were basically economic in character, and that freedom and democracy were essentially a matter of adequate, or even rising, standards of living. Prosperity and full employment of resources will mean larger markets and an increased scale of operations—and the trend toward impersonal social relations will increase correspondingly. I believe that the fundamental weakness of free and democratic society lies in this area.

We all recognize the peculiar suggestibility of the modern "mind," particularly in its urban manifestations. We are aware of the peril of sheer verbalism and sloganeering, and of the emotional appeal to the ill-balanced of the spurious "wholeness" of a dogmatic and totalitarian program. The discipline of totalitarianism appeals because excessive emphasis on specialization has made for lop-sided or warped development of personality, and the totalitarians appeal to this "lack of wholeness" with their emphasis on the warmth of the herd, their stress on youth movements, the discipline of rhythm and marching, and countless other devices.

When we discuss free institutions, we usually devote our attention to the variety of liberties, and specify such things as freedom of thought, religion, and assembly. We seldom speak of the nature of the free man who can be trusted with such freedom. We have drawn on the cultural deposits in our moral banks until the cashier ran out of funds, and now it is becoming apparent that the social cohesion which is essential if free institutions are to endure will have to be created by conscious and rationally directed effort. This is one area in which *laissez-faire* will not work. In fact, free economic institutions depend upon the stability of the social framework within which competitive conditions can continue to exist. Current experience indicates that the stability of that social framework cannot be taken for granted.

Freedom is always based upon shared experience and moral like-mindedness, and it is part of the danger of our present position that we have lost sight of this essential prerequisite. The remedy does not lie in the direction of more verbal instruction. Moral conduct is developed through shared experience. Purely verbal techniques of communication are part of our modern problem. A comparison of modern practices with traditional town-meeting democracy brings out the fact that town-meeting discussion had a fourth dimension in its oratory. The additional dimension was *time*. Men and women listened to one another, and because they knew one another intimately, they evaluated what was said with the yardstick of this *shared* experience over *time*.

If modern discussion so frequently deteriorates into mere argument, it is precisely because the parties involved too rarely measure the validity of what is said by a common moral yardstick. There is no agreement upon the criteria of truth, and the other fellow's argument therefore doesn't "make sense." Under the circumstances a kind of moral fatigue with the whole process of discussion sets in, and another prerequisite of dictatorship has been met.

The problem of freedom is therefore not essentially a matter of standards of living, and in this larger perspective it seems almost ridiculous to say that it is not a matter of reading the classics or even of "cultivation of the intellect." The crucial problems are not concerned with the definition of the rights of free men but rather with the recognition of the dependence of those rights upon the existence of a common sense of responsibility, or, in other words, upon the vitality of shared loyalties.

The crucial question is: What has happened to the loyalties of western man, and what, if anything, can be done about this?

Loyalty is frequently confused with a rather narrow spirit of patriotic devotion to the national government and its symbols. It is really much broader than that; in fact, part of the contemporary difficulty with loyalty lies in its constantly narrowing appeal. We are loyal to our community, our family, our religion, our profession, but it is obvious that contemporary loyalties are limited *by the dwindling role of the family, of religion, and of local and regional appeal.* In a national emergency a society with loyalties that are narrowed in this manner will seek its salvation in sudden sharp stress on the loyalties that remain, and there are likely to be overtones of chauvinism in this process. Chauvinistic patriotism is of course only a veneer of loyalty. It is likely to be intolerant of free personality and, therefore, ultimately subversive of freedom in general.

The remedy is not simple. It lies in the slow, long-run process of rebuilding loyalties of the most diversified sort. Fundamentally, loyalty means the dedication of a person to cause or purpose. In fact, the whole notion of personality is inconceivable without the existence of *purpose.* Training the young or retraining the adult for loyalty is, therefore, not a short-run process of routine drill, or superficial observance of patriotic ritual. It means the creation of opportunities for new loyalties or the reinvigoration of old ones, and this probably will take the form, first of all, of new patterns of direct participation. It is impossible to force people to be loyal, but it is possible to reveal new opportunities for loyalty and to teach examples of various types of loyalty through biography and history in general. Broadly speaking, this means a new emphasis in education on the contribution of personality and on the opportunity for dedicated service to a value or ideal. It probably also means a greater stress on shared experience in skill and rhythm, and a lessened emphasis on purely verbal techniques of communication and exhortation.

The discipline of free men lies in the pattern of diversified and interwoven loyalties that prevails in a free society. Freedom will endure, or rather, society can afford freedom, when men and women are each and every one dedicated to significant purpose in individualized ways that correspond in each particular case to the manner in which their own particular pattern of loyalty has been drawn into personal focus. If these loyalties are worn thin, the society will recover its vitality in an emergency only through central coercion. If a new pattern of plural loyalties can be rewoven to take the place of the shared values that have lost their grip, then a new resilience has been given our freedom.

The greatest asset of progressive society, if it has the insight to use it, is the renewal in every successive generation of the characteristic drive of the young toward dedication to things that go beyond self. The fascists and communists have caught this drive and channeled it for their own purposes. The free and democratic nations have almost created a "youth problem" during the same period by their inability to capitalize on their greatest potentiality. Instead of giving our youth a "sense of belonging" by arranging for their participation in essential economic, social, and political activities, we have managed to close avenues of employment to them so effectively by public and private restrictive practice that unemployment of the young is greater than in any other age group.

Last fall in New York City I repeated a suggestion which I made years ago in Chicago, namely, that some of the deficiencies in our present educational pattern could probably be met by supplementing our present college curriculum with a term of well-planned work-camp experience. I thought of the camps as a substitute for the balance that formerly came from informal educational agencies such as the family, the church, the neighborhood, and so on. The reception that was given to the suggestion gives a measure of the magnitude of our problem. On the left it was promptly labeled "fascist" because the Nazis have used such camps to achieve their own purposes. On the right my suggestion was promptly smeared with the label "communist" apparently on the ground that it carried an aroma of New Deal methods. It seems clear to me that we are likely to deprive ourselves of all effective therapy if we are to discard all ideas or techniques simply because some totalitarian government has already used them. If there is anything to the analysis which I have just presented, it follows that totalitarianism is a response to social symptoms that are also present, although perhaps in a less acute form, in our own community. It is therefore extremely

likely that they may have developed or extended devices which
if used in time and with sufficient persistence may serve to achieve
democratic ends.

We should hopelessly handicap ourselves in the race for survival if we condemned social means simply because they were also
used by others to achieve ends that are not our own. The important thing is to keep our eyes on the preservation and enrichment of the values of a free and democratic society. Anything
that can help us to achieve these more fully should be courageously put to use lest we identify freedom and democracy with
static maintenance of the status quo, and thereby give to totalitarian alternatives the undeserved attribute of progressive recognition of new needs as they arise.

We have gropingly stumbled on some of the essential strands
of the new pattern in our social work with youngsters in the
teen ages, in the scout movement, in the 4-H clubs of the
U. S. Department of Agriculture, in so-called "guidance" and
"activity" programs in the schools, in the enormous expansion
of summer camps as an educational supplement, and in a variety
of public programs such as the Civilian Conservation Corps and
the National Youth Administration. Characteristically enough,
however, the official programs are designed for the underpriv-
ileged as a method of public relief, when the primary problem
is to supplement formal education for *all* our young people in
other than intellectual respects.

If the church has eyes to see, and wishes to avoid a future in
which it loses all social vitality and becomes a purely ceremonial
institution, it might grasp the opportunity which the recognition
of these new educational needs presents. The present struggle
in domestic as well as world affairs is a struggle for the human
soul. Secularization has come to its present excess because the
church too frequently allowed the conflict between the old values
and the critical reason essential to free society to develop into
a stage in which—in the language of Erasmus—the identification
of scholarship with heresy resulted in the identification of ignorance with orthodoxy.

The present need is not for a diminished stress on intellectual
standards. We shall need all the intellectual acuteness and originality we can summon, but we shall be called on to reconstruct
the social and moral framework in which intellectual standards

can be maintained. It will take ability of the first order to recognize the actual and potential religious significance of activities not now recognized as religious. We may find the material for such a rediscovery of and rededication to plural loyalties in unexpected places if our eyes are open to the substance of things rather than to their form. We may, for instance, find more material about the values by which America lives in Carl Sandburg's monumental biography of Abraham Lincoln than in a good deal of conventional moralizing or in certain types of self-conscious patriotism.

Economics and technology have never been ends in themselves, although the "economism" of the 19th century gave us a climate of opinion in which material productivity seemed to be an all-encompassing objective. We are not very far from the time in which an outstanding American social scientist could say that the future of free society as compared to Soviet Russia would be decided by the movement of the index of the physical volume of production. The moral sterility of such an outlook helps to explain the speed and scope of totalitarian success. The workable, that is, effective, immorality of totalitarianism went through our civil as well as military defenses with lightning speed because we had nothing but a moral vacuum to present as an alternative. The reconstruction of the moral basis of freedom, the therapy of the will of our culture, is therefore as urgent in strategy as it is in the larger view of statesmanship.

The discipline of freedom lies in the diversified pattern of the loyalties within which freedom is exercised. We must create new educational instruments that will fill the void left by a declining family and church, and we must somehow restore the perspective to "discussion" that comes from shared experience. If religious imagination is alert and prepared to meet the challenge which a new and unconventional form presents, it may find a striking opportunity to give new relevance to the substance to which it is dedicated.

4

*Is Citizenship Enough?**

IT MAY BE HELPFUL TO OTHERS WHO HAVE A SIMILAR PATH TO GO if I introduce my remarks with some autobiographical details. If the road we have traveled in the last ten decades stands out with some clarity, it may help in distinguishing the static and the dynamic elements in the current intellectual scene.

I became a professional student of economics largely because I was a typical child of my generation. It was the generation to which Charles A. Beard was a great academic prophet. In a sense, my story during the twenties and thirties is the story of a continuous emancipation from the influence of the Beard type of "social science." Economics was to me the answer to practically all the problems that seemed to bother my generation. I was in my late teens at the end of the last war, and the First World War had colored my whole thinking life. It still is the outstanding experience in that life, and I rather doubt that this war will displace it. It left so deep a mark on us in that period that questions about the origin of war and proposals about its control —later on we spoke of the "cause and cure" of war—were the key to all my academic interests as an undergraduate and as a graduate student. And since the thinking of that generation of professors (or, for that matter, still the present one, although not so unanimously) inclined heavily toward assigning the responsibility for most of our major human evils to economics, I inherited the typical academic climate of opinion in that respect. In fact, I became an academic economist for that reason.

As you dig further into economic problems, however, you cannot help discovering that the economics is nothing but a

---

* From *Do We Still Need Religion?* Three Addresses and Discussions by Charles P. Taft, Harry D. Gideonse, Kirtley F. Mather, held in Town Hall, New York, 1942 (New York: Association Press, 1942), pp. 35-49.

veneer—sometimes a very thick one, sometimes a very thin one. Underneath you always find the old problems of human values, the ends that men seek to achieve and the codes by which they live. I have not the time to develop that. Any serious study of the problem of war and peace, which is the one that made me an economist—my special field was international economics— brings out emphatically that economics is not the basic factor in our modern problem, although it is very hard to convince public opinion because public opinion can cite all sorts of politicians, statesmen, and publicists who seem to say that economics is the important source of conflict.

But that proves nothing, except that economic determinism is fashionable, because a politician or a publicist will always talk the language of his day; and if he thinks that a particular genera- tion—the one in which he lives and that he has to persuade—is sensitive to economics (in contrast with political ideals or some other values), then he is likely to stress economics, no matter what his own beliefs may be, because that will be the way to reach his audience or to sell his books. However, this does not at all prove that economics is necessarily the basic motivating factor, for politicians in earlier generations, and in earlier centuries, talked "dynasty." The king had married so-and-so's daughter, and that was a good reason for going to war. Or they talked religion—I merely have to recall the centuries of religious wars in Europe. Or they talked many other things—things that happened to follow the fashionable way of thinking about the causes that made war legitimate. For some generations now, the fashionable way of thinking happens to have stressed economic factors— profits, investments, raw materials, and markets—and so the politicians and the publicists have talked raw materials and markets.

For a while, you may remember—in the last two decades— the whole country talked about modern war as if it were caused by munitions manufacturers, until we ran into this present war and suddenly discovered that this time we were likely to find ourselves at war in the absence of munitions manufacturers. The tragic position in which Great Britain and the United States found themselves in this war—nearer to complete and utter disaster than they have ever been in their history—is largely due to a completely erroneous theory of the cause of modern war.

Clearly, this time even the blind can see that our munitions manufacturers have not had very much to do with it, and that probably has killed the idea, for a while anyway.

I shall not follow that up further with a discussion of a more defensible theory of the cause of modern war, and I simply cite this particular part of my experience as a student because it is relevant to my topic.

The gradual emancipation from the erroneous overemphasis on economic factors is a very large part of the story. The stale and static language of conventional religion is the other part of the picture. It began to make the excessive stress on material factors possible because it seemed to deprive religion of dynamic social relevance. It practically forced us to rebuild from the bottom up. It will help explain, I think, some of the completely worldly ways in which we express things for which an earlier generation used religious language, and it is part of my thesis that the language itself is a large part of our difficulty.

It is precisely because the religious vocabulary has become frozen and because certain ceremonial practices connected with the vocabulary have not remained resilient and flexible that we appear to have developed a far wider gap between the generations with regard to values in religion than in fact exists. The challenge is partly to find new language to express age-old preoccupations. The traditional language has too often become purely ceremonial and, to that extent, dead. A new experience and a rethinking of old experience in which the old problems emerge in new verbal dress will probably reveal much greater basic agreement than some contemporary Jeremiahs suggest, but the new verbal dress calls for *flexibility* on the part of the adherents to the *received* terminology.

Now, if you think about one experience with social problems, you can classify the problems in all sorts of ways, and each and every one of them throws some light on the kind of answers for which you may be looking. I am going to suggest, for the purposes of exposition, that there are just two ways in which you might look at them, mindful of the fact that we could probably find a dozen pairs of alternative ways:

You might say, first of all, that the problems we are concerned about as citizens—social problems, political problems, and so on—are caused by impersonal social forces, by influences that are beyond the power of individuals, by the social trends of the time (that is just one of the fashionable words). In other words, the problems are caused by the economic, social, and technical setting in which men and women find themselves. They are social destiny.

And then, on the other hand, there is the notion that most of the evil that man suffers from is in himself and not in his environment. It therefore follows that whatever you may do about the environment, no matter how wise you are about economic policy, no matter how determined and shrewd you are in your political conduct, in the end, if the "Old Adam" (there you have the traditional language) is still the Old Adam, the evil will simply be magnified to the extent to which the Old Adam has richer and more sensitive instruments at hand with which to do evil.

Here you have your two possible attitudes.

The Old Adam theory, of course, is good old-fashioned Calvinism. There is a good deal to be said for it nowadays. If you will recast Calvin's ideas in terms of modern scientific knowledge about a number of problems to which we have more adequate answers, you will find that Calvinism—modernly implemented Calvinism—has as many valid answers to modern problems as you will find in any other single ism. After all, the notion that the origin of most of the problems you read about in the morning paper lies in "human cussedness" ought not to be so alien to our generation. Of course, if you use Calvin's language and call it "original sin," it sounds a bit old-fashioned; but if you say "human cussedness," which is the same thing, it does not sound alien to modern experience at all.

If you will, then, as I said, be generous to Calvinism and not take Calvin's words literally, but interpret him in the light of our present state of knowledge and in a modern vocabulary, you will find, I think, that such a statement would have a very considerable amount of livable truth in it.

I can almost put an exact date on the occasion when my modern faith cracked. In the middle twenties, when I was thoroughly indoctrinated with the notion that Calvinism was completely passé and that everything was due to environment, that everything was economics and politics, that all you had to do with men was to give them a higher standard of living and give them, by the intelligent use of government, a better political society in order that things would be more wisely ordered, in order that they would have better housing and better health, in order that they would have, in general, more education, and so forth—all the holy words of our generation, you see—when I was thoroughly and deeply drenched in that, I went for a summer to Geneva. There I sat at the feet of a gifted teacher, Alfred Zimmern of Oxford.

Zimmern was a student of the Greek Republic. He had done a grand book on the subject, and lived in a classical tradition that really had colored the whole of his life. He was a Greek of Plato's time who had migrated to the twentieth century. He interpreted the misery of European politics and American politics as he saw it (he frequently came to this country) in terms of Plato and Aristotle, and at first it seemed to me like a performance of *Hamlet* without the Prince of Denmark, because he appeared to pay no attention at all to the things that I had been taught to consider all-important.

I remember an occasion on which we were talking about the relations of employment in certain industries, including an industry in which I happened to have been employed during the preceding summer. There Zimmern came to grips with a situation in which the language was meaningful because of a shared experience. There was behind the words something that had been done, something that had been lived, and for the first time he began to make relevant to me just what the issues were, because up to that time I had not been able to see them. That day, after the meeting was over in the Conservatoire in Geneva, we went into the park. It was two-thirty in the morning before I took Alfred Zimmern to the Hôtel de Russie to restore him to his wife.

I particularly remember one of his final remarks. We were still arguing about this business of the Old Adam versus social trends as the real explanation. I was talking to him about the statistics (the social-trends people always have statistics), demonstrating how obviously if you got higher standards of living—meaning more quarts of milk, better plumbing, and better housing—you reduced juvenile delinquency. I was giving Zimmern obvious facts—and they are facts—about how the tuberculosis rate goes down when housing improves, and so on. Zimmern listened to it all, because it showed that I had not yet got the point. His parting shot to me, as we came to the end of that early-morning conversation, was:

Yes, Gideonse, yes. You can build pigsties, you can build beautiful pigsties, you can build huge pigsties, pigsties like cathedrals. But they're pigsties just the same, Gideonse, pigsties just the same.

The remark did not fully penetrate that morning because it still seemed irrelevant. But as the years went by, it became a symbol to me of my own road to Damascus. It is almost incredible to reflect on the extent to which the secular and material atmosphere of our time has hardened the shell of our consciousness so that we do not even understand the language in which the other position is being stated, because the climate of opinion of our time has become so homogeneous in that respect that any departure from it does not even attract sufficient attention to warrant reflection.

How have we come to be so blind to a moral tradition that is so deeply interwoven with our social heritage? One of the most outrageous distortions of history that you will encounter almost everywhere in contemporary America, and in most of contemporary western Europe where people have any opportunity to think about problems of this sort, is the notion that democracy, the free exercise of citizenship, depends for its vitality on a high standard of living—in other words, that times are hard for good citizenship and for the life of democratic institutions if people are poor. If you were to take a Gallup poll on the corner of Times Square, I think you would find that three out of four would accept the notion that the future of democratic institutions depends upon prosperity.

Now, historically, of course, that is untrue. Historically, in the United States, democracy is related, not to the high standards of living, let us say, of the Virginia plantations, but rather to the low material standards of living of New England—farming on rocks. It is also related historically, very deeply, to what we call the "frontier tradition," which, by any modern standard, represented extremely low material standards of living.

All you have to do, if you doubt that, if you have some ro-

mantic picture in your mind about a farm on the frontier being
a lovely, self-contained economy, with rich cows and dairy
products and fruits, and all of the rest of it, is to read a few
pages of the history of that time from any reputable treatise.
You will discover that life was extraordinarily monotonous;
that diets were so wanting in variety that diseases due to the lack
of diversity of nurture were very common; that childbirth was
a major risk because your next-door neighbor was likely to be
half a day's horseback ride away from where you lived, and he
was likely to know as little about the problems of obstetrics as
you did. So you can see what that did to maternity death rates,
what that would do in general to the material tone of life. And
still that is the period we correctly identify with the period in
which democracy put its roots in the American soil.

On the other hand, to make the argument even stronger, we
find serious questions being asked about the vitality of democratic institutions in our time; and our time is, in all our history,
the time of the highest material standards of living. It is even
true that those of us who are the nearest to physical starvation
—that is to say, those of us who have been unfortunate enough to
be unemployed for a long period of time during the recent years
of depression—even that group, if you look at it in the perspective
of history, is at a higher material level than the human race has
enjoyed up to about a century ago. You can find statistical proof
of that in the fact that our death rate continued to fall to historically unparalleled low levels during the very years of the
depression, and the death rate is a good index of whether
standards of living are adequate at their minimum levels.

No generation, of course, has perspective on itself in that
respect, because it gets accustomed to its own standard of living,
and therefore its low is likely to be regarded as *the* low. It does
not see itself as at the top of an escalator moving upward, as
we in fact historically have been. It is likely to think of itself
on a plateau, perhaps with an escalator beginning where you
are at this time. But if you look at the facts, if you look, for
instance, at the movement of the death rate over the last two
or three centuries, in so far as data can be found to trace it,
you will discover that these sober facts are true.

In other words, questions arise as to democracy's future as
standards of living, materially speaking, improve, and the fun-

damental reason for this disconcerting fact is not obscure. When an economic system begins to produce more abundantly, when it begins to throw off larger returns per capita, it becomes more complex, more interdependent, more delicate; it is therefore more easily thrown out of gear by a mistake here or there, which immediately has widespread repercussions throughout the delicate, interdependent system.

To put it another way, as an economic system begins to throw off higher material standards of living, it begins to be more and more dependent upon a high level of uniform intelligence in its administration, while a high level of uniform intelligence is not nearly so important if the economic system is a simple one. You cannot do as much damage to the simple gadget just because it is simple. But in the delicately balanced and complex organism the slightest little lapse in the coordination of a tax policy and an unemployment-relief policy or a foreign-trade policy can throw the whole thing out of gear.

Moreover, for obvious reasons, democracy does not automatically produce Congressmen and Senators whose knowledge of economics and administrative practice improves as the complexity of our economic life increases. Even if you had a Congress composed of the most competent academic economists, you would have difficulty getting sense out of it, because our knowledge in that area is just emerging out of experience with this new type of problem. So it is uncertain knowledge, experimental knowledge, and we certainly have not yet been able to reduce it to a simple statement. We have not formulated it for textbooks as yet, and we certainly have not got it stated with the elementary-school type of simplicity with which you would have to teach Congressmen these verities. In other words, we have limited knowledge at best, and the little we know cannot yet be made plausible on the political level.

There is another thing I want to say about history, apart from debunking the stereotype that democracy is "fair-weather" government, and it is again something that I think you can understand only if you try for a moment to see our past, not as we are accustomed to see it traditionally, but as our past probably saw itself. That is very hard to do, of course. The best way to try to see the past as it probably saw itself is to go to the books written at the time. To me, one of the most instructive books about the America of a hundred years ago is a book that it is now fashionable to quote rather frequently.

Alexis de Tocqueville was a very wise Frenchman. He had gone through the French Revolution and all the tribulations of the Napoleonic period, and he had shared the aspirations that moved France through that period of tragic experiment. In the thirties, he held a high post in the French service, but found the ground getting rather hot under his feet. France was becoming uncomfortable for anyone with his convictions, and so de Tocqueville had himself assigned the job of making a study of American prisons. He stayed here for quite a while and did a classic study on democracy in America. It is a big "elephant" of a book, but if you have time to read, I do not know of a single book that is more rewarding.

The book is full of prophetic insight about modern dictatorship, and de Tocqueville was very much interested in this problem, which is the heart of our modern problem. He observed Americans in state legislatures, in municipal councils, in New England, in Washington, down South, and on the frontier. He moved around among the trappers and the Indians. Everywhere he observed that, unlike Frenchmen who had also experimented with democratic ideas (1776 and 1789 were part of the same revolutionary impulse, and they sprang from a common French and American fund of political ideas and ambitions), Americans had made a success of their departures from tradition.

The crucial question was: Democracy had failed in France; it had "worked" in America. Why? Frenchmen, he observed, when they got into arguments about a tax bill, or on what to do to the soil or what not, got into great big philosophical arguments about the ultimates of life, about what your religion was, about what you thought of the fate of the universe in which you lived. They never seemed to be able to settle some concrete little problem. To them, it was always a big problem in which you were either a Jacobin or a Bonapartist supporter or a Bourbon restorationist, a clerical or an anti-clerical, and so forth. Inevitably, all argument drifted to that level, and the discussion then became an argument about that, and not about the tax or the land, or whatever was on the agenda. But Americans, by contrast, seemed to be able to get business done. Now why? That was the big problem. Why did it work on one side of the Atlantic and not on the other?

What de Tocqueville builds up is an impressive case for the success of democracy in America on the basis of the fact that America then so obviously had a very strong common moral tradition that did not need to be discussed because it was shared and could be taken for granted, and therefore was the framework within which all the other arguments were conducted. That is to say, you did not have to argue about your fundamental beliefs about the world and the way in which this particular little detail fitted into it. You could take it for granted that almost everybody in the Assembly had the same ideas about that; and therefore everybody had the same moral yardsticks with which to measure what was good and what was bad, what was wise and what was unwise, because you lived in the same moral universe. And de Tocqueville said that the deceiving thing to an outsider might be that if you sat through the debates these basic factors were rarely mentioned. In other words, it did not seem to be important because no one ever said anything about it; but the truth was rather that it was rarely mentioned because agreement on these important matters was taken for granted.

There is a paragraph in *Democracy in America* that might well be pondered by everyone who is concerned with the drift to dictatorships that is so common in the modern world. After studying the relation of successful government by discussion to the general acceptance of a moral code, de Tocqueville asks— and I put his question in modern terms: "Doesn't political freedom depend upon shared values or upon morally likeminded men? And isn't the freedom endangered as moral likemindedness disappears?"

That is a thought. Notice that it says nothing about prosperity or unemployment. It states the modern problem in moral terms. And isn't it true that the modern world has a headache about freedom and democracy because, under the same Constitution and the same Bill of Rights, modern freedom is exercised without the restraint in the exercise of the freedom that came from the shared values, the "moral bonds" of which de Tocqueville spoke?

You can put that in another way, if you please. You can look at it from the standpoint of a comparison of modern democracy —its Town Meeting of the Air, its radio priests, its newspaper columnists that are read from the Atlantic to the Pacific, and all its other impersonal paraphernalia—with the old town-meeting democracy where men—and sometimes women—knew one another well, deeply, personally, and frequently for more than one generation. Every word spoken in the town meeting was understood by everyone who heard it, not just as the word that was spoken, but in the perspective of the shared experience with the man who spoke it, so that you had an additional dimension in the discussion that sprang from the shared experience of the groups over time.

A man might have a silver tongue, and to us might be a great man on the radio or in a syndicated column read from coast to coast because we would not know that man as everyone in the town meeting knew his neighbors. Let us say he was the town drunk, or—which is less fair to him but nevertheless very relevant under those circumstances—that his father had been a ne'er-do-well and had failed three times in running the local grocery store, or something equally significant, so that his eloquence was wasted on his fellow townsmen. On the other hand, there might be another fellow who hadn't the gift of speech at all, whom we certainly would never invite to our microphones but who might be listened to with great care and attention no matter how inadequately he expressed his thought because he was known to be a pillar of society. Let us say he had been an elder in the local church, he had done this or done that, and so the shared experience of the group gave that additional dimension, so to speak, to his eloquence. It is precisely this shared experience that has disappeared in the impersonality of modern life.

That shared experience is the "moral bond" of which de Tocqueville spoke. It is that shared yardstick of the good and the bad that makes language responsible. On the other hand, if the shared values have become thin or are in conflict, the discussion is no longer anchored and moored in common experiences, and we then become cynical of the process of discussion. A sort of moral fatigue within the democratic process develops, and the moral code of freedom is weakened.

We should not become doubtful about freedom and democracy, of course, but we should direct our concern at the impersonality of modern life, in its economic as well as its political, cultural, and recreational phases. The American family, according to the last Census, has, on the average, not quite two children per family unit. I should like to remind you that this has bearing on a child's education because there is nothing that educates as much as your own brothers and sisters, particularly if they are rather close to you in age. The family is far more important as an educational influence than the school, and that informal educational agency has just gone out of the window with the birth rate.

I do not necessarily mean we should all have families of about eight children—there are objections to that, too—but I do draw from it the conclusion that if you remove, for one reason or another, a major educational influence from the life of youngsters —and in this particular case a conditioning influence in the moral area, disciplining you, socializing you—then you must expect disaster if you do not systematically substitute something for it. That is, you must expect disaster unless an educational routine is deliberately planned to take the place of what the brothers and sisters would otherwise have knocked into and out of you. That is how we get our "problem children," and that, by the way, is a large part of the modern problem of discipline and of the little egocentric individuals that we observe around us from the nursery school right up through the colleges and in professional and business life.

The point of all this is that we are misplacing our emphasis when we blame democracy or blame freedom. We are forgetting that freedom and democracy worked, and worked admirably, as long as we could take for granted the common, shared values, the shared moral experiences. The fact that we did not make that explicit in our Constitution and in our Bill of Rights simply meant that it was so obvious that no one had to talk or perhaps even think about it. It means that the responsibility for much of our modern problem of citizenship lies, not in freedom and democracy or in our lack of information about our problems and institutions, but in the anemia and the attenuation, the thinness of the commonly shared moral framework in which we exercise our rights as citizens in a free and democratic society.

In other words, the basic problem is not political. The basic problem is concerned with the change in the shared moral code of a free and democratic society. The moral like-mindedness of the past was largely a matter of inheritance. Now it will have to be reconstructed deliberately and by design. To the extent to which we can build back, in one way or another (and the methods will probably not be conventional because these have lost their grip to a high degree on the very large numbers of us); to the extent that we recognize the problem for what it is and make a dynamic and imaginative effort to reconstruct shared values through shared experience, not just by verbalization, but by the more difficult process of doing things together —exactly in the way in which these values were built up in the earlier period; to the extent to which we do that, our "problem of freedom and democracy" will disappear. It will disappear because the factors that made it a problem were not themselves part of the free and democratic institutions. Those factors were deeply rooted in the gradually waning effectiveness of the moral climate in which freedom and democray were exercised. They were not primarily economic or political but moral.

5

*The Golden Opportunity for Public Education**

YOU HAVE BEEN WORKING IN THE FIELD OF MENTAL HYGIENE NOW for well over a generation, a long generation, and you have made surprising progress, considering how limited the resources in human energy and in money were, and considering the opposition that you have encountered, even from such intrenched vested interests as the medical profession, which made it particularly hard to make a fruitful beginning. If you look over a program such as yours here at this meeting, you see a record of very great progress. It is made possible by a medical profession that has become increasingly aware of the inevitability of a joint attack on common problems by medical men and mental hygienists, and it is also a record that reflects a growing public interest in the entire area. It is true that the governmental interest is especially stimulated by the war-related problems of veterans, but it is a large breach in the dyke.

You have also begun to think in terms of the application of mental-hygiene principles to political questions, such as the relationship of your approach to the study of the forces that make Fascism possible. Personally I would prefer to have such an inquiry cast in terms of the more comprehensive appeal of totalitarianism because the tendency to be destructive of free human personality is not limited to the Fascist side of totalitarian practice. In general, your approach here is encouraging evidence of a widening social horizon, especially if we compare it with the old clinical approach, which dealt with the problems of the individual patient.

However, I am here to argue today that, with all that progress,

* Speech presented at the luncheon of the Thirty-seventh Annual Meeting of the National Committee for Mental Hygiene, New York, October 31, 1946. Published in *Mental Hygiene*, XXXI (January 1947), 14-28.

you strike me as being very busy—and glorying in you busy-ness —in discussing a scheme to change the saloon decorations on a steamer that has a hole in her bottom. From now on I am going to develop that thesis.

The quickest way to get to the heart of the problem is to look at what is happening to young people, to young American people. We talk about young people in terms of "education." We think we "improve" education if we spend more money on it, if we increase the salaries of teachers, and if we do a certain amount of tinkering with the curricula of schools and colleges. Most of our energy is spent in that direction.

Let no one misinterpret what I am going to say here. I am not saying that teachers' salaries or curricula are adequate. But under present circumstances, exclusive concern with cost-of-living adjustments for teachers or preoccupation with a re-shuffling of the curriculum is precisely what I meant when I said that we are concerned with the saloon decorations and not with the hole in the bottom of the steamer. Even if salaries should become adequate, even if New York City should pay its teachers as much as it pays its truck drivers— and you would have to go a long way to achieve such an exalted position—even if you did all that, and even if you made the most statesmanlike adjustments in the curriculum, you would still not approach an understanding of the gap that exists between what the school *aspires to give* young people and what young people in the end *are*—at the end of the schooling. I am referring to the radical shift during the past thirty to sixty years in the composition of the total of all the formative influences that are brought to bear on young people.

Traditionally, we think of these formative influences as, first of all, the family; secondly, the church; and thirdly, the school. Today, those of you who have any familiarity at all with young people will know that these institutions are probably the least important of the formative influences now brought to bear on a very large part of our youth. All we have to think about is radio, and motion pictures, and the pervasive influence of "advertising," with its very clever and shrewdly designed appeal to customers, and particularly to young people, who are not endowed with as much perspective and sales resistance as adults. Finally, there is the educational impact of the general social and economic pattern in which young people grow up. It will be suggestive if we can think of all these influences in their "togetherness" as a formative—that is to say, an educational—force molding our youth.

Let us begin with the last—those social and economic circumstances in which our young people are growing up. America had a "youth problem" for the first time in its history after the depression that began in 1929. Young people were unemployed in larger numbers than any other age group in the population. In the beginning we did not understand the problem, or we doubted its existence. Radicals exploited the unemployed youth group, and it became easy to think that the whole problem was a "Communist" invention.

Adults would react by blaming the young people for "lack of enterprise," or "lack of loyalty," and it was customary to contrast the expensive educational equipment made available for the present generation with the "little red schoolhouse" of more primitive times. Young people were not "appreciative" of the privileges they enjoyed, and it was even intimated that an education which discarded the "fads and frills"—and returned "to the fundamentals"—would soon solve the youth problem.

The facts were inexorable, however, and as the statisticians analyzed them, they began to tell an eloquent story. Adult America had learned to protect itself against "insecurity" by organizing every little economic or vocational sector of the national economy against the competition of outsiders or newcomers. We organized "against competition." We formed trade unions and professional groups, and made it hard for new people to enter the organized fields.

It is easy for a middle-class audience to assume that such activities are limited to bricklayers or automobile workers. It is important to understand that professional or business groups are engaged in exactly the same practice; doctors and teachers are forever "improving" their standards, with the net result that it is harder for newcomers to qualify than it was for the folks who are now engaged in the profession. From a general economic point of view, there is no difference between a John L. Lewis and a Morris Fishbein, except perhaps that the one gets a larger salary and the other has a more extensive vocabulary. They are both walking delegates for a splinter in the national economy—and they represent that splinter as against the log.

It is a daily occurrence in any educator's experience to meet a young man who would like to enter his father's trade—say, for instance, in New York, printing—but who finds obstacles in his way, such as trade-union rules, collective-bargaining restrictions, and other regulations designed to discourage newcomers. These things are not limited to trade unions, even if recent incidents involving Mr. Petrillo's activities in behalf of the musicians have spotlighted the desire to keep even students from getting a hearing.

Within a period of a few decades, adults developed this method of protecting their interests so that it covered the national economy with a network of hurdles against the newcomer. I do not argue that these factors were without benefits of a general social type. I shall leave that thesis for others to argue. Today I am concerned with the impact of such restrictive practices on youth. Essentially I have traced a pattern in which those who have arrived in a trade or a profession organize to establish higher standards, and these higher standards must be met by those who have not yet arrived. Typically, Morris Fishbein does not discuss doctors' incomes. He discusses medical progress and the scientific standards of public health. But then the plumbers talk about sanitation also. The net result for youth is that it is not as easy to be a doctor or a plumber as it was sixty or even thirty years ago. The net result is *restriction;* that is to say, it is harder for those who are not yet there to "get in." It is designed to create greater security for those who arrived early enough to be "included."

All these forces have been accentuated during the war years. To be sure, the immediate symptoms of the "youth problem" disappeared. Young men were at a premium during the war years, and the employment boom created a manpower scarcity.

The final research report published under the auspices of the American Youth Commission opened its conclusions with the statement that "it is perfectly clear that we shall have a 'youth problem' in the postwar period."[1] If this conclusion seems *perfectly clear* to the author of this competent study—and my own interpretation of the relevant data is in complete agreement with his conclusions—then it is even more striking to observe that "youth problems" are almost entirely overlooked in the present plethora of reconversion "plans."

The only agencies that have studied "youth problems" are the American Youth Commission and the National Resources Planning Board. Both ceased to function in 1943. Reconversion planners are busy with public "works"—politicians are concrete-minded in all senses of the term—and with the reemployment of veterans, and I am far from denying that these are vital issues. But if America should once again isolate its fifteen- to twenty-year-olds from normal transition to adult life, does anyone care to predict what the effect may be on the stability of other public arrangements? Can a democracy ignore the role of disaffected youth in totalitarian movements abroad? Is there any evidence to indicate that the present manpower shortages have exercised more than a temporary influence on the social pressures that made "youth unemployment" so characteristic a feature of the period from 1929 to 1939? Or are we, in a community that was traditionally more open to newcomers than any other in the world, gradually, by deliberate organization and regulation, trying to keep our own youth from making an effective transition to the economic responsibilities of adult life?

The answer to these disturbing questions is quite simple. Nothing has been done to change the pattern that gave America its first serious "youth problem" in the thirties— and a great deal has been done to sharpen the pressures that will operate when our present inflationary boom has evaporated. The solid body of evidence gathered by the American Youth Commission under Owen D. Young's leadership has been totally disregarded, and even Dorothy Canfield Fisher's unconventional summarizing volume, *Our Young Folks,* is now merely a college teachers' reference.

Every one of the forces that made unemployment in the "youth" group fully twice as high as the figure for the population as a whole, is still present—and many new pressures have been added to the old. We do not yet see these new pressures because we are still in the postwar reconversion boom and a pleasant inflationary haze conceals most of the disturbing symptoms. I am no prophet, and I do not know whether the readjustment to reality will come in six months or in six years.

It will not last forever, however, and when the great dis-
illusionment comes, we shall find some very disturbing new
factors working against young people. In fact, it can even be
said that the security programs of adults have become a vast
conspiracy against the employment opportunities of youth.

During the war, collective bargaining developed with giant
strides. There are now some fourteen to twenty million adults
covered by contracts which in one way or another include
"seniority" provisions. From the standpoint of youth, seniority
provisions boil down to a protection of the right to a job of older
employees against young employees, or against newcomers. "Share
the work" provisions in case of reduced operations give older
workers a priority in case of recovery. Job-guaranty provisions
give veterans a similar protection, and, throughout the country,
municipal, state, and federal priorities for veterans have created
a stupendous hurdle for the youngsters now in high school.
There are some thirteen million veterans in this particular group.
Their job priorities are priorities over youth. The law does not
say it in so many words, but that is the way it works out. I am
not arguing that the veterans should not have such recognition
of their services. I am simply looking at the result in the spirit
of a clinician. What has it done—together with all the other
restrictive forces—to the economic opportunities of our young
people?

We are in great danger of creating a growing pool of young
people—eager to accept the responsibilities of adult economic
life—who are excluded *by design* from effective and satisfying
transition to adult life. Such a pool of frustrated youth will
ultimately become a dangerous group, irrespective of adult efforts
to "teach" them citizenship and to counteract plausible "isms,"
unless we systematically organize for the equalization of opportunity for the young and inexperienced, who because of their
youth—a country's most vital asset— are not protected in the
competitive struggle of organized pressure groups for adults.
It is no accident that Communists found youth groups peculiarly
receptive to their propaganda in the years immediately preceding
the war. The reason does not lie in the ability of their leadership or in the effectiveness of their propaganda. It is rather
inherent in the treatment we were giving the youth groups

in the formulation of our public and private employment policies.

It is sometimes argued that tendencies to restrict youth employment opportunities are "inevitable" in a "mature" industrial economy. In such matters nothing is inevitable unless we accept it as such, but there is no evidence to warrant such defeatism. England is as "industrial" as we are, and presumably more "mature." English figures do not prove the thesis that juvenile unemployment of American proportions is inevitable. Such unemployment was indeed somewhat higher in England than for the population as a whole, but working-class children moved into employment after leaving school with relatively little difficulty. The reason seems to be a carefully planned wage structure which starts with a low initial wage and rises by smooth, age-related increments to the adult minimum. By contrast, American efforts at government wage regulation—and the same seems to be true of our collective bargaining—have established minimum wages at adult levels, with few or no exceptions for juveniles. Such adult rates are, of course, definitely discriminatory against youth. If a minimum wage is set at a figure designed to displace a minimum of adult workers, it may, nevertheless, have devastating effects upon the employment of younger workers.

If we should take the attitude that the drift of adult policy toward restrictive practices is inevitable—and many take this attitude without apparently sensing its implications—then we should study proposals for alternative public or educational, preferably public *and* educational employment for the youth who will be prevented from making the traditional adjustment to adult responsibility through private employment. If this is the road we must travel, current talk in some quarters about shortening the educational period is nostalgic and reactionary wishful thinking. Such ignorant reaction will beget frustration and irresponsible radicalism. Under these circumstances, imaginative reconstruction and deliberate extension of educational opportunities will be the only conservative alternative.

As things stand now—with a progressive intensification of the forces that prevent young people from making a normal adjustment to the responsibilities of adult life—we are certain to run into major difficulties as soon as the present inflationary wave of spending has ended. The simple extension of present educational programs will not be an answer. Youth will see in such educational provisions a type of "make work" project because it will not gear into the assumption of adult social responsibilities. The creation of a highly educated—in the formal, traditional sense of "educated"—proletariat can be a major factor in the preparation for totalitarian doctrines.

If we are concerned with the development of conditions in which free personality and mature democracy can develop, we should be deeply concerned about a trend to isolate a verbalistic education for youth completely from the adult world of practical experience in which achievement and functional satisfactions develop a "sense of belonging" and a sense "of being needed." Remember that we are thinking of young people with vigorous, healthy bodies. They have all the normal social and biological drives. They want to work and to share in vigorous activities. They need incomes that will permit courtship and marriage, and the establishment of new families. We offer them increasing hurdles in employment, and—at the best—an extension of a verbal type of education that is unrelated to the achievement of a vocational adjustment.

To cap the entire process, we submit youth of this type to the full impact of the major formative influence in American life —which is "advertising" in all its ramifications. It is an educational influence that completely escapes the control of the traditional "formative" institutions, that is to say, of the family, the church, and the school. Just think of the young people that you see around you—the eight-, ten-, fourteen-year-olds—and the way in which their pattern of life and expectancies is set by advertising. Remember, the overwhelming majority of radio programs are pitched on that level.

There is hardly a newspaper or a magazine that is not primarily a medium for the advertising fraternity. Everywhere on the radio and in the press you find the best talent in photography and in color as well as in typesetting skill, the best musical and the ablest theatrical talent harnessed to one dominant purpose. What is the purpose? It is to evoke and refresh new senses of need, new awareness of material want. Read any advertising textbook and you will find a chapter on "the creation of consumer discontent." The purpose is to make people unhappy with what they have and to make them reach out for new products and new services.

It is a bit hard to understand why our conservative friends are concerned about the *Daily Worker* and not excited about people who are spending their whole lives in "creating consumer discontent." We have higher material standards of living than any preceding generation in recorded history. We also have a greater measure of insecurity and discontent than earlier generations, and it would be hard to deny that it is closely related to the continuous assignment of so much of our best talent to the development of critical, negative attitudes toward what we have, and to the cultivation of an ever-expanding array of new wants.

Some of these factors have been an essential element of progress and of commerce in earlier generations, but there were also strong offsetting influences that built up a respect and a liking for stability and routine—such influences as, say, the church and the family. Surely no one is under any illusions as to the extent to which they exercise a comparable influence today. All we have to do is to glance at the divorce rate. It stands at roughly 30 per cent for the country as a whole, and—much more important as evidence of our trend—at from 40 to 60 per cent for currently contracted marriages.

That gives you a picture of what is happening to the basic, conservative institution in our type of social order, which was also traditionally the basic educational agency. It is not an exaggeration to say that the family is going to pieces under our eyes, and at a rapid rate. In other words, the basic traditional formative influence on young people is disintegrating, and no adequate program of remedial reconstruction is in sight.

If we look at the influences that twelve- or fourteen-year-olds at present undergo with regard to marriage, would you be disposed to deny that—apart from a small group that still lives in a family-church culture in which marriage is regarded as a sacrament and therefore endowed with certain sacred sanctions—most of them are undergoing overwhelmingly, the greater part of the time, the kind of conditioning that can best be summarized by saying that marriage seems to be rooted in a sense of smell, as illustrated in the advertising of soaps, perfumes, or deodorants in newspapers, in magazines, and in radio programs?

These are the things that are emphasized day in, day out. If we are realistic about educational influences in our type of world, we must admit that this is the formative influence that is being brought to bear on all our young people most of the time. Let us look a little beyond that and ask ourselves a question about the impact of this advertising appeal on young people who are surrounded by the restrictive vocational influences I have discussed earlier, and "educated" in a school system that does not make a joint appeal to emotion and body and mind, but that has become increasingly verbalistic in its appeal, teaching verbal symbols that are not related to reality most of the time, and therefore giving a spurious impression of certainty of knowledge. What are the predictable consequences when you limit purchasing power and block channels to secure it, while you teach a spurious faith in verbal dogmatism and expose people simultaneously to the appeal of an ever-increasing series of new material wants?

When the readjustment to normal postwar conditions has taken place, and the network of restrictive adult practices has had its full impact on the opportunities of young people, we shall have a generation on our hands that, from the standpoint of mental health, will be in the position of a bird looking at some beautiful ripe fruit behind a plate glass, and pecking at it, and being taught to peck more and more and more, while the plate glass is in the way, and very thick.

I have presented a very large problem to you in the sketchiest outline. My case did not rest on rhetoric or persuasive presentation. I have simply reminded you of a large number of simple facts concerning the social and economic framework in which our young people are "growing up." The facts speak for themselves. We do not often think of them as educational facts because we have a queer habit of thinking of education as the function of agencies and institutions that are labeled "educational." Clearly, however, these facts reflect major "formative" influences. They set the pattern in which our young people grow up. They represent the educational influences by which our youth is "formed."

When the problem ripens—and youth is once again set off as a separate group—we shall probably witness the same political and ideological exploitation that gave the word "youth" itself a subversive flavor to adults in the 1930's. There will be proposals to "solve" the problem by "teaching" patriotism or "history." There will be more or less adequate improvisations by political leaders, such as the National Youth Administration and Civilian Conservation Corps programs in the early period of the New Deal. "Educators" will criticize the political expedients because they will sense the germ of a potential federal educational system in these makeshift agencies, and conservatives in general will nostalgically idealize the "good old times" when schools "stuck to the fundamentals" and young people were "loyal Americans."

It can be granted without further argument that the federal expedients were open to a wide array of legitimate objections—but did anyone propose a more adequate therapy? If we are to avoid another wave of verbal radicalism—the color of its shirts will be an accident of the politics of the time—shouldn't we give some thought *on time* to the mental hygiene of our present practices and procedures?

The general public is aware of a difficulty in the general area of our educational provisions. It responds to various forms of educational quackery, such as the appeal to "return to the three R's," or the notion that if we would only read the classics (in translation) we might turn out another generation of Jeffersons, Madisons, and Hamiltons. It receives very little help from professional educators as a group because the vested interests in specialized scholarship prevent an objective and unblinkered view of the educational process as a whole. Above all, we suffer from an antiquated vocabulary which teaches us to expect "education" only from formal "educational" agencies, and this conventional classification prevents us from seeing the facts as they now are. That is to say, it prevents us from recognizing that the major "'formative" influences in society today are not under any form of educational control. Here and there an administrator—responsible for a more comprehensive view—throws out a challenge to rethink the limits of formal education, but he is promptly squelched by a flood of "expert" opinions which correctly represent the views of intrenched academic opinion.

Would it not be helpful if a group like yours, which is by training and experience better qualified to speak competently on the inadequacy of our conventional perspective in formal education, should devote some of its human resources to study-

ing our young people in terms of the *totality* of the formative
influences that are brought to bear on them? If a sound and
comprehensive study could be made available by such a group
as this, it would be on the books beforehand, and it would not
appear to be still another byproduct of panic in a period of
crisis. Such a report or study would strengthen the hands of
everyone in formal education. It would give a welcome outside
leverage to those who are presently engaged in a struggle with
academic vested interests that are primarily concerned with the
perpetuation of the existing "division of labor."

If we are to recast our educational structure in terms of an
honest evaluation of our needs, we must not tinker with a curricular modification here and there, or with the addition of a
few psychological and guidance gadgets in one place or another,
but we must seek our golden opportunity in a recasting of functions that takes account of the revolutionary shift that has
already taken place in the total picture of the formative and
educational influences that affect our youth.

Every generation has the type of youth it deserves. If we are
to profit from our own experience in the immediate past, we
shall need to formulate a careful and comprehensive policy for
the transition of our youth to adult responsibility in a mature
democracy. The time to build the framework for such "a sense
of belonging" is *now*—before we find ourselves swamped in the
predictable outcome of further drift.

You are rightly rejoicing in the fact that the federal government is awakening to its responsibilities in this field. I share your
satisfaction, but I hope federal funds and manpower will not
anchor your interests too solidly in a concern with the problems
of veterans or with the problems of individual patients. It is far
too important that we should ask more questions about the total
framework in which these symptoms are becoming ever more
prevalent, and ever more common. We are in some danger of
treating mental disease in its symptoms rather than its causes,
as if a medical man were to treat smallpox as if it were a skin
disease.

I have a good example from another field. This may be a bit
provocative to you. When we talk about city planning, some of
the most useful human resources can be found amongst the people who participate in an intelligent way in the real-estate busi-

ness. They know that problem. It is very difficult, however, to use such experienced ability in city planning because so many people in this group have a property-vested interest in urban congestion.

There is a similar possibility in the field of mental hygiene. It is comparatively easy to interest private and public supporters in the treatment of individual patients, and in research concerning such treatment. Funds are available for such work, and careers can be made in it. Professionally, there is a temptation to take the line of least resistance. Questions about the general social and economic framework in which such symptoms increase are not popular, and their study is less likely to afford a handsome professional income than the exploitation of the Park Avenue trade in autobiographical recitations in a social vacuum.

If we had trained brains in abundance, we could afford such conspicuous consumption of psychoanalytical flattery. Socially and politically, the hour is rather late, and if we are really concerned with safeguarding free personality and developing mature democracy, a comprehensive study of the total impact of all the formative influences at work on young people today is overdue.

I want to close these remarks—which are a bit Cassandra-like, and quite deliberately so—with two quotations from *Time*. They bring the subject "up to date"—down to the last minute.

The first is a success story on the part of the U. S. Army. It reports joyfully that it will no longer have to use the compulsions of the Selective Service System because voluntary enlistments are increasing rapidly enough to warrant dispensing with the draft. The army then told the story of its successful drive for volunteers, and *Time*[2] reproduced the most effective army poster. At least one reader looked at it with dismay.

It was a poster in which you saw an attractive young woman sitting in a chair, and an attractive young man sitting in another chair, obviously at leisure, "enjoying life," and both very young. I think the one was knitting and the other was reading a comic. The gentleman wore golf stockings and he was smoking a pipe. Clearly a case of leisure-class appeal. There they sit. How did they get there? Well, the poster makes it very clear. He joined the army at seventeen, and he retired on a pension at thirty-seven.

The appeal was: Join at seventeen if you want to retire at

thirty-seven—if you want to sit in a chair, as these two are sitting, for the rest of your life.

That was the most successful army poster in this Year of our Lord, 1946, in America, which has always prided itself on the self-reliant men and women who founded this country. That is not theory. The army's success with this poster should not be overlooked among the clinical data about the state we are in today.

Secondly, and this will be my final quotation, in the same issue of *Time* there is a long interview with an old American writer, perhaps our most successful dramatist, Eugene O'Neill. It was a very interesting interview. O'Neill was speaking of his own experience with Americans, and with the theater, and then they asked him a question about the "success" of his work, and he spoke as follows—and remember this is not a college president speaking, this is not a bishop or the president of the Federal Council of Churches; this is Eugene O'Neill, thoroughly emancipated secular spirit, quite independent of the stereotypes of conventional American life:

It's very sad, but there are no values to live by to-day. . . . Anything is permissible if you know the angles. I feel, in that sense, that America is the greatest failure in history. It was given everything, more than any other country in history, but we've squandered our soul by trying to possess something outside it, and we'll end, as that game usually does, by losing our soul and the thing outside it too. But why go on—the Bible said it much better: 'For what shall it profit a man if he gain the whole world and lose his own soul?' There is a feeling around, or I'm mistaken, of fate, Kismet, the negative fate, not in the Greek sense. It's struck me as time goes on, how something funny, even farcical, can suddenly without any apparent reason, break up into something gloomy and tragic.[3]

I rest my case with that.

6

Free Science and
the Security of an Open Society*

MAY I BEGIN BY MAKING IT QUITE CLEAR THAT I DO NOT SPEAK OF science with the professional authority of a scientist. It is true that I was engaged in chemical research almost a generation ago, including joint authorship of a few papers read at meetings of the American Chemical Society. But that was a long time ago, and I do not even claim the ability to understand the papers read at current meetings of the same type.

I am speaking of the problems of free science as a student of the type of society in which science has prospered in the past. I am speaking quite specifically from the standpoint of such experience as may be acquired in the discharge of administrative responsibilities, which include keeping scientists happy as professional workers, as teachers, and as research men. I am also speaking from the vicarious experience which may result from discussions with others who have had comparable duties. My problem here today can be formulated in the following question: What are the cultural conditions in which free science has prospered and developed? How should we administer a structure—public or private—in which the full potentialities of science are realized? And what are some of the hazards that we must consider in this area as we look at the problems we face in America today?

It is a commonplace to observe that scientific and technical changes have consequences in the social and moral fields which are no part of the design or intent of scientific workers. Ideological conservatives are always reminding us that social change has been a part of the experience of the human race since Adam and Eve left the Garden of Eden. It is true, nevertheless, that there

---

* From *Education for the Preservation of Democracy*, a Report of the Thirteenth Educational Conference, New York City, October 28 and 29, 1948 (Washington, D.C.: American Council on Education [©1949]), pp. 23-29.

are questions of relative speed of change: any one who gives a little thought to the possible consequences in the economic, political, legal, and even constitutional fields of the military, as well as civilian, implications of atomic fission is likely to conclude that we face an enormous acceleration of social change in the next few decades. We could contemplate the possibility with more equanimity if we could take international peace for granted. However, military or scientific disarmament is improbable if suitable security safeguards are not provided by such limitations of national sovereignty as are inherent in minimum provisions for international control and supervision. Such international security provisions do not appear to be in the cards for this generation, and although this is a stupendous challenge to the moral and intellectual genius of our time, I shall not deal with it any further here.

As a social scientist myself, I also wish to state quite explicitly another limitation in the definition of my present problem. It is clear that we might bridge the widening gap between scientific and technical change, on the one hand, and the moral, social, and legal framework of society, on the other hand, by a more intensive study of the problems and techniques of adjustment that are requisites of minimum assurance of stability. The various social sciences may have a great deal to contribute in this field—as is obvious from even a cursory study of the work of men like William F. Ogburn—but we are politically unprepared for the acceptance of these intellectual possibilities. The same legislators who press for large federal subsidies for additional physical and technical research refuse to appropriate funds to study the social and economic byproducts of the progress in the physical sciences. It is difficult to understand the difference between the advocacy of and the study of social change, and the likelihood of radical social change is increased by the unwillingness to promote scholarly study of the social implications of unplanned and cumulative scientific and technical change. Many of our best legislative minds still confuse social science with collectivist propaganda, and unconsciously help to promote the latter by their refusal to support the former. We may deeply regret such a refusal to listen to the voice of reason, but a realist will admit that the problem of the survival of a free society in the immediate future will have to be tackled with a full awareness of the intellectual and emotional limitations of the legislative mind.

Science has been—and will continue to be—a major factor in the defense of an open society. There is today an enormous public interest in the physical and biological sciences. It expresses itself in public appropriations that may even be in excess of the research and creative potentialities that are immediately available. It springs from admiration of the role played by science in World War II, and from concern about the role science may play in a possible World War III. It is part and parcel of the fear of sabotage and espionage, and it expresses itself in the elaboration and enforcement of a variety of "security" provisions. Some of these provisions or procedures attract public attention, such as the stories in the *New York Herald Tribune* about the scientist whose "loyalty" was questioned because his landlord found a copy of the *New Masses* in the family garbage (which could happen even to a rabid "red baiter" with some slight concern for documentation), or his colleague who was deemed unfit for national service because he had "a relative who was married to a Communist" (which could happen in the most patriotic family). Others do not attract public attention, but their experience is part of the atmosphere or climate of opinion in which scientists work. In the present Cold War, concern about sabotage and espionage is certainly legitimate. Concern about procedures designed to protect the national interest in science that may "throw the baby out with the bath water" is equally legitimate and, in my judgment, vastly more urgent.

In our defense of the vital interests of a free society, it is time to be sure of our first principles—to shed the husks and to preserve the kernel.

We live in an age of fear and propaganda. Some fifteen years ago a great President reminded us that we have nothing to fear but fear itself. Today we live in a climate of opinion in which the drive for security—born of fear and propaganda——has become almost hysterical, and in which we forget that we have just come victoriously out of a war with totalitarianism because a free society can mobilize resources that have been destroyed in closed societies by totalitarian practice.

Fear could lead an open society like our own to destroy its most precious assets in a struggle with a closed society of the Nazi or Soviet type. This is not beautiful theory or wishful thinking, but the very essence of our own experience in the recent war. The Germans were engaged in atomic research, and German science was no negligible competitor. Atomic research happens to be in a highly theoretical field in which Americans have not normally been interested in the past because of our drive to applied science and technology. But our doors and windows were wide open rather than closed. In accordance with the principles of an open society, we took men and ideas from all over the world, and as ideas from Italy, Hungary, France, Scandinavia, and even Germany played into the customary open and above-board process of scientific interchange and reciprocal criticism and enrichment, we ended up with the ideas and the technical execution before the other side did. *We did not achieve leader-ship because we observed rigorous security regulations.* The opposite is true. We led because we followed the true principles of an open society and encouraged quite consciously an open process of exchange of ideas. Most of the ideas came from abroad, and many of the men were citizens of other countries or even refugees from our own enemies in the war. Security was imposed in the final stages during the war, but, to repeat, we won our leadership because we followed the principles of free society and free science—and our enemies lost because essential men and vital ideas did not get a full chance to play into their own research programs.

It is vitally urgent to make no mistakes about these matters now. From my own observation of the security regulations now in effect, I doubt whether we are getting the benefit of the strength of our own position. It is one thing to mobilize scientists in wartime when everyone is ready to give patriotic service. It is quite another thing to impose controls in peacetime on a professional group which has a tradition of achievement that calls for the exact opposite. It appears, for instance, that special security folders are kept on scientists who have at any time worked on defense research. Should such security regulations actually result in discriminatory treatment regarding, say, the issuance of passports—even if the scientist is wholly patriotic—simply because of time-consuming bureaucratic procedures for checking security, scientists will hesitate to accept government employment. They will hesitate because delays in the processing of their passport applications may cause some to suspect their patriotism. It is hard enough in peacetime to induce creative scientific talent to engage in applied research. All the professional traditions and academic motivations are in the direction of basic research, and additional frustrating limitations or moral hazards will tend to restrict personnel choices to those who are moved exclusively by salary or seniority considerations. It is no reflection upon some of the able people now in the civil service to remember that the civil service has a tendency to select those who like their routine routinely administered. The challenging spirit of a creative mind is likely to be frustrated in such a setting.

Modern wars are won by "big" industry, backed by "big" laboratories and "big" science. No one who reads James P. Baxter's official history of the role of science in our war effort—*Scientists Against Time*[1]—can fail to be aware of the crucial importance of the relationship, or to overlook the extent to which it was the "open" and competitive character of our scientific life that contributed vital ideas from all over the world. I have already stressed the international interplay of men and ideas that made the atomic bomb possible. Perhaps I should not forget the vital role of Alexander Sachs's intellectual salesmanship in persuading President Roosevelt that a gamble of several hundred million dollars might be rewarding. The fact that an economist for a New York banking firm could know as much as he did of recent scientific developments is itself due to the climate of opinion of a free and open society, which lends itself to such relational cross-fertilization in scholarship, industrial applications, and public service.

The record of our scientists in the war effort is vaguely appreciated by the general public. But there is little understanding of the type of cultural conditions in which science flourishes, and almost no conception at all of the extent to which a continuous flow of achievement depends upon a constant and open process of interplay of ideas, experiments, and discussions. Those who talk about closing doors and keeping secrets—one Brooklyn patriot has even proposed that we "should keep our borders closed, coming and going, to domestic and foreign professors"—should ask themselves who would have had the key ideas in atomic fission if foreign professors had been kept out of the United States. Do these patriotic obscurantists realize that radar and penicillin came from England, DDT from Switzerland and Germany? What would be achieved by preventing the Library of Congress from publishing its *Monthly List of Russian Accessions*—as seriously proposed by congressional statesmen from the Republican (Taber) as well as Democratic (Rankin) side— except that our scholars and scientists might be kept ignorant of significant Russian contributions?

Security does not spring from control and regulation. It comes to a free society because the open exchange of new truth and knowledge affords a leadership that in a world of incredibly rapid change can spring only from a rate of progress and growth which keeps one step ahead of the "secure" and "regulated" conditions of the police state. Scientific information is like a fish that has been caught—it doesn't improve by efforts to keep it well preserved. We grow in science by casting our nets out anew all the time. Our true security lies in the maintenance of this process of casting out the net again and again, and it does not lie in preserving the "security" of the fish that were caught yesterday. The totalitarians had a theory that a state that was "totally" prepared for war would inevitably conquer the "unprepared" democracies. But the record shows that such early "total" preparation froze the economic and technical structure in a stage of development that was inferior to that of a society in which a large section of economic, scientific, and technical life remained open to experiment, exchange, and discussion. It is this same society in which, after mobilization, a vast array of new ideas and practices gave a resilience to an eventual war effort that would not have been available if "total" mobilization had been ordered in an earlier stage of preparedness to provide national "security."

There are, therefore, two conditions which a free society must meet if it is to maintain the leadership in science which we now enjoy. The first is the preservation of the conditions which have given us that leadership in the first place. The second is the development of a form of administrative organization that will preserve professional incentives and establish working conditions which will insure the quality of public service in scientific work.

If the government wants to secure the services of the ablest scientific personnel, it must arrange for employment conditions that evoke a creative response on the part of first-rate men. President Conant has recently stressed the fact that ten second-rate men cannot take the place of the one first-rate man in this field. If we need the services of the cream of the profession, we need employment conditions that will attract them. When scientists observe the treatment received by men like Lilienthal and Condon in scientifically illiterate congressional committees, they draw certain conclusions as to their own desire to submit to comparable abuse. The congressional assumption that you can overcome such difficulties by appropriating large sums of money for research ignores the fact that high scientific ability cannot be purchased like lard or pig iron, but must work under conditions that evoke a maximum use of creative potentialities.

Ours is not a totalitarian world in which men can be ordered around from trade to trade. We would not think of selecting a Secretary of Agriculture or of Labor who was personally unacceptable to farmers or to organized labor. When will our public men learn that the quality of scientific achievement depends upon the selection of men who can evoke a creative response from professional people? Are we, in a spurious pursuit of security, going to throw the greatest resources of an open society away because we fear the operation of the very principles that have given us leadership?

In a world of dangerous national and ideological competition, there is no security in provisions that make for secrecy about *past* achievements. The only security that is worth while lies in the *preservation of the conditions that have given us leadership thus far,* and those conditions call for open and creative interchange of all the true talent, irrespective of race, creed, or national origin. The way to defend an *open* society is to keep it *open*—let's leave the closed doors to folks who believe in them as a matter of principle.

7

*Political Education**

YOUR INVITATION TO ADDRESS THIS MEETING WAS "A SIGN OF THE times." I have been asked to discuss what in my judgment is wrong with our "political education." Why has this country been relatively successful in "shooting war"—and so tragically unsuccessful in diplomatic war? Have we neglected part of our tradition? Could the right type of political education help to save us from disastrous political defeats? What type of education?

It is quite an order, but it is obviously a responsible question. I shall range widely in my reply and there will be little originality in my reasoning, although some of my arguments may have acquired a new cutting edge because we have neglected them so disastrously in recent decades.

In my response you will not expect me to discuss details. The question is obviously directed to the core of the matter, and we must—in the favorite image of my former colleague at the University of Chicago, T. V. Smith—change the venue from the day shift of specificity, on which modern scholars and scientists delight to labor, to the night shift of generality where the philosopher in each of us likes to roam.

My reply can be summed up in one sentence: Our political education is weak because we no longer understand our own tradition. As a result, our political behavior and our political education are rooted in a misconception of the nature of freedom as well as of men. We have drifted into a preoccupation with the contemporary and the secular which blinds our eyes to the stark fact that in the running tide of world and domestic affairs our moral anchors are dragging. A spurious pursuit of objectivity

---

* From *Education in a Period of National Preparedness*, a Report of the Sixteenth Educational Conference, New York City, November 1 and 2, 1951 (Washington, D.C.: American Council on Education [© 1952]), pp. 27-46.

and "scientific method" has dehydrated the experience of the race as we pass it on to our young people by eliminating or underemphasizing the great imponderables of human history— the irrational, the tragic, and the evil—because they are regarded as an expression of value judgments and do not lend themselves to measurement. We end up with a collection of empty verbal shells, unrelated to experience, either our own or that of our ancestors, while our totalitarian adversaries kidnap our vocabulary, and official propagandists for the Voice of America develop stomach ulcers worrying about the conflict between historic reality and contemporary verbalizing. To cap it off, some American intellectuals tend to assume that a little psychiatric assistance would solve most political problems—including the irrational behavior of the Russians, which is pontifically demonstrated to be due to the way in which they wrap up their babies in childhood—while education, or propaganda, is regarded as the cure for the "ignorance" of our political leaders. Taking it all together, the political behavior of our leaders in the national capital is a model of responsibility if we compare it with the chaotic and unprincipled character of contemporary discussion, and in the modern jargon of David Riesman's *The Lonely Crowd*,[1] we may perhaps ascribe this reassuring fact to the dominance among middle-aged political leaders of the "inner-directed" who have not yet been sufficiently diluted by the peer group psychology of the rising generation.

Let me check these general statements with a few specific examples related to two key concepts in our political life: the idea of *freedom* and the idea of *democracy*. Who has not met the American enthusiast for the idea that the present "disintegration of colonialism" in the Far East is a victory for the ideas of freedom and democracy as we understand them in this country? Who has not heard the ideological propaganda—in the face of the fact that there are more Indians or Indonesians in jail now than ever happened under British or Dutch rule— that Indian or Indonesian liberation is a victory for "'freedom" in "the spirit of 1776"? What was 1776? Was it not the adoption by a young nation, which was a part of one of the most advanced political communities in the world and which was richly endowed with some of the most mature political philosophers of its generation, of the responsible idea that certain enumerated crucial liberties of the mind were beyond the scrutiny of government, be it the government of a tyrannical king abroad or a willful democratic majority at home? What is the meaning of the Bill of Rights— which the Founding Fathers were forced to incorporate as an explicit amendment to the Constitution before they could secure its adoption—if it was not a specific declaration of the limits beyond which a democratic majority was not trusted to go in its legislative treatment of "civil liberties"? Do men who begin their most basic legislation in the field of freedom with the words "Congress shall make no law" regarding freedom of religion, of speech, of the press, or of assembly, write in the sloppy modern assumption that there is nothing wrong with democracy that more democracy cannot cure? Or are they rather saying quite explicitly that democracy is a good thing *within limits,* and that the limit is transgressed when it is used to curb certain strategic freedoms in the regulation of which majority rule is specifically rejected? Is this the idea of "democracy" which is now spreading throughout the world—or is it rather the Rousseau idea of a "general will" that will "force men to be free"?

In other words: If "freedom" is merely the flag that covers a cargo of unqualified nationalism, is it not clearly a danger to peace and to "freedom" in the Bill of Rights sense of the term, and is not the currently fashionable idea of democracy as unqualified majority rule—correctly described by Thomas Jefferson in his *Notes on the State of Virginia* as "elective despotism"— the exact opposite of our own historic conception of majority rule qualified by a Bill of Rights? And have not some of our most popular slogans—"making the world safe for democracy" and the "Four Freedoms"—helped to confuse these basic issues here and abroad? When "'freedom" and "democracy" are taught as absolutes, they result in cynicism in young minds as soon as realistic historic experience demonstrates the need for their reciprocal qualification, and the issue is further confounded if still another group tries to implant the stereotype that freedom is primarily an economic concept glorifying private enterprise in whatever its contemporary form may be. It is not necessary to accept these apologies for a specific set of private interests to see a peculiar form of the current degradation of the democratic dogma in the present confusion of the idea that all men are created equal with the vote-catching temptations of the slogan that they should be kept equal.

It is a specific form of modern political heresy to describe our constitutional government as "an optimistic bet on human nature." The idea of "democracy" is qualified in our American experience by the realistic theory of human nature which our Founding Fathers took for granted. They were not all Calvinists, but even those who were Unitarians—take, for instance, Thomas Jefferson—lived and acted in a framework in which they assumed that human nature had elements of determinate evil in it as well as potentialities for transcending it. They *therefore*—and the "therefore" is important because it points to the political significance of a reasoned view of the matter—had a profound distrust of the consequences of trusting even a good man with unlimited power. The result was the elaborate provision for the separation of powers, the so-called "checks and balances," which in their present extreme interpretation sometimes constitute a major obstacle to effective and efficient as well as responsible government.

Government itself is—in the words of Madison in his famous fifty-first essay in *The Federalist*—"the greatest of all reflections on human nature. If men were angels, no government would be necessary. If angels were to govern men, neither external nor internal controls on government would be necessary. In framing a government which is to be administered by men over men, the great difficulty lies in this: you must first enable the government to control the governed; and in the next place oblige it to control itself."

The government described in *The Federalist* by Hamilton, Madison, and Jay was clearly an act of faith in man's ability to govern himself, but it was faith in man fully aware of his historic limitations, conscious of what John Adams had called "the efforts in human nature toward tyranny." It is not necessary to accept the dogma of the total depravity of man, or of original sin, to follow the reasoning of the Founding Fathers, although it is charcteristic of the method of discussion adopted by many of our contemporaries that the mere use of terms such as "elements of determinate evil in the nature of man" is sufficient to close their minds. The theory of man involved goes back way beyond Calvin and Luther to St. Augustine and the Old Testament prophets. Perhaps the argument would be more convincing if we avoided the worn vocabulary of traditional theology and ascribed the responsibility for the news in, say, the past decade's headlines to innate "human cussedness," and anyone who has had a chance to observe a child in its earliest ages is welcome to the view that all of the cussedness in adults is due to environment, diet, or psychological conditioning, to use only a few of this generation's favorite escape mechanisms. It is—to use Barbara Ward's words[2]—a curious modern paradox that "the most revolting forms of cruelty, the most appalling exhibitions of the lust for power, and the most frenzied search for material gratification have, in our own time, coincided with an almost complete rejection of the idea of sin." We can perhaps ascribe this parochialism of our generation to the general acceptance of economic determinism, to the popularity of various sects of "depth psychology," or to an eclectic combination of both of these fashionable philosophies, which some folks apparently can manage to achieve without incurring intellectual indigestion.

Human perfectibilism in one form or the other is certainly near the core of most of our modern political—or educational—fallacies, and it may well be that the theologian's tendency to overemphasize sexual escapades in the catalogue of sins has made it incumbent on this generation to rediscover the moral experience of the race. Any reputable religious history will reveal the fact that the traditional list of seven deadly sins begins with spiritual pride—the denial of God as an ultimate source of moral authority. Modern man, under the influence of a misunderstood "higher criticism" and a misinterpreted achievement of the physical sciences, resents the fact that political power should not suffice to remedy the results of his own weakness—which he is likely to describe euphemistically as "ignorance"—and in his impatient rejection of an imperfect morality he sets up an ideal of perfect bestiality. Pascal foresaw it all in his classical formulation that "man is neither an angel, nor a beast, and the human tragedy lies in the fact that those who assume he is an angel end up behaving as beasts."

Those who cite the experience of the race are labeled as traitors, degenerates, or reactionaries, and, as Michael Polanyi said, "by inflaming the mob's resentment of all historic, moral, or cultural authority, the structure of society is pulverized and its homogenized masses are made subservient to the arbitrary rule of the Bohemian,"[3] that is to say, of groups who had never accepted responsibility in the peaceful functions of civil life and who accepted support from hitherto politically indifferent peripheric masses. The great modern tragedy is the number of men who, obsessed by hate—of class, of race, of group—are ready to torture and "liquidate" their neighbors in order to achieve the Utopia of their dreams: an Aryan paradise, a "classless" society, a "mass democracy." Again in Barbara Ward's words, "The more convinced they are of the utter infallibility of their political creed, the more ready they are to kill their opponents for daring to stand in the way of the realization of Absolute Perfection."[4] "Freedom" in this context—as in Hitler's use of the term in German election campaigns in which it served to combat the Versailles Treaty, or in almost any Asiatic country today where it is simply a symbol of hatred for the "white" and a synonym for unqualified national sovereignty—has become a symbol of nationalist totalitarianism in which minorities are "forced to be free" in accordance with Rousseau's prescription, which included the death penalty for heresy from the civic religion, and in which the word "freedom" has come to represent the exact opposite of the values we seek to safeguard in our Bill of Rights.

The belief that the power of the state is *limited* by conscience and by law is the core of our political faith. It is, in our tradition, the essential idea of the Declaration of Independence and of the Bill of Rights, but in our colonial history and in the tradition of Western Europe it can be found in many earlier formulations. When the medieval priest and lawyer, Bracton, wrote that "the king is under God and the law," he was striking a blow at the foundations of royal, and therefore of state, absolutism. The whole meaning of William the Silent's *Je maintiendrai* ("I shall uphold and preserve") lies in its relation to the preservation of the laws and privileges against the royal drive toward absolutism. A modern American textbook in political science such as John H. Hallowell's *Main Currents in Modern Political Thought*[5] is anchored in the text that "conscience is the keystone of the whole liberal structure." Are not these basic ideas—the moral and philosophical core of our political tradition—swamped in a flood

of misinterpretation in which the Declaration of Independence
becomes a focus for anti-British sentiment in the twentieth century and in which a plethora of "current events" details almost
leads to a situation in which an act of Congress, or of the United
Nations, might change the syllabus and the curriculum?

How much of our smooth "integration" of the social studies
is achieved by virtue of what we choose to omit? How much of
our instruction in "history" is a concession to contemporary
politics—either of the author or of the taxpayer—and merely a
projection into the past of the values which some of us in the
present seek to pursue in the future?

We can detect the symptoms of a pathic condition today in
the "classics" of yesterday. Few of us are deceived today by a
collectivist such as R. H. Tawney, who lost his perspective on
"things as they were" when he tried to tell us that capitalism was
the social counterpart of Calvinist theology, or by a nationalist
collectivist such as Charles A. Beard, who told us in 1932 in
A Charter for the Social Sciences in the Schools,[6] published
under the auspices of the American Historical Association, that
"national planning" and social insurance systems were objectives
which the American nation seemed "to have set for itself,"
according to American history. It would have been understandable if Mr. Beard had argued that these were desirable objectives
for the future. It was obviously quite another matter to distort
history to make it yield the truths that suited Mr. Beard's current
political prejudices. In Beard's work the American Historical
Association Commission had carried us quite as far from Ranke's
wie es eigentlich gewesen ist as Henry Ford's dictum that "history
is bunk." As a veteran of that battle who published a careful
analytical study of Beard's report under the title "Nationalist
Collectivism and Charles A. Beard,"[7] in which all the nationalist
and isolationist implications were identified that became so
dominant in his later work, I can assure you that a generation of
scholars and teachers who sense a threat to their most cherished
prejudices are in no way superior to some of our contemporary
senatorial inquisitors with their musky techniques.

Today it is no longer necessary to argue the point. In these
cases, clearly, history no longer served to elucidate the present
because it had become a political tool with which to conquer
the future, and Tawney's as well as Beard's subsequent political

record has helped to open our eyes. An unpleasant question should remain in our minds as the final residue of the experience. Almost all of us here today may agree in our view of the utter irresponsibility of a Senator McCarthy, but it is surely sobering to the "liberals" amongst us that almost all of the *Chicago Tribune's* most venomous accusations of Franklin D. Roosevelt's conduct of the foreign policy of the United States can be documented with relish from Charles A. Beard's disgraceful political pamphlets published as "histories" of the "coming of the war." Is this not the same Beard whose textbooks were praised only a year or so ago as models of the "new" history? How much responsibility for the political education of that student generation do the teachers have who selected and prescribed these texts? This record of bias is now itself recorded history. How clearly do we see the slant in the contemporary output? If the social studies are to become an intellectual weapon with which we seek to ratify or validate our conception of the present or of the future, will we not have committed a "treason of the intellectuals" which matches the worst European examples cited in Julien Benda's classic essay?[8] And, on the other hand, if history or the social studies should degenerate to the status of a subject that is inoffensive to all pressure groups, is it not a certainty that it will have dulled the cutting edge of the ideas which historically are at the core of our achievements?

True history is, of course, concerned with making the past—including specifically the ways in which it differed from the present—intelligible to the present, but true history does not do so selectively as a tool with which it permits the present to mold the future.

If conscience is the keystone to the whole structure of free society, we might take another look at the extent to which we stress moral responsibility in the exercise of our freedom as teachers. It is surely a mistake to allow all our political education to be cast in the framework of the "conflict" between the "free" world and the "Kremlin" world—as serious a mistake as to present the period of the "religious wars" in the image of the conflict between Rome and the Reformation. There were certainly religious factors in the fanaticism of that period, but to place all the blame on Luther or on the iniquity of Rome is surely to overlook, in Herbert Butterfield's words, that "the real seat of the tragedy lay in the ideas which Luther and Calvin and the Popes held in common and held with equal intensity— the idea that society and government should be founded on the basis of the one authoritative religion, that all thought should be dominated by religion, and that within this religious society no heresy or blasphemy or abomination should be allowed to rear itself up in defiance of God."[9]

Similarly, there are certainly basic issues at stake between our free society and the area dominated by the Kremlin, but a historian of the future may well be inclined to stress that the real tragedy of our generation lay in the overwhelming over-emphasis by both adversaries on "economism," the destruction of the community in the sociological sense by technology and the state, a conception of human nature as indefinitely plastic material for psychological and propagandist manipulation, the use of human beings as means rather than ends, and even the practice of regarding religion as an instrument to serve political ends. My principal interest in this paper is precisely the iden-tification of the alien elements that have crept into our own structure and are destined to destroy its foundations if the present trend toward so-called "peer group psychology" is not arrested. I have no doubt that our national survival is at stake in our struggle with the Soviet government, but I have little doubt either that some of the tendencies I have traced may quite as effectively destroy free government here without the assistance of any exotic foreign ideologies or military power. As teachers we also know that there is less risk of a rebound into cynicism "on the morning after" if we present a conflict in power politics *as such* and do not camouflage it unduly with ideological absolutes that do not correspond with experience.

Fundamentally, I have been saying that political education in a free society must be moral education, or, in more controversial language, religious education. We are really concerned with the morale of free society. The morale of a free society is not the same thing as its morality. It is rooted in determination based on intensity of vision and clarity of purpose. It reveals itself in fortitude in the face of adversity. These are precisely the weak spots in our present picture, and they are directly related to our tendency to develop the state and church issue to ridiculous extremes under the intensifying pressure of legalistic conceptions of education that overlook the nature of the human beings with whom we are concerned.

There is a prodigious amount of nonsense in much of our current talk on the role of religion in education, and some of it is reflected in recent Supreme Court decisions. I shall not discuss these issues; it suffices for my present purpose to state the obvious fact—recognized so eloquently in the Report of the Educational Policies Commission, entitled *Moral and Spiritual Values in the Public Schools*[10]—that the idea of the separation of church and state can never mean that public education, or more broadly nonsectarian education, should be neutral about the moral basis of a free society. The law may forbid sectarian instruction, but the primary function of the public school is to strengthen the quality of citizenship in a free society. Public education is not neutral when liberty is at stake. Since liberty is itself dependent on the vigor and vitality of the faith of free men and women, it follows that public education is vitally interested in the growth and depth of the shared values of free society.

The contemporary appeal to young people and to "intellectuals" of both fascism and communism is deeply rooted in the destruction of community which has produced the anomic (normless) individual, the youth "without a sense of belonging," the uprooted intellectual and the "mobile" industrial worker, and the "art for art's sake" artist with nothing but a cash nexus to his society. They all sought the restoration of community in their response to the social appeal of the totalitarians, but they found a strengthened state that destroyed the free associational vestiges that remained. Those who see in our government only a constitutional text, while they overlook the free associational society and the moral philosophy which were its context, are supplying another example of the proverbial performance of *Hamlet* without the Prince of Denmark.

Contemporary liberals are fond of quoting the words of Jesus, "And ye shall know the truth, and the truth shall make you free" (John 8:32), but this is hardly an appropriate cover for the type of libertarian abuse that claims freedom to do "as you please" and even advocates—as is the case with the Academic Freedom Committee of the American Civil Liberties Union—that student groups that are found to be untruthful to college authorities about their off-campus affiliations should not be suspended or subjected to "any other disciplinary action." Thus we have come to the point where moral indifference to untruthfulness is advocated as a defense of freedom by a group of educators of whom we should have been able to take a minimum of historical and moral literacy for granted.

Liberty in the classic sense—in the sense in which the "truth" can make us "free"—means obedience to the moral law. "Stand fast therefore in the liberties with which Christ has made us free" (Galatians 5:1). It is to be understood in the sense of the old hymn, "Make me a captive, Lord,/And then I shall be free." Is it necessary to stress that this is the opposite of much current use of the word "freedom"? And that "laissez faire" in moral matters can be as disastrous to genuine freedom as "laissez faire" in any other area of social policy?

Liberty is like health: we take it for granted as long as we enjoy it. We value it when there is a threat we might lose it. But we enjoy it only if we live in liberty, as in health, in a way that is compatible with their preservation. There are principles of hygiene that must be observed if health is to be preserved, and there is a similar discipline of freedom. Freedom is not just "doing as you please," but rests on the cultivation of practicable purpose, and is rooted in awareness of this purpose in the light of the nature of man himself. The more powerful the instruments which a growing mastery of nature makes available to man, the more urgent the need for a true knowledge of the nature of the man who is to use the instruments. The so-called "advanced ideas" about evil being due to material circumstances, low standards of living, and the backward state of the technical arts, fly in the face of the experience of a generation with the highest standards of material living in the history of man, which is now anxiously asking whether human life itself may not cease to exist within another decade or so. The greater the power of man, the more terrible the consequences of his weakness. The problem is clearly not the control of nature or the control of material circumstances. It is the control of man.

Totalitarianism is one answer to the demand for such control. In studying the problems to which it has given rise—and of which it is itself merely an expression—there is nothing more stale than the views of the "moderns" of yesterday who, in rebellion against the discipline of religious and humanist tradition which they have never understood, militantly attack the unmanned trenches of a deserted battlefield of a war that lives only in the history books. There is a sharper cutting edge to the insights of the Old Testament prophets or of Shakespeare, not to speak of Plato and Aristotle, than there is in the empty echoes of nineteenth century materialist secularism such as that of Harold Laski who, in the face of the bankruptcy of everything he had taught for a lifetime, could still proclaim in a lecture in New York City shortly before his death that "we must begin with the assumption that the sole method open to mankind by which he can improve his lot is an increasing mastery of nature."

Even the developments in atomic energy had not yet taught Mr. Laski that to call for increasing mastery of nature in the absence of increasing moral restraint is, in fact, to intensify the pressure making for totalitarian political control. Our Founding Fathers showed that they understood this when they established a new Constitution that reflected their full awareness of the political temptations to which man is susceptible. A realistic view of the nature of man is the basis of all the great common insights of the Old as well as the New Testament. It is reflected in all our great religious and humanist literature. Shakespeare knew it when he let one of his characters say that "appetite, a universal wolf,/So doubly seconded with will and power,/Must make perforce a universal prey,/And last eat up himself." The remedy is not—as Mr. Laski said—"more will and power" but— as this generation is learning in blood and sweat—it lies in a controlled "appetite." The kingdom of this world can flourish and grow strong only so long as it sets its sights by standards that do not come from laboratories, dictators, or even democratic majorities.

Modern politics all over the world is still blinded by the light of dead stars. We talk about the "right" and "left" of Victorian days, although it is plain to the untutored eye that the extreme "left" and the extreme "right" have merged into indistinguishable black reaction.

The Communists are still peddling their old bag of divisive tricks, trying very hard to promote anti-Americanism, anti-Negroism, anti-Semitism, anti-Christianism, as well as all the old class struggle ideology, but the running tide of postwar politics has found a new channel that gives a bleak and shrill sound to their stale echo of nineteenth century agitation. Everywhere we sense, in a vague and groping way, that the remedies do not lie in purely economic programs but that communist as well as fascist totalitarians have been able to subvert liberty, irrespective of rising material standards, because freedom is secure only in a world of spiritual checks and in political institutions that are rooted in a realistic theory of man.

American and European politicians still think in the framework of a dead ideological past when they apply economic yardsticks to every program, or prescribe economic remedies for every problem. In view of the toughness of the Old Adam it is just as silly to predict the early extinction of man as it is to assume that the only barrier to the perfectibility of man is the absence of a little more technology, or of a more varied diet, or of some improved plumbing gadgets. The new trends in politics—and they can be found all over the world—supply the first healthy reaction against the dominant materialism of the Western as well as the Soviet world.

In the depths of the depression, an author in the *New Republic*, who was anxiously admitting that something had gone sour with the great Soviet experiment, proposed seriously to save the "ideals" of the revolution "by taking communism away from the Communists." In a similar spirit, a serious interest in political education—which is always, in the classic sense of the term, "conservative," that is to say, responsible for continuity—may well lead us to inquire whether we should "take conservatism away from the conservatives." We have plenty of "conservatism" in contemporary America in the sense of defense of the status quo, private enterprise, and "constitutionalism." If my experience is typical, teachers receive a ton of such propagandistic print for every ounce of so-called "liberal" literature. It has a common emphasis upon "liberty" but it has—as Reinhold Niebuhr has well said in a trenchant article in the *Yale Review* of March 1951 —about the same relationship to classical liberalism as Herbert Hoover's book entitled *The Challenge to Liberty*[11] has to John Stuart Mill's book, *On Liberty*. In this literature, "freedom" has become an ideological façade behind which a certain type of economic vested interest seeks to preserve its "liberty" against a more broadly based political power, and this type of conservatism is primarily concerned with establishing the stereotype in the public mind that the most effective methods democracies have developed to refute Marxist prophecies of doom are themselves a malignant malady of free society. Politically and intellectually incompetent, they even confuse Keynes and Marx, and drive youth to more extreme positions since accommodation and adjustment are precluded. It is characteristic that the position has become so ossified that vigorous intellectual restatements of the economic possibility of using political power to restore competitive controls—such as Henry C. Simons' *Economic Policy for a Free Society*[12] and David McCord Wright's *Democracy and Progress*[13] and *Capitalism*[14]—are rejected as "socialistic," a position that would on further analysis lead to sticking the same label on Alexander Hamilton, Abraham Lincoln, or Woodrow Wilson.

American conservatism has become so heavily "economic"— in the narrow sense of a commitment to the orthodoxy of the McKinley period minus the Sherman Act—that it presents itself quite unwittingly in the form of a Marxist caricature of itself. In Niebuhr's words:

Such a community predicates its operation upon the containment of the various egoistic drives, individual and collective, within the nicely circumscribed balances of a competitive market. In this realm, life is neither noble, tragic, nor demonic, and the purposes of life are never incalculable. Realists in this world readily assume the force of human selfishness, but they also believe that it is confined to the desire for gain. Hence they are oblivious to the dynamic of the idolatrous political religions of our day, whether Nazi or Communist. The idealists of the same world find its chief moral glory in the fact that it repudiates the overt use of force—of which bourgeois culture has a horror —but they do not comprehend the endless complexities of power and the covert forms of force in a human community. Economic power—as distinguished from political and military power—is, in fact, so lacking in the symbols of force that it is easy to describe its operation in purely moral terms, and to hide, either sentimentally or hypocritically, the power elements in economic competition.[15]

The failure to understand "power" is characteristic. Somehow the American climate of opinion has been drenched with the idea that power is evil *in* and *of* itself. The idea would have been unintelligible to the generation that wrote *The Federalist.* Historically, power and policy are always inextricably interwoven, and there is "power politics" in any situation—including the election of a Faculty Executive Committee or the officers of a Ladies Aid Society—in which the answer is sought to the question: Who is running things?

Perhaps our rigorous separation constitutionally of civilian and military responsibilities has contributed its share to the weakness of our political tradition in this respect. The obvious and desirable purpose of the separation was to insure civilian supremacy in the use of military power. It is a measure of the political illiteracy of the present generation of American "conservatives" that they can combine a general plea for freedom and for "constitutionalism" with the acceptance of the slogan that we should "free the military from State Department control." Our constitutional separation of *function* has led to a separation of *thought* which is hardly exaggerated in the statement that we seem to insist that policy ends at the point where the use of force begins. The political vacuum in which our Joint Chiefs of Staff operate is a current example, and congressional insistence in the Korean issue upon clarifying political questions by testimony from military sources is another indication of the deep-seated confusion that surrounds this area in our political life.

Historical illustrations abound. Our military leaders may differ in many ways as widely as, say, General MacArthur and General Eisenhower, but our "separation" of civilian and military responsibilities led to a situation in World War II in which it could be said that it was more or less characteristic of all our military leaders—Marshall and Eisenhower as well as Leahy and MacArthur—that they were inclined to think that the test of war was "victory" and *not the achievement of the war's political objectives.* The same thing could even be said of Franklin D. Roosevelt, who was an admirable civilian commander-in-chief but whose most serious political error in the management of the war may well be involved in his war slogan of "unconditional surrender"—a statement of a military and not of a political objective.

Nothing is more striking in comparing our military memoirs

of World War II with Churchill's account than the unreasoned American assumption that the purpose of the entire military effort was "to win the war" while Churchill never lost sight— although he lost most of his arguments with American spokesmen —of the crucial fact that military victory should be a means of achieving our *political* purposes. Whenever Churchill urged this basic argument on American military or political leaders, they had a tendency to regard his efforts as an attempt to introduce impure political motives into a strictly military matter, and in their reaction to such arguments they had a tendency to feel quite righteous about the purity of our military purpose. Our experience since World War II has shown us how empty a purely military victory can be if appropriate and relevant political objectives are not achieved by the military action.

Political education should clarify the historic role of power, including in the concept the efficiency of the political structure, the force of ideas, religious commitments, scientific achievements, and anything else that contributes to the strength and stature of a nation. Power has always been inextricably involved in the formulation of policy, in peace as well as in war. The "fleet in being" is an important political fact in peacetime and, on the other hand, the absence of American military power after Potsdam was a vital *political* fact in all our postwar issues with the Kremlin. Policy and principles are not one thing, and power another. Peace as well as national survival is dependent upon the continuous and realistic reevaluation of their inevitable togetherness. "Power politics" is likely to be most dangerous in a community in which "power" is a specialty of one group of technicians, and policy the realm of another. "Power" can be "tamed" only if its use is anchored in a clear grasp of moral priorities and in a realistic theory of man, including an awareness of the basic axiom that policy commitments should not extend beyond power means.

Reinhold Niebuhr's succinct summary is well worth quoting in full:

In any event we will be undone if we do not constantly overcome the two temptations of nations in our situation. One is the temptation to flee from the responsibilities which are inherent in our power. There is no safety for us in such a flight, for our power diminishes at every point when irresponsibility prompts us to sacrifice friend or ally to a ruthless foe. Furthermore, we have gone too far, culturally, morally, and religiously, to find it tolerable to gain our security at the expense of a nascent community of free nations.

The other temptation is to overestimate the degree of our power, more particularly our moral authority, in the calculations of world politics. This is true not only with reference to our position in the more intimate circle of our allies and friends in the Western community. It is also true in our relations to a world of uncommitted, or only partly committed, nations, who fear aggression and are therefore prepared for a general defensive alliance. But they are not prepared to accept us as the arbiters of their destiny or as the guides of their political pilgrimage.

The first temptation assails us in moods of despair; the second in moments of desperation. It is no sign of weakness if even strong nations learn to measure the limits of their power and the contingent character of their moral values. This kind of humility is an absolute prerequisite for our leadership if we are to engage successfully the shrewd and calculating foe who confronts us, and if we are to prevent both the spread of Communism and the outbreak of an atomic war.[16]

Now that destiny has cast America prematurely in the role of the world's leading military power, the need for responsibility, balance, and continuity is forcing a realignment in social and intellectual forces. There are healthy signs of reorientation in almost every branch of American life. In economic matters the Committee for Economic Development has been concerned about the elaboration of a program of research and education that must have deplorably subversive characteristics to conservative observers who are dismayed at the solid and enthusiastic support its activities are receiving in influential industrial and political circles. *Fortune* magazine is often the spokesman for a responsible political and intellectual reorientation that is reflected in part in Russell Davenport's writings, and specifically in *U.S.A., The Permanent Revolution,*[17] which presents in book form the contents of a special issue on "The American Way of Life" with special emphasis on the "problems of free men."

Intellectually, too, there is evidence of considerable reorientation. The rising influence of Reinhold Niebuhr is characteristic. It is not an exaggeration to say that he has become the successor of William James and John Dewey as the most read—

and cited—philosopher of our time. There is more relevant political education in Niebuhr's *The Children of Light and the Children of Darkness*[18] than can be found in a ton of civics textbooks. It is instructive to compare the naïve rediscovery of absolute evil in the European existentialists, evil "without mixture and without remission" in a "horrible, irreducible purity," with the deeply rooted continuity of vision and tradition in Niebuhr's work. In the former we find the combination of abysmal pessimism and contempt for man that is so characteristic of totalitarianism and perfectibilism on the rebound, while the latter is typical of the reasoned faith in man's potentialities for strength and charity that springs from a realistic view of his limitations as revealed in historic experience.

In Peter Viereck's writings we find an eloquent restatement of true conservatism in terms that come to grips with the weaknesses in our intellectual armor. In a classical formulation that cuts across all the conventional and sterotyped lines, he defines his terms in *Conservatism Revisited:*

The conservative principles *par excellence* are proportion and measure; self-expression through self-restraint; preservation through reform; humanism and classical balance; a fruitful nostalgia for the permanent beneath the flux; and a fruitful obsession for unbroken historic continuity. These principles together create freedom, a freedom built not on the quicksand of adolescent defiance but on the bedrock of ethics and law.[19]

Political education is a matter of compelling events as well as of textbooks and educational programs. *The Federalist* is the record of such a compelling historic experience. The new responsibilities of world power are another. Leadership calls not merely for sweetness and light, but for toughness and shrewdness in pursuit of moral purpose. To ask us to broaden our perspective and—in the language of a leading Harvard pundit—to remove our "cultural parochialism" by including the culture of China and India in our educational programs may be excellent platform rhetoric, but it raises the issue of just what the culture of the Far East is today, as well as the more crucial question of the ends America is to serve as a responsible wielder of unparalleled power. American power has never been mere force or wealth. We have had a specific faith of freedom that has given a moral edge to every significant expression of America's political purpose. We find it in George Washington's statement to the Constitutional Convention in 1789 that "the preservation of the sacred fire of liberty, and the destiny of the republican model of government, are justly considered as deeply, perhaps as finally staked, on the experiment entrusted to the hands of the American people." We hear its reiteration in Abraham Lincoln's words in 1858, "Our reliance is in the *love of liberty* which God has planted in our bosoms. Our defense is in the preservation of the spirit which prizes liberty as the heritage of all men, in all lands everywhere." We see it in a Kantian framework in Woodrow Wilson's words on May 17, 1915, "The interesting and inspiring thought about America is that she asks nothing for herself except what she has a right to ask for humanity itself."

These men did not broaden their perspective by absorbing the culture of India and China. They served the world as well as their country by plain speech drawn from the Western liberal tradition—a tradition (need we remind ourselves?) which is the only one in which liberty in our sense of the term has been a historic reality.

America today is in a unique position. If we shed the excrescences of limited political rivalry and separate the essential from the peripheral, if we remove the moss and varnish that cover the true grain of the original handhewn beams, we will find that America's best political service to the world of nations today will be its own rededication to the moral foundations of our liberty—a form of cultural parochialism that may serve as well today as it did in the days of George Washington, Abraham Lincoln, or Woodrow Wilson.

I have no objection to American students reading Confucius —it may even be a good idea for students in China, if Mao Tse-tung will let them. But if America is to make a contribution worthy of its past to the present world conversation about the rights of man, we must be mindful of the inexorable teaching of history that no culture has ever survived that had severed itself from its own roots. The creative energy of free society in America—its moral drive—has been embedded in our religious tradition with its Christian, Jewish, and Greek origins. If political education is to serve the ends of free men, we must recognize that a social science that is not committed to the search for a moral framework for the cultivation of freedom and justice has signed its own death warrant. We might fruitfully turn a new leaf and inquire with Burke, who in a comparable period (1791) asked in his *Appeal from the New to the Old Whigs:* "This is the true touchstone of all theories which regard man and the affairs of men—does it suit his nature in general, does it suit his nature as modified by his habits?"

If we do, we shall—in the language of First Corinthians—hear no "uncertain sound" at the core of our own tradition. "We are in the making still."

8

*On Rethinking Liberal Education**

IN THE RISING TIDE OF VOCATIONALISM—AND OF SHEER NUMBERS —the defense of liberal education has been conducted as if it were merely another of the vested interests struggling to preserve its prerogatives and perquisites in the colleges as the traditional home of lost causes. Ivy League college presidents address their alumni, and a cheering, gregarious spirit of self-approval is generated. The principals of "independent schools" meet, and congratulate themselves that they are not as other men. Esoteric books are written about the "spirit" of liberal education—and even the average college professor in the humanities fails to recognize his daily practice in their eloquent chapters about the "basic values of free society" and the "capacity for discriminating perception," while teachers of freshman composition and mathematics search in vain for even an awareness of the recurring problem of each year's new invasion by lovable but illiterate barbarians who have to be taught the elements of grammar and arithmetic.

Meanwhile, enrollments in the humanities—and more recently the social sciences—continue to fall, while we preach sermons to the converted, or splinter our dwindling ranks by philosophical civil wars between "rationalists," "neohumanists," and "instrumentalists." At the same time, the shrinking resources of private educational institutions and their superior talent for public relations have led to the temptation of identifying private and liberal education in the face of the fact that some of our strongest programs of liberal education are today conducted under public auspices. A similar confusion has been created

* From *Strengthening Education at All Levels,* a Report of the Eighteenth Educational Conference, New York City, October 29-30, 1953 (Washington, D.C.: American Council on Education [© 1954]), pp. 30-52.

between mass education and general education which obscures the fact that some of the most vital programs reestablishing the essential goals of liberal education are today conducted under the label of general education.

Meanwhile, a tidal wave of increasing enrollment is rolling along through the elementary schools, and within a decade all of the country's colleges will be swamped with huge increases in the number of applicants for admission. There are no corresponding increases in graduate enrollments holding out the promise of a new supply of college teachers to match the increasing undergraduate enrollment. There are no indications of improved financial or professional incentives to induce such increases in graduate enrollment. We are clearly drifting into predictable chaos and critical dilution of standards from which only a miracle can be expected to preserve or to recover a qualitatively strong pattern of intellectual achievement.

There are no miracles in sight. There are, however, a number of green shoots on the old tree, and I am selecting them for emphasis because they hold out the promise of "a tide in the affairs of men," which, if we "take the current when it serves," may afford us a new and perhaps final opportunity to argue the case for an education broad and historical in perspective that may be the condition without which free society will be incapable of survival.

There has recently been an abundance of new evidence that a case for liberal education is being prepared in the citadels of its traditional vocationalist adversaries or competitors. *Fortune* magazine of April 1953, in an editorial entitled "Should a Businessman Be Educated?" raised the basic question whether "business itself" is not "largely to blame" for its current experience that "overspecialization is robbing business of potential top-management material." Business—the editorial went on to say—can create its own "specialists" after it hires them, but "what they need and can't create is men with a decent general education." The editors went on to discuss some statistics they had collected about current trends. Out of 227,029 men who got their first degrees from 1,306 colleges last year, "less than a third took courses that by any stretch of the definition made them products of a general education," and the percentage of liberal-arts—basic-science majors declined from 43 in 1940 to 35.7 for the class of

1952. The editors also quoted some of the statements of leading management personalities, including that of Irving Olds that "the most difficult problems American enterprise faces today are neither scientific nor technical, but lie chiefly in the realm of what is embraced in a liberal-arts education." Shouldn't the "home office" be sending some changed instructions to the recruiting officers who visit the campus to interview the graduating seniors?

Similar sentiments are expressed by other business leaders, such as, for instance, Clarence B. Randall, who, in his fresh and cogent "survey of the intangibles which command one American's loyalty" entitled *Freedom's Faith*, says:

> The weakness of technical education as a preparation for a business career . . . when it is not balanced by participation in liberal disciplines, is that it leaves in the mind of the student the impression that all problems are quantitative, and that a solution will appear as soon as all the facts have been collected and the correct mathematical formula evolved. Would life were that simple! Unhappily, the mysteries of human behavior from which come our most complex modern problems do not lend themselves to quantitative analysis, and there is no mental slide rule which can be distributed as a substitute for straight thinking.[1]

The new search by business, and by government, for talent that has developed—in the contemporary personnel jargon—a potential capacity as a "generalist" is matched by the new Air Force ROTC curriculum, where the very title stresses its "generalized" character which on further scrutiny turns out to be a "liberal arts" emphasis, rather than, as the ROTC literature explicitly states, a premature vocational preparation for "military specialties." A recent statement on pre-legal education published as a Statement of Policy by the Association of American Law Schools emphatically endorses a renewed stress on liberal education, and this fall the thorough report by A. E. Severinghaus, Harry J. Carman, and William E. Cadbury on *Preparation for Medical Education in the Liberal Arts College*[2] has once again made the dependence of high-grade medical achievement upon a solid general education, "with more attention to the human and social aspects," one of its principal recommendations. Those of us who read such literature as part of our professional chores know that the mere publication of "reports" does not necessarily change the practices even of the authors of such documents, but there is no question that such recommendations strengthen the position of liberal arts colleges in their approach to the professional schools. Even in teacher education, there is encouraging evidence of a return to liberal education from the methodological sterilities of a predominantly "teachers college" orientation. Experience here ranges—quite contrary to the stereotypes of the scandal-mongering "best sellers"—all the way from the Ford Fund projects to a completely reorganized teacher education program at Brooklyn College, which is essentially a vocational inlay in a substantially "liberal" education.

With the appearance of this new evidence of appreciation for the contribution of general education in the achievement of vocational objectives, the moment seemed to be opportune for the College English Association to take the initiative in organizing, under the creative leadership of its executive secretary, Professor Maxwell H. Goldberg, an institute at the Corning Glass Center from October 15 to 17, 1953, with the announced general theme "Business and the Liberal Arts: An Exchange." As the guests of Corning Glass Works and Steuben Glass, Inc., an industry that combines esthetic elements with the most advanced chemistry and technology in the manufacture of glass, a group of leading teachers of English, chairmen of English departments in colleges throughout the United States, a few college administrative officers, and a strong sample of top-drawer American business leadership met to explore some of the problems in which an awareness of a joint interest is now developing.

Since the purpose of the conference was to clarify both the college and the business representatives' understanding of the nature of this joint concern, it was unavoidably a limited group in which there might be some hope for a fruitful discussion. My participation in the meetings convinced me, however, that the nature of these discussions is charged with the broadest possible interest to American education as a whole, and I am therefore devoting this address to some of my personal impressions, and to the suggestions which they led me to make to the officers of the College English Association.

Perhaps I should first identify the authors of this initiative.

The College English Association is primarily a group of some two thousand teachers of undergraduate courses in English. Negatively, I think it is fair to say that they are to be distinguished from the graduate professors because their primary interest is in the improvement of college teaching and not in what is euphemistically described as "research and publication." Positively, they are interested in the teaching of literature as a "humanity," and they have accepted more responsibility than most professional groups of this type for the interpretation of their professional aims to a larger public. The Executive Secretary of the College English Association formulated that concern rather succinctly in an article in the *CEA Critic* for November 1952, in which he said:

People say the swelling demographic tide will resolve our crisis. Perhaps that of *employment*. I doubt if it will resolve the crisis involving the continuation of our humanistic discipline itself—at least as we have traditionally known it. That crisis is far deeper. The crux is this: *without letting go of our long-cherished humanistic ideals and regimen, can we so modify them that, maintaining their integrity, they will become freshly essentially relevant to our radically altered civilization?*[3]

The concern about interpretation appears clearly in the final point of a summary program for the College English Association, which reads as follows:

A free society supports us, and we must enjoy its confidence. We owe it our best professional efforts and advice. It must know what we are doing, why we are doing it, and why we feel our work is advantageous to our students and our times.

But, like a lawyer's clients or a doctor's patients, society will judge our success largely by its own satisfaction. This is healthy and stimulating.

We must be sure our society understands us, but we must be sure we understand our society.

The discussion at Corning made it quite clear that there is a wide area of joint concern about shared problems between business leadership of the type that was represented at the conference and educators who think of the liberal arts tradition in a living and creative fashion. Discussion helped to clarify the nature of this joint concern, and in fact much of this clarification really resulted from the translation of the language in which each group habitually expressed itself into the vocabulary and concepts of the other. Words have a way of getting stale and shopworn, so that like a worn-out coin they need to be sent back to the mint, and the conference at Corning was characterized by its reminting of the verbal currency.

It is clear that when business complains about the absence of potential skill as a "generalist," it is concerned with the absence of intellectual qualities which liberal education has typically staked out for itself as its own special domain. We usually describe these as perspective, widened horizons, analytical ability, enlarged opportunities for comparison, or—if you please—vicarious experience, which is really another way of getting at perspective and horizon. This—if we can learn one another's language—is potential skill as a generalist. Civilized beings are those who, as Whitehead put it in his *Modes of Thought,* survey the world with some large generality of understanding.[4]

There seemed to be general agreement at the conference that diminishing returns had set in as far as technical or vocational specialization was concerned. The fact was cited that a survey of seventy-six corporations revealed that lack of specific skills accounted for only a shade over 10 percent of the discharges in industry while character traits accounted for almost 90 percent. Character traits also represented the factors preventing promotion in over three times as many cases as did a lack of specific skills. Albert L. Nickerson, vice-president of Socony-Vacuum Oil Co., Inc., gave an address in which he said:

A company hires the whole man and can never fully isolate any one aspect of him; we naturally look closely for poise, self-confidence, tact, capacity for leadership, judgment, and the ability to express himself. . . . We need people with convictions reasonably and deeply held, the sane judgments which come from emotional stability and the imaginative comprehension which comes from understanding the whole condition of man.[5]

William H. Whyte, Jr., put it even more sharply in his address: "The technician . . . is fit only to be a lackey, not a leader. He can't conjure, he can't speculate, he can't dream."

A similar emphasis can be found in Randall's *Freedom's*

Faith, where after a vigorous discussion and defense of academic freedom—including the businessman's right "to participate in that freedom" if he thinks the professor "is plain dippy"—we find a call for "purposeful thinking" rooted in "a strong sense of immediacy and urgency" that will not be limited to the development of "intellectual agility." Mr. Randall goes on to say:

Universities must teach students not only to think, but to feel: They must deal not only with the mind but with the heart. The disciplined brain becomes a dangerous tool indeed if coupled with undisciplined emotions, and until we bring clarity and control into that dark area of human behavior we shall have no sound hope for the future. The leaders we seek for the next generation are those who will be as sure in their handling of the emotional storms that will blow about them as they are clear in their thinking.[6]

The discussions also made it clear that there is broad concern about some of the human byproducts of an exclusive business concern with economic productivity. There was agreement with a recent statement of an efficiency engineer pointing to a new form of waste in excessive preoccupation with economic efficiency. Intelligent adjustment to change calls for experience in the exercise of choice. A large corporation, we were told, must have an organization that permits great decentralization of authority and responsibility for the reason that if it does not *de*centralize, it will tend to *over*centralize. If there is no choice or diversity of patterns, management becomes restricted in the exercise of its judgment and the organization becomes inflexible and bureaucratically rigid while it loses its capacity for survival, which is rooted in an intelligent adjustment to the certain requirements of change. This was sometimes formulated as the need for "distributing the responsibility for making decisions."

There was also a good deal of emphasis on profits as a yardstick of efficiency in the use of resources—and this is a formulation which even modern collectivists with their concern about the merging of collective and competitive controls would find more acceptable than the traditional assumption that profits are not in need of a social justification. There was great stress on the nature of man as the residual limiting factor in business judgment—"the job of management is in the most fundamental sense the job of developing people"—and there was frequent mention of the "community development" problems in industrial location, the social and political byproducts of migration, such as the human relations and interracial problems involved in the Puerto Rican and Southern Negro movement into our large cities.

Throughout these meetings there was an abiding concern with the future of business enterprise, and with its growth and development in the light of domestic and international political experience. Perhaps this could be formulated in one summarizing question: What is the general climate of ideas in which free enterprise can continue to function effectively? And isn't this a question of joint concern since the associational freedoms, which in de Tocqueville's classical formulation are the core of a free society, depend for their support on the creation of income that is not politically and bureaucratically controlled?

It is clear that these discussions—conducted sometimes in stereotyped language on either side and sometimes in a mutual effort to translate the clichés of either side of the argument into the stale and worn phrases of the other—helped to create a new awareness of common objectives. There is sometimes a fatal disconnection between formal language and life. Here in the fullness of time, discussion was restoring a cutting edge to language which had become barren because it no longer seemed relevant to our own experience.

The classical definition of a free society as a society characterized by the presence of responsible choice, the classical liberal insistence upon dispersed controls and the separation of powers, and even Acton's "Power tends to corrupt, and absolute power corrupts absolutely"—all these were emerging as new insights growing out of industrial experience and awakening a new interest in the declared and traditional objectives of liberal education. Could there be anything but cheer to a humanist in this new interest in the nature and the whole condition of man, since the study of literature is clearly the most effective method known to human culture of acquiring vicarious experience concerning the nature of man? Here clearly an acre was ploughed up that holds out rich promise of rewarding crops in the future, if the conversation could be broadened with imagination, with tact, and with persistence. It would of necessity be an empirical process in which we would have to hold purposefully close to actual experience, and it would be fatal to resort too early to preconceived and dogmatic formulations, but there was clearly the promise that a new and vital restatement of liberal education might emerge from the rediscovery of its essential characteristics in the baffling frustrations of contemporary experience. If the process had a confused and opaque quality, it also had a suggestive and earthy resemblance to some of the richest chapters in American intellectual history. Here, too, a shared process of clarifying the formulation of the questions we address to our shared experience may bring results only if we ruthlessly purge ourselves—on either side—of vulgar vested interests, either in a material form or in preconceived verbal formulations.

We have obviously come a long way from the time when the American business community could almost unanimously cheer the insight and the statesmanship of Yale's William Graham Sumner, who asked himself in 1883 the question: What do the social classes owe to each other? and answered in book length: Nothing. Today the human measure is applied and, although the name was not used, there would be a better understanding of a Brandeis who used to irritate both the liberals and the conservatives of his time by his refusal to accept the popular myths of Big Government or Big Business while he insisted that the correct test of any social system or economic proposal was the type of man it tended to produce. The development of the individual is "both a necessary means *and the end sought*"—Brandeis told a correspondent—and since our society "substitutes self-restraint for external restraint . . . the great developer is responsibility. . . . Our objective is *the making of men and women* who shall be free, self-respecting members of a democracy—and who shall be worthy of respect."[7]

This is, of course, classical American doctrine, frequently expressed by Abraham Lincoln, who used the word "responsibility" at least as often as the word "liberty," or by Emerson, who spoke of the true test of civilization as "not the census, nor the size of cities, nor the crops,—no, but the kind of man the country turns out."[8]

All of this is music to the ears of the humanist, but before we indulge ourselves in smug complacency, we might well direct some questions at our own practice as contrasted with our preachments. There is a danger that we might overlook the plight of the humanities in our present concern with the plight of vocational education or of business leadership. It is pleasing, and deeply encouraging, to see the evidence of a new awareness of the vital necessity to a free and productive society of a dynamic program of liberal education. Also, if I may express it somewhat perversely, it was heartening to a seasoned administrator, who has a long academic record of participation as a teacher in the development of such programs as Columbia's Contemporary Civilization course and the initial College program of the University of Chicago, to share in a venture which included so many teachers of the humanities who consider themselves "humanists." But, and it is a very large "but," do we ourselves *live* by the values we so frequently *preach?* And if we are to take advantage of the opportunities that may be offered by the reorientation of others, is it not urgently important to reconsider our own position?

Are we in fact teaching the humanities, and the social sciences, in a humanistic spirit? What light do the humanities—honestly now and in the family circle—throw on such problems as urban migration, community development, and the responsibility of free men? What light do our courses and programs—not as they should be taught but as they *are* taught—throw upon the clarification of human value judgments? Haven't I recently read in an *Atlantic Monthly* article by one of our leading university "humanists" that "values" is a "vogue word," which English teachers should instruct us to avoid because it "almost always means nothing but temporary vacancy of mind"?[9] And isn't "detachment from value judgments" one of the most fashionable borrowings from the natural sciences in a good deal of our "humanistic scholarship"? Can you "clarify" value judgments—and the inevitable tension or polarity between them—by teaching your students that true scholarship calls for eliminating them? How can you cope with the modern heresy that maturity and adjustment can be found in "security" if humanists and students of human society do not insist that a realistic view of the nature of man is the basis of all the common insights of the moral and literary tradition of free society, and that the only maturity that is compatible with the responsibilities of a free society is a man's ability to cope with unavoidable insecurities within himself?[10]

Do we really develop character traits? How and where? Or do

we just in a simple way *assume* that we do so—as an unplanned
byproduct of activities designed to achieve something else? Just
exactly where and how do present humanities courses sharpen
perception, discipline emotion, and help to clarify and balance
values? And is it not quite possible that we might improve the
quality of our marksmanship in attaining these noble objectives
if we asked ourselves some searching questions about the nature
and location of our target and the adequacy of our instructional
weapons?

Is it not in fact true that a very large number of our teachers
in the humanities or the social studies have no reasoned general
conception of the liberal education in which they merely have
a vocational vested interest in the narrowest possible sense of
the term? Can they specify the particular value of a liberal
education as distinguished from other types of education? Or
do they often simply mean that they prefer their own vocational
routine to that of others? Or—only a bit more broadly—do they
mean that they prefer the traditional collection of disconnected
subjects rather than some new one? Or is it rather true, as
Professor C. J. Ducasse has recently said in an excellent article
on the role of philosophy, that "college teachers commonly have
only vague answers if any" to such questions as: What do the
traditional components of a liberal education have in common?
What specific role do particular subjects play in a liberal education? How relatively important or unimportant may be the
role of one subject as compared with that of another? And are
there reasoned priorities in the claims for inclusion between
new and old subjects that are intellectually more respectable
than the number of votes cast in a faculty, which may simply
reflect the status quo rather than a reasoned view of the type
of education the college should be giving in contrast with the
program that is in fact in operation?[11]

There is likely to be warm response—and there was at Corning
—to an eloquent plea that the humanities contribute to vicarious
experience and to "the full awareness of all that it means to be
a Man," but before we righteously gloat at the current disarray
of our adversaries, we might well ask ourselves just how the
taxonomic and recondite erudition that is so often camouflaged
as "humanistic scholarship" contributes to the achievement of
these aims? Do we in fact teach the humanities in a humanistic

spirit? How often do we merely teach techniques, or grind the life out of literature between the millstones of historic "scholarship" and academic Philistinism? Or teach *Hamlet* by the "card index method"—as I discovered recently in an excellent academic high school? How often do we successfully teach our students the essentially humanistic distinction between privacy and loneliness? Why did the solitude of Abraham Lincoln's youth lead to an outcome that differs so sharply from the "peer group psychology" of the "lonely crowd"? Do our humanistic and social studies programs have any bearing on the rising tide of "other directedness" and "peer group psychology" reported by David Riesman? What do we contribute to the "sources of responsibility," including the moral and religious development of our students? Is not moral education, as Whitehead insisted, unthinkable without the habitual vision of greatness? What relation does the habitual vision of greatness have to our present instructional materials or methods?

These questions are not new to the members of the College English Association, for it has been an awareness of these weaknesses in humanistic education that has characterized their individual and corporate activity. But they are real questions, and they must be faced before we can expect to have the present "moral bellyache" about the educational needs of a free society result in significant new support for liberal education.

During the current year Columbia University is celebrating its two-hundredth birthday, and it has taken the occasion to initiate a world-wide discussion of the "right to knowledge." Does the chosen theme—"Man's right to knowledge and the free use thereof"—state the core of free society's intellectual problem? Would it not focus more directly upon the real difficulty of our time if the theme had been formulated to read: "Man's right to knowledge and the *responsible* use thereof," thereby emphasizing the supreme intellectual obligation of clarifying the *sources of responsibility* in a free society? And isn't the real problem emphasized by omission rather than by explicit statement when Columbia University opens its program for the ambitious convocations with the citation from the Gospel according to John (8:32): "And ye shall know the truth, and the truth shall make you free," thus following the contemporary liberal tradition by dropping the opening words of Jesus' statement, which reads in

full: *"If ye continue in my word, then are ye my disciples indeed;
And ye shall know the truth, and the truth shall make you free"*?
Even if we allow for subsequent explanatory statements that
"the responsibility inherent in such free use" [of knowledge]
was "so obvious" that "its inclusion in words would have been
gratuitous,"[12] the question remains wide open whether contemporary academic and nonacademic practice, at home and abroad,
does not make it crystal clear that the exaltation of rights and
the minimizing of responsibilities is precisely the reason why a
challenge to free scholarship and to liberal education has arisen
in the twentieth-century world. The clarification of the sources
of responsibility is the primary challenge to free society in the
struggle with its totalitarian adversaries.

The problem of a vital restatement of the role of liberal education is clearly *moral* and *human* in the broadest sense of the
terms, and it calls for restoring the study of the nature of man
to a central place. The errors and heresies of our generation of
liberals—yes, and of humanists—have in this respect been as
subversive of freedom as the worst excesses of "economism" on
the part of our conservatives. Our social institutions are deeply
rooted in a realistic conception of the nature of man, and just
as economic progress depends upon the extent to which the
strongest, and not merely the highest, forces of human nature
can be utilized for the increase of the common good, so our
conception of political and intellectual freedom has not been
simply "freedom period," or the right to do as you please, but
rather self-control as contrasted with external control.

What shall we say of a recent address by one of our leading
liberal humanists based on the thesis that our freedom is endangered today because we have lost our faith in man, and that
faith in the one rests of necessity upon faith in the other? Is not
this a pernicious confusion of the essential difference between
the French Revolution, with its perfectibilist illusions about
the nature of man, and the American Revolution, which, in its
faith in dispersed controls and the separation of powers, was
deeply rooted in a realistic view of the nature of man? Clearly,
the new opportunities for a revitalized liberal education will call
not only for an awareness of the errors of "presentism" and
"vocationalism," but also for a critical and persistent view of
the philosophical illiteracy and plain historical ignorance that

have gradually distorted liberal and humanistic scholarship itself. The challenge to revise the error of our ways is a double-edged sword, and if we are to take full advantage of the present possibility of a turning of the tide, liberal education will have to scrape some of the barnacles off the bottom of its own ship.

After we have placed such reservations in the record, it still remains true that we are apparently in the presence of a changed set of circumstances in which, if the case is presented with integrity and imagination, the whole subject may well be reviewed in a new spirit of objectivity without the usual appearance of a mere conflict between old and new vested interests. It would also be desirable, before we go much further, to widen the group involved in the present conversations among representatives of the colleges, business, and industry. There is plenty of evidence that there is a new group of leadership in American organized labor that is arriving at a comparable interest in the relation of education to the vitality of free institutions. Names like Reuther of the United Automobile Workers and Dubinsky of the International Ladies Garment Workers occur readily to my mind, and it is perhaps not necessary to remind this audience of Will Herberg's influential book on *Judaism and Modern Man*,[13] which was born out of a concern with the moral vacuum created in New York trade union circles when Marxism declined in its appeal as a secular "religion." There is potential strength here for a new initiative in public and in adult education, and it should be brought to play upon the problems that were tackled so fruitfully at Corning.

There are two reasons for thinking that time is not on our side in these matters—one concerning the business leaders and one concerning the academic group. We have considerable evidence that the personnel on the side of industry and business that is now deeply concerned with "horizon" and "breadth" is largely an older group which was itself trained in a wider perspective that helped to create awareness of the educational deficiencies of the oncoming generation. There was deliberate exaggeration in the statement, but one of the leaders in this group at Corning spoke of there "being nothing but technicians below the level of the senior vice-presidents." An observer who is aware of the educational trends in technical education during the past generation will not be surprised—clearly another gener-

ation may be on the way which is blissfully unaware of its
own limitations.

A similar problem exists on the academic side where enrollments, fiscal trends, federal support for defense-related research,
and scholarship incentives, have all contributed to a thinning of
the humanistic ranks, both quantitatively and qualitatively. At
a recent commencement at Brooklyn College, we graduated
twenty-three majors in physics, and at the time of graduation
twenty-one of them had received some type of scholarship or
fellowship assistance for their graduate work, including one
student who had earned a C record at Brooklyn College. On the
other hand, there was practically no fellowship support for a
larger group of majors in philosophy, history, and other humanistic subjects, and this group included many of our highest
aptitude students. This has been a national trend, and if the
colleges, in the face of declining enrollments in these subjects,
are compelled to appoint inadequate manpower in terms of
dedication and initial quality, we will soon have a large group
on the faculties, endowed with tenure to the ripe age of retirement, who will themselves tend to discourage students of the
proper caliber from entering the profession. If present trends
continue, there may be a barren age ahead of us—and in a few
years it will be difficult to reverse these trends. As things stand,
time is of the essence.

There are three channels through which we might promote a
widening and deepening interest in the present possibilities for
restating our case. If we take the questions which seemed to
be common denominators of interest as our theme, I think they
would be formulated as follows: What is the general climate of
ideas in which free institutions can continue to develop? How
can education contribute to the formation of men and women
who are fit for the responsibilities of free society? If we could set
some competent committees to work on the clarification and im-
plementation of these questions in the field of teacher education,
the liberal arts college program, and the graduate program of
training college teachers, we would, I think, contribute a desirable note of specificity to the discussion. My own preference
would be for a separate committee assignment in each of these
cases—and perhaps for several committes with the same assignment. At this stage it might be preferable to aim at a composition

of these committees that would reflect a measure of philosophical homogeneity rather than "statesmanlike balance" of opposing views. There is plenty of compromise in the status quo, and discussion in the present stage is more likely to be fruitful if it is nourished by the presentation of reasoned and sharply articulated alternatives.

I would be particularly concerned about the field of graduate instruction, in which the vested interests of research and publication have often become a clearly defined hazard to the values of liberal education. There is perhaps no area in American intellectual life in which there is a wider gap between practice and preachment, and graduate schools have a determining influence upon the selection of the next generation of teachers. A properly motivated student may overcome a good many financial hurdles. But if we combine financial hurdles and economic disincentives with a training process which sifts out and eliminates the students with a natural aptitude in our direction, we are close to a set of conditions which forecast a complete sterility in a few decades. There are, I know, exceptions to all these generalizations, and it will be precisely the function of such a program of reasoned evaluation to spotlight the growing points that hold out promise for a new vitality in liberal education.

If we compare the usual statement of humanistic values and liberal arts objectives with the actual operation of our graduate schools, or if we compare the generalized statement of graduate school aims with the criteria that are used in the selection of men for advancement or in the support of research, it would not be unfair to paraphrase an old historic slogan to read, "Millions for research and not a cent for understanding." From 60 to 80 percent of graduate school students are destined to be members of liberal arts college faculties. What would we say about a medical or engineering faculty which deliberately sacrificed the future professional needs of three-fourths of its students to the laissez-faire vested interests of the individual members of its own faculty? Or, if it is argued that these professional needs are most effectively served by deliberately ignoring them, is it not a rather obvious intellectual responsibility to document such a startling thesis in a responsible and scholarly fashion?

There is one additional major concern that developed in my mind as I participated in the Corning program, and since it is confirmed by experience throughout the country, I think it may deserve some mention here. For rather obvious reasons, it is difficult today for college administrators to discuss their problems without mention of budgetary aspects. Equally apparent, a search for new support for the idea of liberal education is partly and quite legitimately motivated by the need for new sources of financial aid. It is an error, however, to present the problem of preserving liberal education as if it were a challenge to industry to preserve privately supported higher education. In the first place, *if* we really make our case for the identity of the interests of liberal education and of free society, the support will tend to take care of itself. And in the second place—and this is important to a municipal college president—there is *no evidence* whatsoever that liberal education at present is more effectively or more frequently pursued under private than under public auspices.

More than 50 percent of America's undergraduates today are enrolled in public colleges. If we are to be realistic in our evaluation of present fiscal and economic trends, we shall probably agree that the figure is not likely to decline. I do not say this to belittle the importance of private education. I regard its survival as crucially important from the standpoint of the quality and the diversity of the whole of American society. But it would be a fatal error to assume that mass education and public education, or that vocational education and public education, or that liberal education and private education are synonymous. There is as much diversity in American public education as there is in American private education; and sometimes it is a diversity within the *same* system of public education. New York City's City College in Manhattan has made major adjustments to degree programs in vocational education. Right across the river, Brooklyn College—established and supported by the same City of New York—has rigorously kept its entire undergraduate student body matriculated for the baccalaureate degrees within a pattern of liberal education. This diversity is a matter of deliberate choice, and I think it would be easy to prove that many private institutions have made substantially greater concessions to vocational pressures than a large number of colleges that are publicly supported. It would also be rather easy to prove that the graduates of public liberal-arts-and-science education stand up quite well by national standards. Our graduating class at

Brooklyn College of ten years ago earned eighty-one scholarships and fellowships in thirty-seven different graduate and professional schools, while the report for last year shows two hundred and twenty-one scholarships and fellowships in seventy-nine different institutions.

Recently a study by two members of the faculty of Wesleyan University traced the collegiate origins of the younger generation of American scholars.[14] The yardsticks were national, and in order to equalize the results for six hundred small and large institutions, they were calculated in terms of the number of scholars per thousand recent graduates. This was a study of quality, not quantity. And the yardsticks which were used did not in some respects fully reflect the achievements of our own student body. Under these circumstances, it would be reasonable to expect that some of the country's excellent small private colleges would be high up in the final list of the top fifty colleges —and they were. But—and it is a "but" that is directly relevant to my present argument—when they were measured by these national yardsticks, Queens College and Brooklyn College were twelfth and thirtieth, respectively, in the final list of the country's leading fifty institutions, and if we remember the size of these institutions, these two municipal colleges accounted for as many scholars as sixteen other institutions in this top list of fifty. Brooklyn College was listed immediately following Amherst and Williams. If we throw the figures for the four New York municipal colleges together—which would be justifiable in a study that classified the University of California as one unit— and if we look at the *total* number of scholars (and not at the statistical index measuring the number of scholars per thousand graduates), we find the College of the City of New York in its corporate capacity leading the country as a source of the nation's new scholars and scientists, with Harvard in second and the University of California in third place (the total figures are 292, 288, and 272 respectively).

I cite these figures in some detail because I am familiar with them. A study of other public institutions would probably lead to similar conclusions. The data certainly prove that public education today is a major factor in the country's qualitative achievement in liberal education. Liberal education is concerned with a quality product, and a quality product is just as costly in public as it is in private education. Quality or excellence is not only a classical liberal objective, but in the quantitative thinking that dominates contemporary world politics—in which Americans are a minority—quality may well be the determining factor in national survival. Since more than half of our human educational resources on the college level are engaged in public higher education, it is crucial to remember that the financial pressures bearing on public education are just as heavy as those that are brought to bear on private education. Recent New York State data show an annual cost per student for all colleges in the state that averages around $1,000. But the figures for the New York municipal colleges average $668 per student, with Brooklyn College at the bottom of the scale, averaging $587 per student. I am not proud of these figures—they measure in a rough way the acute pressure on public education of tendencies that are too frequently discussed as if they were exclusively a feature of the country's private colleges.

The protection of the quality of liberal education is emphatically a matter of joint interest to public as well as private education, and it is a serious error in professional judgment to permit the development of a false impression in this regard. But, I repeat, it is an even more serious mistake to give the discussion of budgetary factors priority over the discussion of the primary interest of the national community as a whole in the preservation of an educational structure that aims first of all at the development of men and women fit for the responsibilities of free society. If we establish our case convincingly for the latter, the support will take care of itself. And in any case, at any given level of financial support, there are qualitative improvements open to creative and courageous leadership if we continue to ask ourselves clearly and persistently: How do we rate the priorities of the educational needs we now serve and those we are at present unable to meet, and is the lowest need now met more urgent than the highest need not met?

If the "unexamined life" is the basic sin, according to the classical humanist and Socratic position, then the Corning conference has some virtue to its credit. Clearly the discussion is back to fundamentals, and to their persistent testing by discussion.

We are concerned with the establishment of cultural yard-

sticks which will help us to assign valid priorities in the commitment of our educational and intellectual energies. We are asking
a classical liberal and American question when we inquire into
the nature of the man who can be trusted with freedom and who
will be fit for the responsibilities of a free society.

We are not concerned with the elaboration of a technique of
turning out smoothly polished spare parts for the industrial ma-
chine, or of a method of expressing the values of the humanistic
tradition in words that will appeal to the business community or
to reactionary politicians who do not even understand the nature
of the free society they are presumably concerned to defend.
Neither are we concerned with the preservation of the vested
interests of industry or academy. We are not denying the validity
of vocational or technical education for competence in the most
specialized fields for employment which our current economic
system holds out to the huge enrollment in higher education—
although we would like to emphasize rather than to blur the
distinction in objectives of these proliferating programs—and we
are certainly not arguing that liberal education as it is, or as it
should be, can "train" students for business. "Utility," as Professor
John Ciardi pointed out at Corning, "is not the problem of the
liberal arts," and "business would be in a bad way indeed" if it
were to depend on liberal education to supply it.[15] We are concerned with the contribution liberal education can and should
make to the development of responsible and responsive personality, and this is in many ways the most crucial problem of
free society today.

We are in a very real sense engaged in a *conservative* quest,
and in the present climate of opinion I use the controversial
word deliberately because it expresses my meaning. If we choose
to be more tactful toward prevailing stereotypes, we might say
that we are concerned with establishing the conditions of an
"enduring individualism." Even this statement of the goal is
deeply conservative—not in the sense of preserving the status quo,
which is rejected for varying reasons by all concerned, but in the
sense that we are concerned about preserving or reestablishing
the conditions in which a free society can continue to exist, that
is to say, a society that will be characterized by the presence of
responsible choice.

The times are ripe for a bold and imaginative leadership.

There are new beginnings around us everywhere. They abound in recent literature. They are evident in the concerns of the not-so-silent younger generation, which has found sterility and frustration in the educational drift as well as in the "advanced" ideas of the recent past. If we are to benefit from the lesson of the Hutchins' Great Books episode, which began in a similar burst of enthusiasm for revitalizing liberal education, we might fruitfully focus on the fatal insistence of its promoters that it was "irrelevant" that "the students will not like it,"[16] since "young men have not lived long enough to know why temperance and wisdom are good."[17] The question to which we should seek an answer is precisely the student's inquiry cited by Chancellor T. R. McConnell of the University of Buffalo in an able survey of the meaning of general education: "Why is it that our courses in philosophy never seem to have anything to do with things that matter to *us*?"[18]

The present opportunity lies precisely in the changed motivation which we would overlook at our peril. The question is not: How can we return to a *past* pattern of liberal education? The present challenge is rather: How can we make liberal education indigenous by rethinking its moral and intellectual content so that it will be relevant to the needs of free society in America today?

There is little danger today, however, of the ivory tower complacency of twenty years ago. There is a general awareness that we must take advantage of a running tide if our ships are not to be beached. There is even a danger that, in our present concern with the weakness of technical and vocational education, we may find so much easy consent to our general thesis that a smug tendency may develop to overlook the size of the group that is comfortably at ease with the fleshpots provided by the astounding material productivity of our economic system in the present phase of its development without realizing that the fleshpots themselves—as well as our effectiveness in the technology of national defense—are derived from and deeply dependent upon the freedom of science which developed as a byproduct of traditional liberal education.

Let us not forget the danger, characteristic of educational initiatives of a humanist inspiration, that the early converts to a new insight might easily become a closed community rich in mutual admiration for its own wisdom and perspective. I therefore close with a very Christian prayer, pronounced some years ago by a Protestant bishop at a clerical conference in Canada which had not been too responsive to the bishop's efforts to lift the discussion beyond the vested interests of the participants.

When the bishop was asked to offer the final prayer, he said: "May the Lord grant that we justify the esteem in which we hold ourselves. Amen."

9

*Academic Freedom: A Decade of Challenge and Clarification**

"THERE IS," SAYS SIDNEY HOOK, "MORE SLOPPY RHETORIC POURED out per page about academic freedom both by those who believe that they are supporting, and those intent on criticizing it, than on any other theme with the possible exception of democracy."[1] Another generation has discovered for itself that freedom is not inherited as a youth acquires property rights in a house from his parents. Freedom can only be inherited in the sense that every succeeding generation has the opportunity to hammer out for itself, on the anvil of its own experience, the framework of unavoidably interwoven rights and responsibilities within which freedom in the sense of self-expression and freedom in the sense of self-control can be for such a generation a working faith.

ORTHODOX CASES OF ACADEMIC FREEDOM

In recent years we have, of course, had our normal quota of orthodox academic freedom issues, cases in which a teacher is dismissed because he addresses a Wallace-for-President meeting, or in which a trustee interested in dairy farming argues that a campus supporter of the removal of fiscal handicaps for oleomargarine is unfit to serve a state university. There have not been more issues of this type than in any other decade, if the reports of the American Association of University Professors are a trustworthy guide, and even a valiant and responsible spirit of professional self-policing could hardly be expected to eliminate these altogether in our sprawling system of higher education with its decentralized and varied controls. Our preoccupation with the

---

* From the *Annals of the American Academy of Political and Social Science,* CCCI (September 1955), 75-85.

issues—false and real—of Communism in education has even tended to promote underemphasis, in recent years, of a few startling abuses of academic freedom of the vulgar variety.

One of the many merits of Russell Kirk's "essay in definition," entitled *Academic Freedom,* lies in the balanced discussion of the two "most shocking" cases of the violation of academic freedom in recent years, that is to say, the effort to impose the views of professional "educators" upon the rest of the faculty by President Minard W. Stout of the University of Nevada in the so-called Richardson case in 1953, and Chancellor Hutchins' removal on less than a day's notice—in the fall of 1950—of Mr. W. T. Couch as director of the University of Chicago Press.[2] The feeble and belated intervention of the American Association of University Professors in these cases may itself have been due to the Association's preoccupation with the issues presented by membership, past or present, in the Communist party. It is not without interest that the national officers of the organization did not take a hand in the Nevada case until it appeared that some members of the Board of Regents might attempt, without any foundation whatsoever, to insinuate that there was a "Communist" or "fellow traveler" angle to the case.

There is nothing new about the "orthodox" cases of academic freedom in recent years. Arthur O. Lovejoy's authoritative article on academic freedom in the *Encyclopaedia of the Social Sciences* and an able summarizing article on "Academic Freedom" in the *Annals of the American Academy of Political and Social Science*[3] by Henry W. Tyler and Edward P. Cheyney can still be cited as the best sources for historical and philosophical documentation, with appropriate stress upon the valuable and creative role of the American Association of University Professors in the formative years.

NEW ISSUES

The new issues in academic freedom arising from membership in the Communist party came to the fore in the late thirties in New York City, and received their earliest formulation in connection with the Rapp-Coudert investigation of public education in New York City from 1940 to 1943.[4] To the country as a whole these remained "special New York City" issues until the University of Washington dismissed several professors in 1949 on the ground that they were guilty *as members of the Communist party* of violating the principles of academic freedom and therefore of "conduct unbecoming a teacher."[5] The classical formulations of the principles of academic freedom by the American Association of University Professors contemplated no such development. Neither the 1925 nor the 1940 "statement of principles"[6] foresaw a hazard to academic freedom in the ideological commitments of the teachers themselves. They speak of the university or the college as the party that "may not place any restraint upon the teacher's freedom of investigation" or "impose any limitation upon the teacher's freedom in the exposition of his own subject in the classroom or in addresses and publications outside the college."

The 1940 "statement of principles" postulates that the "common good" of institutions of higher learning depends "upon the free search for truth and its free exposition." Recent experience has demonstrated with tragic emphasis that political organizations as well as the federal government itself may place more effective restraints or limitations upon the teacher's freedom of investigation or his freedom of exposition than were ever contemplated by colleges or universities themselves.

The struggle for academic freedom takes a new form as the intellectual, ideological, and cultural landscape changes. The essence of the tradition must be restated and redefined by every generation in the light of current facts, current challenges, and current abuses. Those who live in an atmosphere that is comparatively static will abide by the received verbal formulations. Those who live in a climate of opinion deeply affected by new developments—such as, say, in the modern scene, a university with a real experience with Communist infiltration or a large number of teachers in the physical sciences affected by federal security regulations—will find little help in a parrotlike repetition of the old words and phrases. If they are to be a living chart—and not an empty verbal shell covering an alien content—their meaning must be defined anew in the light of developing experience. In such a period of restatement and redefinition, it is inevitable that there will be an interval of confusion and even chaos arising from the differences in thought and emotion evoked by old and new verbal symbols, and only a process of sharing and analyzing the new experience will contribute to a basic clarification of the issues involved.[7]

After six years the initial storm of confused and essentially uninformed comment and discussion has settled down to a professional agreement that covers a remarkably wide area. In recent years authors who are as far apart in their basic philosophical views as Sidney Hook and Russell Kirk have arrived at a reasoned view of freedom under professional responsibilities in the face of the new challenge of totalitarian discipline of scholars that is in all essentials in agreement with the statement on "The Rights and Responsibilities of Universities and Their Faculties" unanimously adopted by the Association of American Universities in 1953.

It may serve a useful purpose to compare the definitions of academic freedom which have been formulated in the light of the new experience. Sidney Hook deserves a great deal of credit for the tenacity of purpose and the clarity of mind with which he has sought to make the general public as well as the academic profession understand the full meaning of the experience to which New York City was exposed earlier and more intensively than the country as a whole. In developing the thesis that it is our moral obligation in a free society to tolerate dissent, no matter how heretical, and not to tolerate conspiracy, no matter how it may be camouflaged, he offers the following definition:

What is academic freedom? Academic freedom is a specific kind of freedom. It is the freedom of professionally qualified persons to inquire, discover, publish and teach the truth as they see it in the field of their competence, without any control or authority except the control or authority of the rational methods by which truth is established. Insofar as it acknowledges intellectual discipline or restraint from a community, it is only from the community of qualified scholars which accepts the authority of rational inquiry.

Like every other freedom, academic freedom, although it has an intrinsic value, is not absolute. It must be judged by its consequences on a whole cluster of other freedoms (values). The *justi-fication* of academic freedom must therefore lie in its fruits.[8]

Russell Kirk, who offers a sympathetic and reasoned criticism of Hook's definition, accepts the definition of W. T. Couch that "academic freedom is the principle designed to protect the teacher from hazards that tend to prevent him from meeting his *obligations in the pursuit of truth,*"[9] and then suggests that it should be anchored in a commitment, made in a spirit of dedication, not of suspicion,

. . . to adhere to the Truth, according to the light that is given to the teacher; a promise to conserve the wisdom of our ancestors and to extend the empire of knowledge as best a teacher can; a promise to guide and awaken the student, but not to indoctri-nate; a promise to abide by the principles of social order, as ex-pressed in the country's constitution; and a promise always to put freedom of the mind above material advantage and the passions of the hour. What the Hippocratic oath is to the physician, such an oath ought to be to the teacher, and more; and no further oath ought to be required by any authority.[10]

Some of the key paragraphs of the unanimous statement of the Association of American Universities reflect both the con-sensus of professional opinion— unchallenged by any responsible governmental authority—and the nature of some of the problems inside and outside of the profession itself. After a statement of the "unique" role of the modern American university, the defin-ing paragraphs read as follows:

A university must . . . be hospitable to an infinite variety of skills and viewpoints, relying upon open competition among them as the surest safeguard of truth. Its whole spirit requires investigation, criticism and presentation of ideas in an atmos-phere of freedom and mutual confidence. This is the real mean-ing of "academic" freedom. It is essential to the achievement of its ends that the faculty of a university be guaranteed this free-dom by its governing board, and that the reasons for the guaran-tee be understood by the public. To enjoin uniformity of outlook upon a university faculty would put a stop to learning at the source. To censor individual faculty members would put a stop to learning at its outlet. . . .

Timidity must not lead the scholar to stand silent when he ought to speak, particularly in the field of his competence. In matters of conscience and when he has truth to proclaim the scholar has no obligation to be silent in the face of popular disapproval. Some of the great passages in the history of truth have involved the open challenge of popular prejudice in times of tension such as those in which we live. . . .

Appointment to a university position and retention after appointment require not only professional competence but involve the affirmative obligation of being diligent and loyal in citizenship. Above all, a scholar must have integrity and independence. This renders impossible adherence to such a regime as that of Russia and its satellites. No person who accepts or advocates such principles and methods has any place in a university. Since present membership in the Communist party requires the acceptance of these principles and methods, such membership extinguishes the right to a university position. . . .

"Academic freedom" is not a shield for those who break the law. Universities must cooperate fully with law-enforcement officers whose duty requires them to prosecute those charged with offenses. Under a well-established American principle, their innocence is to be assumed until they have been convicted, under due process, in a court of proper jurisdiction.

Unless a faculty member violates a law, however, his discipline or discharge is a university responsibility and should not be assumed by political authority. Discipline on the basis of irresponsible accusations or suspicion can never be condoned. It is as damaging to the public welfare as it is to academic integrity. The university is competent to establish a tribunal to determine the facts and fairly judge the nature and degree of any trespass upon academic integrity, as well as to determine the penalty such trespass merits.[11]

The stress in all these definitions on key words such as "truth," "conscience," and the "discipline of the community of scholars" springs from the new awareness of the hazard to free scholarship that may be inherent in the acceptance by individual teachers of political discipline in matters of learning and academic organization. Thus the national clarification of standards and values arrived at a conclusion which matched the decision of the New School for Social Research in New York City in its adoption of a bylaw many years ago stating that "no member of the faculty may be a member of any political party or group which presumes to dictate in matters of science or scientific opinion."[12] This is a reflection of a new tough-minded liberalism which refuses to permit the destruction of free institutions by their totalitarian abuse, and is morally rooted in the acceptance of the ideal of the search for truth as the evidence and your conscience may teach you to see it, not as a political party or ideological discipline may force you to twist it.

COMMUNIST PARTY MEMBERSHIP

The significance of the new formulation of academic freedom is its insistence that fitness to teach must be decided primarily on intellectual and educational rather than on political grounds, and that membership in the Communist party is relevant because of its educational and intellectual, rather than its political, implications. There is no issue concerning teaching about Communism or about Communist ideas—every student in a free society should be exposed to their study and their criticism. Least of all is it a matter of fear of meeting such ideas in open discussion since actual experience with members of the party who are members of a faculty reveals a deliberate and disciplined policy of concealing their identity and of teaching "at the least risk of exposure." The rejection of members of the Communist party as members of the teaching profession is not a matter of ideas but a question of professional *conduct*.

When the nature of the Communist party is understood—and even the carefully nurtured ignorance of some of our more extreme libertarians begins to yield to the wealth of evidence concerning the party's insistence that all members must "at *all* times take a position on *every* question that is in line with the policies of the party," that they must "display a thorough readiness to accept party discipline," and that inactive or "bad" members are expelled because they do not have "any latitude or discretion in the matter"—it becomes plain as a pikestaff that membership in the Communist party is *prima facie* evidence of *professional unfitness* to teach. Sidney Hook has summarized a large amount of the relevant evidence from party documents, official hearings, espionage cases, and so forth.[18] It has taken several years for the evidence to convince some of our liberals, who are frequently more hostile to anti-Communists than they are to Communists, but it is now quite generally agreed that "membership" in the Communist party is not in any significant sense similar to membership in any other legal party.

To be a registered Republican or Democratic voter—which is presumably the meaning of "membership" in such a case—does not imply the assumption of iron discipline in executing the party leaders' orders even in intellectual matters as politically remote as biology, the history of philosophy, or the theory of music, whereas "membership" in the Communist party really means that the individual becomes the *agent* of the party—this is the phrase Lenin always used to describe "members"—in every field in which it is seeking instruments to achieve its power purpose. While excesses may have occurred under the doctrine of "guilt by association," it is misleading to speak of party membership in these terms, since this would be true of membership in the free society's sense of the term, whereas membership in the Stalinist sense means a dedicated commitment to accept the discipline of the group, *which is active co-operation and not association.*

There is no warrant, either, for the confusion of past and present membership in the Communist party since the academic agencies have been as insistent upon the protection of the rights of teachers who proved the bona fide termination of their membership as have the senatorial investigators. Justice Douglas, in his dissent from the United States Supreme Court's decision declaring the New York State Feinberg Law constitutional, spoke of "the threat" of the New York City procedure as raising "havoc with academic freedom" because "youthful indiscretions" and "misguided enthusiasms" would "become the ghosts of a harrowing present." The law—and the procedures—make it very clear, however, that Justice Douglas' fears have no closer relation to the facts than his views as to the real nature of the Communist party.

CONFUSIONS

There has been a good deal of distressing evidence of abuse of intellectual freedom in the years of clarifying discussion and experience that have led up to the present emergence of a new consensus. In the exaltation of rights and the minimizing of responsibilities, which have been so characteristic of free society in recent generations, it is possible for a distinguished professor of sociology in one of our major universities to tell the *New York Times* that "freedom is either unqualified or it does not exist"; it is possible for a distinguished professor of history to say that after a decade of incessant snooping only "two real live Communists" have been found in American colleges and universities although evidence available to any newspaper reader would have told him of over a hundred such cases in his own city; and—to cite only one further example from a wealth of similar evidence of professional irresponsibility—it is possible for four distinguished academic personalities to sign a letter to the *New York Times* in which they speak of "faceless informers" who are used to convict New York City teachers of perjury although the record conclusively shows that no teacher has been convicted of perjury without an open trial in which the witnesses against him were subject to public cross-examination, and in which there was always the opportunity for an appeal to the State Commissioner.

Meanwhile, Robert M. Hutchins—and others of comparable standing could be cited—tells the world that "everywhere in the United States" university professors are "silenced by the general atmosphere of repression,"[14] and that the "entire teaching profession of the United States is now intimidated."[15] In lectures to Swedish and Canadian universities he made similar statements about the position of "intellectuals in America."[16] Although these statements correspond as little with the facts as his description of John Dewey's influence, they lend credibility to the views of Bertrand Russell, who tells his audiences that American professors of economics are considered "subversive" if they "know" what the doctrines of Communism are, or that if the Federal Bureau of Investigation in its "perpetual snooping" should hear a teacher quote with approval some remark by Jefferson, he "would probably lose [his] job" and find himself "behind bars."[17]

To an American reader, it is of course clear that Mr. Hutchins and Mr. Russell were acquainted with selective samples of the American teaching profession, and Sidney Hook's comment is surely relevant that:

... the facts are that no professor who was in the habit of speaking up five years ago has been silenced, many who were silent five years ago are speaking up, while those who were silent five, ten, fifteen years ago and are still silent cannot be regarded as victims of a reign of terror. It is not necessary to picture the situation as ideal—or to deny the episodic outbreaks of intolerance towards professors with unpopular views (when was the U.S. free of them?) to recognize Mr. Hutchins' statement as a fantastic exaggeration, and no more accurate in its description of the situation than a characterization of the state of academic freedom at the University of Chicago under Mr. Hutchins would be if it were based only on Mr. Hutchins' outrageous dismissal of Mr. Couch.[18]

Every year the annual crop of assorted nonsense about "dangerous thoughts" and "radicalism," which is produced as an inevitable byproduct of a free society by folks with whom "liberals" do not agree, frightens those who are easily intimidated and makes it easy to confuse the distinction between real and imaginary threats. Cultural vigilantes occasionally make fools of themselves by insisting that Robin Hood is a "subversive" book —the fact that they failed to convince the Indiana school authorities of the validity of their claim is not usually mentioned. Ignorant politicians sometimes make themselves ridiculous by describing the Tennessee Valley Authority or unemployment insurance as "Communistic," or a group in Congress, which needs to be reminded of the vital distinction between conservatism and reactionary radicalism, apparently assumes in an "investigation" of the foundations—without, however, securing the support of the House as a whole—that it might be an appropriate function of Congress to decide whether an empirical or a philosophical approach is more rewarding—or even patriotic—in scientific research.[19]

None of this irresponsible conduct on the part of nominal conservatives disproves the fact, however, that there is such a thing as a real Communist conspiracy, with all of its unpleasant links to conspiratorial conduct, to anonymous and scurrilous libel of colleagues, to perjury, and even occasionally to espionage and murder. The fact that spurious patriots exploit the public concern about real professional abuses, as defined by any reputable academic body, by casting doubts upon the members of scores of more or less innocent "front" organizations which were deliberately designed to enroll the idealistic and the gullible does not explain away the indisputable fact that perjury is intolerable in a teacher, irrespective of his or her political associations. It is not morally edifying to hear a plea for the avoidance of relevant testimony by a college professor on high grounds of "conscience" when the preceding day's testimony clearly *and admittedly* included evidence of perjury by the same individual at an earlier session. These only *appear* to be political issues. They are in fact *ethical* questions that strike straight at the core of the viability of a free society.[20]

It may seem to be a pity that so much energy has been spent in recent years on the clarification of elementary values in academic and in free society. In a larger sense, however, the rethinking of the philosophical foundations and the moral prerequisites of free society may be strategically more vital than the development of our foreign policy or the perfection of our armament.

In recent years the most glaring weaknesses in the tradition of academic freedom have not appeared as a result of the arguments of its enemies but have been revealed in the philosophical and historical illiteracy of some of its advocates. The record at the University of California, the University of Chicago, and Harvard University makes it clear that our enemies may be sufficiently strong to win an occasional battle but they do not win the war. In New York City's municipal colleges academic freedom is as real as it is anywhere else in the country or in the world, in spite of a determined effort to make it appear otherwise by some misguided "liberals" and fellow travelers. Harvard University is a citadel of strength in the defense of intellectual freedom in spite of Senator McCarthy's envenomed attacks, and Mr. Hutchins' prophecy that donors would "hesitate to give money to the university" has been emphatically disproved by the munificent gifts Harvard received immediately after the most vicious phase of the campaign of attack.

The best-known congressional representatives of the idea that there should be no rules inhibiting a congressional investigation have encountered a firm check in public opinion as well as in the restraints imposed by their legislative colleagues. If we examined the report of the subcommittee of the United States Senate Committee on the Judiciary, which has handled most of the cases related to education, we would find a statement of rules and objectives that is in line with the best democratic and professional tradition, including the provisions of the statement of the Association of American Universities. The detailed cases described in this committee's report of July 17, 1953, under the title, *Subversive Influence in the Educational Process,* indicate a form of unprofessional conduct which would be so defined by any reputable academic authority, and in any case the committee has left the final judgment concerning such evidence to the discretion of the appropriate educational agencies and authorities.[21]

The philosophical and political illiteracy of a defense of freedom which is anchored in a plea, by a founder of the American Association of University Professors, that scholars act "as the agents of the people," and that their responsibility "is *not to the truth*" but "to the people who need the truth,"[22] or the argument just cited that "freedom is either unqualified or it does not exist,"[23] points to a weakness in the prevailing theory of a free society which promises to be far more dangerous than any of the attacks by outsiders that we have experienced thus far. Such views are a characteristic byproduct of a rising secular religion of democracy, in which it becomes possible for intelligent men to teach that "there is nothing wrong with democracy that more democracy will not cure." These men do not understand that they are thereby denying the basis in political principle of the Bill of Rights, and that they are incidentally undermining the philosophic basis of the distinction between the so-called "people's democracies" of the Soviet type and our own variety, which is anchored in the limitations imposed upon what Jefferson called "majoritarian despotism" by the Bill of Rights.

This situation is perhaps an unavoidable outcome of a century of scholarship in which students of jurisprudence have glorified "positive" law in continual efforts to prove that the very idea of natural law was a hoax, in which sociologists have spent their energy demonstrating that the very idea of community —and its related values and moral standards—is ideological in character, and in which psychologists have treated "conscience" as if it could be illuminated by conditioning experiments with rats and—of course—dogs. Academic life has been crowded with scholars who have spent their lives eagerly sawing off the branches upon which they themselves—or their colleagues—were sitting.

Freedom is anchored in the relative autonomy of the associational liberties, the significance of which de Tocqueville and Burke understood so well, and this is, of course, the reason for our renewed interest in their views. When scholars accept the status of "agents of the people," the door has been opened to all forms of populist, majoritarian, or totalitarian control. The philosophical vacuousness of certain types of contemporary philosophy and social science may constitute a greater hazard to free society than any of the conspiratorial activities of the more easily recognized enemies to which we are devoting so much of our attention.

FREEDOM AND RESPONSIBLE CHOICE

Freedom is not the absence of restraint or the right to do "as you please." It is the presence of responsible choice. It is anchored in a capacity for self-control. Free society and its opposite cannot be distinguished by the absence of authority in the one case and its presence in the other. It is, rather, a question of inner checks in the first case and external control in the other. This is not merely a question of intellectual understanding; it is essentially a matter of moral commitment. Just as de Tocqueville taught that "despotism may govern without faith but liberty cannot," we must learn to see that a free society is not an "open" society but, on the contrary, a society strictly committed to a distinctive set of beliefs which are widely regarded as obsolete in the free world today, and perhaps most commonly among scholars.

It was the fall of liberty in Europe—or the threat of its loss —that aroused a new consciousness of the basic beliefs on which these liberties rest. But—as Michael Polanyi has reminded us— "the beliefs remain nevertheless logically prior to these liberties"[24] and "the coherence of science must be regarded as an expression of the common rootedness of scientists in the same spiritual reality."[25] To Polanyi, "the principal belief . . . underlying a free society is that man is amenable to reason and susceptible to the claims of his conscience."[26] Free men can never be nihilists. Free men are always—in the moral sense—committed men. The problem of freedom lies in the understanding of the nature of their essential commitment.

There is a jungle of philosophic and semantic confusion crying for systematic cultivation here. The quest for total "objectivity" is so deeply rooted in the best of our Western tradition that it will call for a major reorientation to recognize its relationship to the moral insecurity and normlessness that are the intellectual breeding ground of totalitarianism. There is nothing novel about the cultural pattern, however, to anyone who is aware of the Jewish, the Christian, and the Greek sources of our culture. Aristotle knew that anomic libertarianism was an immediate predecessor of despotic government, which conceals the symptoms of normlessness by imposing an iron framework to prevent disintegration.

The problems of academic freedom are in this sense merely a special example of the larger problem of restoring the vitality of free society in general. Ranging all the way from the quest for a philosophical foundation for our foreign policy on a world scale to the need for an indigenous restatement of the theory of general education on the local campus level, we can only escape the confusion of a congeries of conflicting material and power motives by a recognition of the need for clarifying the order of our priorities in the moral or philosophical field. To refresh the sources of responsibility is the primary challenge to free society in its struggle with domestic obscurantism as well as with its totalitarian adversaries in world politics. In this emphasis we are merely returning to the theme of John Dewey's remarks in 1915 as the first president of the American Association of University Professors, in which he described issues of academic freedom as not more than "an incident of the activities of the association *in developing professional standards,* standards which will be quite as scrupulous regarding *the obligations imposed by freedom* as jealous for freedom itself."[27]

10

Colonial Experience and the Social Context of Economic Development Programs*

IN AN ADDRESS ON NOVEMBER 1, 1953, BEFORE THE WORLD AFFAIRS
Council of Northern California, the Assistant Secretary of State
for Near Eastern, South Asian, and African Affairs made some
carefully formulated statements about "colonialism" that have
been widely interpreted as evidence that a new maturity has
emerged in our official attitude towards the so-called underdeveloped countries. The title of Mr. Henry A. Byroade's address
was itself significant: "The World's Colonies and Ex-Colonies:
A Challenge to America." And although Mr. Byroade made it
clear that "old style colonialism is on its way out," and that
"nothing can restore it," editorial comment on the speech was
far from wrong when it selected his statement that "premature
independence can be dangerous, retrogressive and destructive"
as the significant new policy note. To the United States in recent
years experience in the Near and Far East has been a hard and
pitiless teacher. National independence—the State Department
spokesman explained—is not "a magic solution" to all the difficulties of "our friends" in previously colonial countries. "Premature independence" has not served the interests of either
the United States or the free world, and "least of all" has it
served "the interests of the dependent peoples themselves." While
we continue to favor "eventual self-determination for all peoples,"
we place a new stress on "evolutionary development to this end,"
and our own experience in recent years has strengthened an
awareness of the large gap between the talk about "economic
exploitation of dependent peoples" and the fact that economic
relations between European countries and overseas territories
were "often beneficial to both parties."

---

* From *Economics and the Public Interest*. Robert A. Solo, Editor (New
Brunswick, N. J.: Rutgers University Press, 1955), pp. 247-67.

Our experience has not been merely political. We have also learned that there has been a significant "development" factor in colonial experience just as some of the enthusiastic advocates of postwar international monetary schemes had to learn that there was an impressive measure of achievement in international monetary coordination in the nineteenth century even if no one bothered to formulate the "rules of the game" in the twentieth-century form of an international treaty. In the same way, experience with modern "development schemes" has taught the lesson that there had been a considerable measure of "development" in the nineteenth century—the vocabulary was new but the practice was as old as the voyages of the Phoenicians.

Five years have elapsed since President Truman launched the "Point Four" program in his inaugural address, calling for "a bold new program" to make available the benefits of our store of technical knowledge and to foster capital investment in areas needing development. Since that time we have witnessed the usual ups and downs in enthusiastic and critical discussion of the proposal, and we have acquired some scattered and instructive experience. American conservatives have criticized the proposal as if it involved "a hand-out" of billions of American taxpayers' dollars "incompetently" distributed for the purpose of financing consumption abroad, and some of the discussion in other countries has encouraged this misrepresentation by confusing projects to enlarge consumption abroad with proposals for genuine investment and development. Meanwhile, a large number of technical assistance projects have been initiated in various branches of the American Government, in the International Bank, and under a variety of United Nations auspices. Professor Walter R. Sharp of Yale University has recently published a study pulling together impressive evidence of the vitality of the idea, which is after all a natural outgrowth of some of the basic lessons taught by the economic development of the American economy itself.[1]

A recent memorandum on *United States Foreign Development Programs* for the Advisory Committee on Underdeveloped Areas of the Mutual Security Agency (dated December 8, 1952) has made it clear that our accumulating experience has now prepared us for a more realistic evaluation of the positive contributions of colonial experience. The authors of the memorandum stress the point in varying ways that "development" is not merely a matter of dollar expenditures, of loans and subsidies, or even of resources and skills. Productivity—and reciprocally, "poverty"—are seen as primarily dependent upon an *institutional framework* in which social, political, and administrative factors are appropriate for the advancement of productivity. It is stressed that development programs cannot be effectively carried on a year-to-year basis, that loans must be visualized—as illustrated also by colonial experience—in terms of reinvestment of both principal and interest and that "the most important principle of operation is *a sense of permanence and continuity*." The lessons that have been learned are illustrated by the gravitation toward the *community-development approach,* which is so evident in our growing experience, and by the administrative emphasis placed upon the "principle of jointness" rather than the traditional separation of powers, and on the *"country program"* approach "to which all types of U.S. activities in the economic development field have gravitated sooner or later."

Now that the stereotypes of "1776 and all that" have been qualified by American experience, it may be useful to stress that Dutch, English, French, Belgian, and even Italian experience in colonial development can be cited in all its diversity to document the more recent U.S.A. (and UN) conclusions. Specifically, what are the lessons from colonial experience for the United States—or for a projected World Development Authority—concerning the direction and the organization of development programs? Can we profit from such lessons without enflaming all the passions of "anti-colonialism" which are frequently the most effective political cement in development countries?

Indonesia will be used as an example, partly because it illustrates colonial experience at its best, partly because its recent history demonstrates so eloquently the hollowness of the usual "anti-colonial" cant about unilateral "exploitation," and also because the recent historic experience is clearly irreversible and does not permit even consideration of the reestablishment of the preceding regime. The data are not cited to argue that some earlier colonial regimes should be reestablished—in this case or in any other. They are cited to prove that there was a *valid, general* experience with development programs in many of these "colonial" cases, and that colonial development at its best was not unilaterally concerned with a purely economic exploitation of one people by another—and that we may play into the hands of enemies of the free world if we overlook this experience.

Indonesia is today a lawless country, the ports of which are so characterized by theft and banditry that insurance companies hesitate to cover shipping contracts. "Banditry"—an evil that was characteristic of the Far East until Western governments established order in the nineteenth century—is so common that the government in Djakarta prefers to "reorganize" the Defense Ministry rather than permit its military authorities to discharge their normal responsibilities. Foreign capital, which was formerly available for development at rates only slightly in excess of the rates prevailing in the Netherlands, is now unavailable at any rate corresponding to calculable future returns. Disinvestment at panic rates prevails where reinvestment of capital and interest was the rule. Foreign technical personnel (engineers, doctors, scientists, administrators), formerly available on a career basis at rates slightly higher than prevailing rates in the Netherlands, is now hard to find at rates that are appreciably higher than even American figures, except for a category of international adventurers ("Nazi" engineers, refugees, etc.). Java, which grew in population from four to forty-five million in one preceding century of Dutch rule and which became, and remained, self-sufficient in food supply during that period of feverish growth, now imports rice from abroad. Djakarta spends even-dollar exchange to secure rice from places as far away as Louisiana, U.S.A. Here is a clear case where "the institutional framework for development" has been shattered, and where "the sense of permanence and continuity" has disappeared. What were the elements in "colonial" policy that permitted the unparalleled development in Indonesia during the century ending in 1940?

The idea of "development" does not appear in Indonesian colonial experience until the nineteeth century. Up to that time, "trade" was centered in local products that were found on hand (stress on the spice trade, etc.). With the introduction *by the Dutch* of rubber, copra, palm oil, tea, sugar, sisal, and all the other "typical" Indonesian products, the problems and policies of development appear. The "interests" are more clearly defined and the conflict emerges between the cultural integrity of the native civilization and the plantation drive for profit. A Dutch cabinet that came into office in 1901 specifically formulated the emerging policy (the so-called "ethical" or trustee policy). Plantation concessions were to be judged in terms of their impact upon the integrity of the village culture. Cultural policy was formulated which would avoid centralized and uniform bureaucracy. There are some fifteen to twenty clearly recognizable racial groups in the islands, and some two hundred local dialects. Malay was fostered as the common language of Dutch administration—it ultimately became the official "Indonesian" language —but Dutch administration made the protection of the local culture a central objective. Natives were to be judged in courts in which their customary law was to be the standard—not Dutch or Western law, but so-called "adat" law. "Adat" simply means native custom; we would say "common law." Since law as such might easily disintegrate under the impact of impersonal Western market forces, Leyden University devoted some of its best scholarly resources to the study, adaptation, and codification of "adat" law. Van Vollenhoven, known to the world as a great international lawyer, was an authority on "adat" law and codified the customary law of the natives, including among other things the principle that no Dutchman or Westerner was ever to be a judge in any of the "adat" law courts.

Landownership was never to be vested in non-Indonesians, much to the displeasure of many foreign and Dutch investors. Provision was made for small, subsistence landholdings for the natives when leases were granted for plantation cultivation, and "estates" were heavily taxed—up to 45 per cent of earned profits —to develop public works, sanitation, irrigation dams for rice culture to supply food for the native population. The central ideas were "federal" or "pluralistic" rather than "central." They were concerned with the *institutional framework as a whole* before economic development was permitted or encouraged. Negatively, they included discouragement of Christian missionaries and, positively, they provided for scholarly development of Moslem resources, including the establishment of Asiatic and Arabian culture as a field of academic study at Leyden University (Snouck Hurgronje). They included emphasis on education on the village (dessa) level in vocational and agricultural subjects rather than the introduction of the Western stress on literacy, which was socially irrelevant but available for those who sought it.

Western influences regarded the protection of the local culture as "reactionary," and such capitalist as well as liberal influences —in the Netherlands and in Indonesia—were stimulated by Communist infiltration and by the Japanese occupation during World War II. Djakarta now follows a policy that aims at bureaucratic centralization, uniformity of rule, and "verbal literacy" as an educational objective—and the evidence of disintegration of culture, removal of customary restraints, and general proletarianization abounds. The modern form of Asiatic "nationalism" is not an alternative to communism, but its most fruitful preparation. Meanwhile the basic pillars of economic development have crumbled away: foreign capital has disappeared and foreign technical assistance has become costly and short term in character. Communism may depend more on empty minds and empty souls than on empty stomachs, but in Indonesia it flourishes on a combination of empty souls and empty stomachs—and an American foreign policy designed "to strengthen the free world" by the promotion of a premature independence for Indonesia has materially strengthened the likelihood that an area that is vital from the standpoint of strategic raw materials might be lost to chaos (or to the enemy) in case of developing world conflict.

Naïve enthusiasts for the idea that the "disintegration of colonialism" represented a victory for the "revolutionary dynamic of 1776"—and they can be found in both American political parties —are beginning to have second thoughts. They are coming to understand that there is a difference between the American experience of a young nation which was a part of one of the most advanced political communities in the world and which was asserting that certain crucial liberties were beyond the scrutiny of government (be it the government of a tyrannical king abroad or a willful democratic majority at home), and a feverish Asiatic majoritarian totalitarianism that is trying to make "freedom" synonymous with nationalism unqualified by the Bill of Rights. We are also beginning to appreciate the fact that airfields in Morocco or naval oil depots in Sumatra have a determining influence in global strategy, and that they may be strategically more significant in defending the freedom of the people of Morocco or of Indonesia than the slogans of Moscow's "anti-imperialist" propaganda might suggest.

Free political institutions, an adequate flow of capital, and the availability of technical personnel on a trained career basis, all *depend upon a moral and social context* without which political and economic development is inconceivable. There is a curious inability to understand the vital importance of the social context of freedom—both in America itself and throughout the world. Freedom, democracy, civil liberties, parliamentary government, all these words describe institutions that derive their meaning and their viability *from a social and moral context*. They are not ideas that can be transplanted in the absence of the social and moral prerequisites for their birth. Americans sometimes talk about the "export of freedoms" without appreciation of the historic fact that freedom—that is to say, the presence of responsible choice—is viable only within a framework of shared values. If a national culture is in a state of disorganization, the import of economic, political, and personal "freedoms" may undermine the last vestiges of social authority, and we may then witness another example of the classical Aristotelian cycle in which libertarianism is the immediate predecessor of despotism. On the other hand, the American revolution of 1776 is too often seen abroad as a symbol of triumphant nationalism, although the essence of our Bill of Rights is clearly the idea of a specific constitutional declaration of the limits beyond which the national will may not go in its legislative treatment of certain enumerated crucial liberties of the mind. In this sense, modern nationalism with its totalitarian intolerance of minorities is the exact opposite of the doctrine of the American Declaration of Independence and the subsequent Bill of Rights, and it is not at all surprising that Communist propaganda finds it possible to use such modern nationalist movements as convenient channels for the achievement of its own imperialist purposes.

There is a sad irony in the thought that America with its commitment to ideas such as federalism and cultural pluralism should pursue a policy that naïvely assumes the preeminence of economics in the explanation of almost any type of cultural or political problem, while the Russians, who are supposed to believe that only a change in the mode of production can bring about basic social and political modifications, in fact ignore economic change in their tactical approach to marginal countries. Instead, they concentrate on the political instrumentalities through which power can be seized and a new structure of social hierarchy and order substituted for the social disorganization that gave them their opportunity.

The strength of communism in its impact upon the non-communist world lies in its understanding of the role of the *political* framework within which economic and cultural decisions can be made. The weakness of the free and democratic world lies in its stress on personal and political liberties without a corresponding emphasis on the reconstruction of the shared community values upon which these liberties depend for their realization. "Nationalism" by itself is one of the most subtle enemies of freedom *in the Bill of Rights sense of the term,* and the perverse modern identification of the word "freedom" with extreme nationalism, which began with Hitler's "Freiheit und Brot," is simply another warning against the semantic confusion which is the first objective of any totalitarian attack on a free society.

There is a gold standard governing the verbal currency of political controversy, and there is a semantic equivalent for Gresham's law as well. Words are not crystals, transparent and unchanging. They are rather—as Justice Holmes once said— the skin of a living thought and they may vary greatly in color and content according to the circumstances and time in which they are used. When variations in meaning are deliberately introduced in order to confuse the debate, it is time to return to the classical sources, which in their relation to the cultural ideal of a free society will invariably reveal an explicit or implicit reliance upon the inner checks of moral constraint. External constraint or police power—whether native or foreign is here immaterial—can only be replaced by freedom in this classical sense where the shared values of a society can be trusted to ensure sufficient social cohesion by reliance upon the internal constraint inherent in the cultural discipline itself.

We have written the final chapters of the history of "colonialism" in the sense of the exploitation of one people for the benefit of another, except in the sense in which the people of the Moluccan Islands are now exploited by the people of Java, or the people of Hyderabad by the people of India as a whole. With the exception of the areas and peoples controlled by the Soviet Union, such relations will now have to be placed on the basis of reciprocity and mutual benefit, and those who have only recently drunk from the heady cup of nationalist independence will need to ask themselves how they can find adequate substitutes that ensure a reciprocal respect for one another's interests and for the economic and social development that was often one of the undeniable byproducts of the colonialism of the past.

It is politically fashionable to speak, say, of the "wealth" of Indonesia which was "exploited" by the Dutch— and many other examples could be cited—but the sober fact is that the so-called "cash" crops of Indonesia were introduced by the Western agricultural science of the Dutch "exploiters." Copra, coffee, tobacco, rubber—and even quinine—all these were imports to Indonesia as a part of a systematic development program before they could become profitable exports. The wealth that was "exploited" had to be introduced with the aid of foreign capital and technical assistance. There is much in the present record to suggest that it cannot even be preserved at the old level, and least of all expanded, if a suitable respect is not maintained for the interests and for the skills of those whose cooperation is essential for the "development" of such resources. The point is valid irrespective of the nationalities that may be involved, and the only substitute for the old imperialist constraint—or police power—will be the development of the internal discipline or inner constraint which is the moral prerequisite of freedom everywhere.

There is a sense—and the example of Turkey is suggested—in which the most important requirement for economic development is a religious reformation which will give adequate moral recognition to material and physical motivation. How can traditional determinism of the Egyptian Moslem variety or the deep-seated Indian respect for physical and material renunciation be reconciled with the respect for work and the material motivation that are the conditions without which a program for economic development will never get out of the blueprint stage? It is easy to draw up programs of educational reform designed to serve the economic needs of a country—there are shelves of such reports in India—but how can a democratic government make such reforms effective rapidly if they call for a change in the values of the people themselves? Even the simpler forms of economic development—such as the adaptation of techniques of advanced agriculture to the specific requirements of local soil and climate—call for major educational changes modifying native habits of disdain for practical and laboratory work.

Will the expenditure of imported dollars reduce the gap between desirable educational objectives and prevalent community values? Or is some form of outside prodding unavoidable if educational stagnation is deeply rooted in the shared values of such a community? Have the insights of Max Weber and R. H. Tawney concerning the moral origin of Western economic institutions nothing to contribute to our thinking about the economic development of countries in which exactly the opposite religious attitudes prevail? Or is it perhaps naïvely assumed that such moral factors are simply a byproduct of economic stimulation? Is there any evidence anywhere to bolster up the notion that the type of self-control and caution that are indispensable for direction and supervision are automatically generated by a sufficiently generous flow of purchasing power? At a minimum these questions suggest that *time* itself is one of the essential ingredients of the type of cultural change that is contemplated in some of the more ambitious United Nations pronouncements in this field. None of the older forms of colonialism were as culturally aggressive and subversive as the currently fashionable "economism" which explicitly assumes that a free society can be built by a flow of foreign financial grants matched with a vague desire for material improvement.

The "principle of jointness" and "the sense of permanence and continuity," of which the Mutual Security Agency memorandum spoke, are well illustrated in the Netherlands experience in Indonesia, which is typical rather than exceptional. The stream of capital at—for the Far East—exceptionally low rates of interest was dependent upon specialized banking experience and confidence in the sanctity of contract which was insured by Netherlands sovereignty. "There were no Abadans in Lord Palmerston's day," but in a world in which Abadans are a predictable political risk, capital will have to carry the additional charges inherent in the political rapacity of nationalist politicians who need to be taught a refresher course on the sanctity of contract by painful domestic or foreign experience. Handouts from the United States Treasury are not a long-run remedy for the confiscation of British or Dutch investments, and it is no consolation to remember that the people of Iran or of Java are the most tragic victims of their leaders' blindness to economic and political facts. Would Nehru, Sukarno, or Naguib invest Indian, Indonesian, or Egyptian capital in countries in which earlier investments by their own nationals had just been stolen? The Indonesian example—both the flow of capital at low cost *before* and the cessation of the flow of capital at any cost *after* the establishment of the Indonesian Republic— suggests the conditions for a restoration of productive cooperation in the future. It may be necessary for security reasons to bridge the gap temporarily with aid and subsidies, but economic development on a continuous and dependable basis will call for new forms of restraint and discipline sufficient to induce a competitive comparison with other possible uses of capital available for such purposes.

Recent developments in the Philippine Islands and in India show a concern for ensuring appropriate conditions to induce foreign investment, including—in India—the assurance that foreign majority stockholders of oil refineries will be able to "control" their investment and that no projects exist for "nationalization." In an atmosphere in which "Abadan" is financial shorthand for a major investment hazard, such assurances may need to take an appropriate legal form under international auspices. United Nations experience in Southeast Asia suggests that these examples may be indicative of a major shift in the political trend in countries with a recent "colonial" experience.

A new flow of foreign investment will depend first of all upon the creation *in the borrowing countries* of a political climate favorable to such investment. There are no political mysteries or serious intellectual problems here. The International Chamber of Commerce has clearly stated the rules of the game—they can be simply restated in ordinary language. There must be assurance by the borrowing country that the foreign property will not be stolen or "expropriated." There must be assurance that the lender will be able to collect interest on his investment and that he will be eventually repaid as far as the principal is concerned. And the lender must be free to develop his investment with technical and administrative skill that may have to be imported with the capital, although it will surely be necessary to provide for the training of native personnel as part of the development program. In our current fashion of rediscovering the achievements of private action in the past in the elaboration of the details of present public programs, it is too easily forgotten that the private investments of the nineteenth century brought with them the complete array of technical personnel and managerial skills. Technical assistance, although it was not so described, and the export of "know how" were born long before "Point 4."

In a recent article Chester Bowles speaks of Asiatic experience with colonialism in the following terms:

As colored peoples they associate their unhappy past with the rule of arrogant white men who rarely bothered to learn their language, paid scant attention to their rich culture or their history, and quite obviously considered them second-class human beings.[2]

He points to the commendable new instructions to learn the Hindi language which are now given to all U.S. Embassy employees in India, and he speaks of a prospective "six-week indoctrination school" in which all new U.S. employees in New Delhi will be introduced to Indian cultures and problems. These practices are new and commendable innovations in the American foreign service, but the remarks about "colonialism" suggest that Mr. Bowles is apparently unaware of the established traditions of the old colonial services in which—as, for instance, in the Netherlands—no new employee was ever *sent to* Indonesia without at least *two years* of prior training in languages and culture at the University of Leyden or the University of Utrecht. There were some "arrogant white men" who remained ignorant of native language and culture, and *they* are in independent Indonesia *now*. They were not in the colonial government's service but engaged in private business—and they are carrying on such activities at present. The public services, however, were typically the custodians of native culture against the eroding pressures of Western business practices, often also engaged in by natives or by Chinese middlemen.

It is instructive to compare the hit-or-miss recruiting of present

"technical assistance" programs with the regular career basis of
the earlier colonial service. Young people were recruited at the
universities with the incentive of academic training at government expense. Such doctors or engineers were then, after five to
seven years of university training, committed to a period of
(usually) ten years of required service in the colonies. After that
period they were free to leave the public service, and a large
number remained in either public or private practice. In this
manner specialists who knew the country and its problems were
continuously recruited from the very best groups of scholarship
students in the metropolitan centers, and a regular flow of
training and research emerged that centered on the specific
problems of the area. In this way, Leyden became a center for
tropical diseases, and Delft a training school for Indonesian
irrigation engineers. Young men were induced to enter the
service because it was a dependable and secure life career with
attractive pension systems, etc. This should be compared with
the present one-, two-, or three-year contracts and the corresponding lack of incentive for specialization. Salaries that are double
the usual rate in the Netherlands are now insufficient to draw
mediocre talent, whereas in the past scales that were only slightly
in excess of the European salaries sufficed to draw the best talent
into a life career.

Here again a promise and a policy that has some validity *over
time* is the essential difference. It is not merely a matter of dependable scholarship incentives in recruiting and attractive salary
scales in subsequent service. A capable public health officer—or
irrigation engineer—will be rapidly demoralized if corrupt or
lax government is not prepared to enforce the technical policies
that are required for dependable results—and the demoralized
conditions in Java rice culture are merely one example. It is possible to conceive of a high-grade international technical development service with a regular flow of able talent from the world's
universities, although such a service with rotation, say, from Indonesia to Egypt, would inevitably lose some of the valuable byproducts of geographical "identification" that were so frequently
characteristic of the Indian or Indonesian service under British
or Dutch supervision. It is much more difficult to see how able
talent could be *retained* in such a civil service if adequate local
administrative support were not forthcoming. Can sanctions be

developed that would help to ensure such support? And is the "single country" approach compatible with the development of such sanctions? Or is it better to strive from the beginning for a maximum use of budgetary and human resources to develop the largest possible program of student exchanges to ensure native cadres in the specialized branches in all "development" countries?

Many of our problems are "problems" only because we are committed to seeking solutions that are compatible with our ideal of a free society. It is clear that many of these difficulties evaporate if we postulate development along totalitarian lines— as illustrated in China or in Poland today. It is possible that such a trend is inherently unavoidable because of the "majoritarian totalitarianism" of modern nationalism in its Far Eastern and Middle Eastern forms. If we are committed—for ideological or for security reasons—to the strengthening of the *free* world, the social implications of economic development will need continuous and imaginative stress, and policy will have to vary with the special context of geographical, human, historic, and moral factors. If the aim is to build and maintain a society hospitable to freedom and growth, the requirements of growth—and specifically of economic growth—are *social* in the broadest sense of the term, and they tend to make much of the present-day economist's technical, logical refinement of narrowly defined economic postulates about as irrelevant to the solution of a policy-maker's problems as the logical positivist's views on ethics are to a nursery school teacher in downtown New York.

This is not the vulgar complaint about economists who "do not agree." We may recall Winston Churchill's story about his request for advice from the six leading economists in England. He received "seven opinions—two from Mr. Keynes." It is easy to imagine seven from Mr. Keynes—all sound but based upon different presuppositions. It is not necessary to question the logic or the quality of training of many contemporary economists when we question the *relevance* of their postulates and therefore of their policy conclusions. In many "growth" situations Adam Smith's or John Stuart Mill's postulates—and, therefore, conclusions—are even today more relevant than those of many contemporary Keynesians. Keynes himself would not be included among the Keynesians, for he knew how to shift his postulates around, and how to keep himself and his reader aware of the significance of the change in postulates in the evaluation of the relevance of his conclusions.

In studying the potentials for growth and development, it is easy to recognize the importance of natural resources and population. Then there are relevant knowledge and education. There must be saving from current consumption, or investment from abroad. There must be an open attitude toward innovation and enterprise. There must be a government prepared to maintain law and order, and to give a promise some validity over time. There must be freedom to criticize and to challenge. Freedom of intellectual enterprise is an essential part of freedom of enterprise as a whole. And there must be a moral potentiality for developing the types of persistence, discipline, and restraint that are related to and essential for a stable combination of all these elements.

There is very little academic discussion in English of these elements in the problem of growth and development.[3] David McCord Wright's *Capitalism*[4] has an admirable chapter including the strikingly pertinent statement by Alfred North Whitehead that *a race makes progress which combines reverence for its symbols with courage in their revision.* Enterprise does not flourish where the status quo is sacred and unchangeable. Freedom cannot even be born where there is—in Lord Acton's words —a "belief in the function of ghosts to make laws for the quick." Neither does enterprise flourish in chaos and disorder. We need a fortunate polarity of freedom and order, and a mere flow of dollars is the least likely method of achieving it.

It is impossible to build a society out of nothing but transition and mobility, and we in America could supply some gory details concerning the need for social reconstruction where excessive mobility has eroded social cohesion to the point of normlessness, or what Durkheim's sociology called "anomie." It is equally clear that growth and development do not arise in the stalemate of indefinite repetition of a historic ideal. As Whitehead has said, "Without adventure civilization is in full decay." The export of dollars—or of competitive free enterprise—could *by itself* do more harm than good if it were not accompanied by a deliberate effort to reconstruct the social context in which fredom might be meaningful.

Exactly the same objection can be raised against a public program of rapid economic development which ignored—or simply assumed—the social and moral context of such change. Professor S. Herbert Frankel of Oxford, in a sharp critique of the United Nations Report on *Measures for the Economic Development of Under-Developed Countries,* has put his finger on the basic weakness of the type of "development" thinking that emphasizes almost exclusively the need for "foreign capital." In a richly documented warning against oversimplification of the problem of structural change, he summarizes:

For structural change is a vast process of slowly evolving social and economic re-orientations. It is not at all like the switching of factors of production to making one product instead of another; and it cannot be adequately discussed in terms of mere "planning" decisions. To postulate major structural readjustment is to imply that the goal of change is known; whereas this is precisely what is not known—unless we are to trust to the intuition of the artist-planner. . . . Human beings are not a medium of artistic expression, except for tyrants. . . . Development depends not on the abstract national goals of, and the more or less enforced decisions by, a cadre of planners, but on the piecemeal adaptation of individuals to goals which emerge but slowly and become clearer only as those individuals work with the means at their disposal; and as they themselves become aware, *in the process of doing,* of what can and ought to be done next. . . . What is involved is neither just another ready-to-hand goal of action, nor the transfer of a new set of techniques, but the necessarily slow growth of new aptitudes, and of new ways of doing, living, and thinking.[5]

Freedom is first of all the presence of choice—in values, in politics, and in economics. It calls for an intellectual understanding of the choice as well as for the development of a moral will to choose. Historically freedom emerges when internal checks can be substituted for external constraint, and, conversely, freedom is endangered if a free community's shared values are no longer sufficiently vigorous to create the moral cohesion on which the discipline of free men rests. When you pulverize a rock, you have dust. When it rains on dust, you have mud. That, in brief, is the problem of any society in which mobility erodes the shared values which hold it together while no alternative source of co-

hesion is developed. That is how even a free democracy with
rising material standards of living may become what Walt Whitman called a society of men with hearts of rags and souls of
chalk. Many forms of modern nationalism or collectivism are
blind efforts to hold together a society that has been pulverized;
in other words, they are attempts to organize a community that
has literally been *dis*organized.

Political freedom depends not only upon constitutions and
forms of political organization. It calls for a sociological and
moral context in which dispersed economic controls are compatible with social cohesion, and a blind imitation of such competitive controls in a society in which the cultural context cannot
be taken for granted merely holds out a temptation to political
despotism which creates, as it were, an iron framework to prevent
social disintegration. Modern collectivism is not social in the
sense of being rooted in community.

The contemporary appeal of totalitarianism—and of a good
deal of modern nationalism—has its roots in the destruction of
community which has produced the normless (anomic) individual, the alienated man. In their quest for restored community
they respond to the social appeal of the totalitarians but find a
strengthened state that obliterates the free associational vestiges
that are still left. The "community development" schemes of
the Indian economic plan, with their deliberate stress on the
reconstruction of the diversified village societies *as social wholes,*
are an encouraging sign that the democratic leadership in New
Delhi is beginning to understand that economic development
by itself may intensify the vulnerability to totalitarian appeal,
and it is deeply encouraging that American aid in India—both
public and private—has chosen these features of the Indian economic plan for special support.

Americans—and foreign observers—who see in our economic
philosophy merely an *economic* mechanism overlook the free
associational society and the moral heritage that are its context.
They also overlook the peculiar noneconomic byproducts of
excessive social mobility that are an urgent problem even in
America itself. They will court disaster if they do not simultaneously develop a sociological program to reconstruct the community while they aim to rely upon the impersonal checks of
deliberately dispersed economic controls. This is not a problem

to refer to specialized sociological agencies while the economic aspects are developed in a typical, modern conveyor-belt fashion by a financial institution—these are two aspects of the *same* thing and they should be treated in their inevitable and unavoidable togetherness.

The text of this essay has really been a long elaboration on the following warning paragraph from the United Nations Report of 1951 on *Measures for the Economic Development of Under-Developed Countries:*

Economic progress will not occur unless the atmosphere is favourable to it. The people of a country must desire progress, and their social, economic, legal, and political institutions must be favourable to it. . . . Progress occurs only where people believe that man can, by conscious effort, master nature.[6]

We may question—as has been done in these pages of comment —the simple assumption that "progress" is merely a question of "mastering nature." If development of men and women fit for the responsibilities of free society is a major objective, the mastery of man or the development of self-control is at least as essential as the capacity "to master nature." But we can clearly not rely on a process of pumping in dollars—and letting political and social history take its course. Even the dollar pump will run dry in short order under such circumstances, and the social and political consequences in the so-called underdeveloped countries will speak eloquently for themselves if we are sociologically blind enough to act on such a narrow economic basis.

Colonial experience with "development" at its best is one long endorsement of the "principle of jointness," of the "community development" approach, of the "country program" approach, of the need for "a sense of permanence and continuity," and of the need for a continuous concern for the "institutional framework" that may be appropriate for economic development. Colonial experience also suggests that a very considerable effort may be required to maintain—or rather to restore—the momentum that had been established in the past. We are not discussing a brand new idea in our "development programs," but we are considering new ways of doing a thing that had in many parts of the world been done very effectively under forms of political administration that were frequently misunderstood and that have now

been discarded. In many parts of the world new national governments are "living off capital" that was invested in the past.
"Disinvestment" is now so widely practiced as a response to the
new political hazards that an investment program will have to
be large indeed to restore the development momentum that was
taken for granted before 1939.

As a nation Americans are peculiarly sensitive to the accusa-
tion of "imperialism," and the rediscovery of some of the virtues
of the nineteenth-century colonial development programs is
likely to intensify the ideological slogan-mongering in this direction. It is characteristic of this tendency that Communist
propaganda has selected the Indian "community development"
program as its favorite channel of attack on the economic planning of New Delhi. For some time to come American foreign aid
will unavoidably be interwoven with American foreign policy
as a whole—and it is hard to visualize a great expansion of
United Nations administration of funds contributed by American taxpayers during a period in which Russian or "neutralist"
votes may veto our own conception of the best methods of
strengthening the independence of politically marginal countries.
In the long run, however, development programs call for guidance and even direction in areas that definitely encroach upon
national autonomy, and it is probable that such influence will
be more acceptable if it is exercised by the International Bank
or by other United Nations agencies rather than by the representatives of a single great power. There is—as Jacob Viner has
said in one of the rare American academic studies of this difficult
subject— ". . . not much actual evidence as yet to aid judgment,
but it is possible that recipient countries might take contractual
obligations to a multi-national agency more seriously, and treat
them as less susceptible to unilateral deviation, than obligations
to a single government which might have political and other
reasons for refraining from pressing vigorously for adhering to
pledges."[7]

It is difficult to expect Western countries to develop public
policies for the development of Asia or of Africa that reflect an
awareness of the economic impact upon the social and political
structure of a society when such considerations still have an
element of novelty in their own domestic development. There
are few examples even today of an effective translation into public

policy of the insights we may owe to our present understanding of the assets as well as of the liabilities that are inherent in the complex historic experience which is described as the "Industrial Revolution." In a similar way it is almost impossible to expect a sudden understanding of the need for qualified sovereignty in countries that have only recently experienced national independence in the political sense of the term. Western nations with a long experience of sovereign independence are gradually learning that self-sufficiency is a myth, and a political hazard to their national survival is producing new forms of integration in which aspects of national sovereignty are surrendered or merged in various types of international organization. It is probable that the painful experience of accepting the discipline of the facts of life will be easier for the formerly dependent peoples of the world if it comes in the form of multi-national limits to national sovereignty rather than in bilateral arrangements that evoke the memory of forms of colonialism, irrespective of the wisdom or the degree of objectivity with which the process may now be interpreted.

11

*The Challenge of Soviet Education**

THIS IS A REPORT BASED ON OBSERVATIONS BY A TEAM OF SEVEN
American college and university presidents who were invited
to visit universities and research institutions in the Soviet Union.
This visit was one of the first arranged under the new cultural
exchange agreement between the United States and the Soviet
governments, and in November of this year a group of seven
U.S.S.R. university rectors will come to visit American universities.

My report of this visit will follow closely the actual path of
our trip: the institutions and the regions which we visited, the
programs we observed, our conversations with Soviet officials and
professors, and here and there I shall make some comparative
remarks about American conditions and equivalents. There is,
I think, a great need for a comparative study of the realities of the
Soviet system in all of its strategically vital aspects. In the past
we have been forced to rely excessively upon information that
was colored by ideological or material preconceptions. Either
a blind, dogmatic "hold the line and all will be well" or an
equally oversimplified faith in "negotiation" for its own sake
colors the stream of American comments about the Soviet Union,
if it is not some form of reactionary industrialist opinion based
on faith in the possibility of "doing business with the Russians."

First of all, let me say something about the nature of our
assignment. It was heavily focused on universities, professional
and technical institutions, and scientific research institutions.

---

* From an Address at a Freedom House luncheon, broadcast over Station
WMCA, and published as *A Freedom House Report,* September 30, 1958.

When we arrived in Moscow we had quite a little struggle to make clear what we wanted to see. And I want to add immediately that we finally succeeded in getting to see everything we had listed, with one exception—the educational institutions of the Communist party itself—and our request in this respect was "for the record" since we did not expect it to be granted. The resistance we seemed to meet was largely based on the feeling that, typical of Americans, we were trying to overdo it. We wanted to see too many things, which, judging by our travel schedule, was perhaps a legitimate objection. But when we insisted we wanted to see not only Moscow and Leningrad, but also the southern part of European Russia and Central Asia, where there were two universities we wished to visit, those arrangements all came through, even if it meant rearranging airplane schedules and making privately chartered plane trips possible in areas "East of Samarkand."

The result, of course, was a very strenuous, typically American schedule, with plane shifts and transfers at two o'clock in the morning in places such as Tashkent in Uzbekistan. The Soviet government went to considerable trouble to make this possible, and an almost compulsive sense of hospitality seems to be characteristic of the way Russians treat foreign visitors. This hospitality takes in the whole range of the world. All of Asia is with you all the time in the Soviet Union. In all your hotels you find Burmese and Indians and Chinese and Indonesians and East Germans—East Germans, by the way, in very impressive numbers. The visitors seem to travel typically in groups, known as "delegations." There is a special ceremony or ritual about the treatment of foreign delegations, and they seem to be drawn from the entire world. Very many of them have all their expenses paid by the Soviet Union. Many of them, of course, are Intourist visitors who pay their own way, or they are Soviet workers who are rewarded for some type of competitive or "incentive" achievement by a variety of "all expenses paid" travel.

The typical official delegation gets the clear green light on transportation, on hotel accommodations, on the available recreational opportunities—the choicest seats in the opera or for a symphony orchestra are reserved for the foreign visitor. If we compare this with our American practice with foreign visitors, we will have some inkling of the rather compelling weakness in our own arrangements in this developing pattern of worldwide cultural exchanges.

I spoke a moment ago of the "ritual" or the "ceremony" of the Russian treatment of the visiting "delegation." The story of the Russian banquet with its toasts has often been told. The reality lives up to the most colorful descriptions. In travel arrangements the Russians do not favor the individual adjustment. In general, they like to keep people in groups. The need for interpreters and for automobile transportation are two strong arguments in favor of group travel, and the foreigner's typical inability to speak Russian is, of course, another factor that explains the emphasis on guides.

I must say for myself, however, and for my colleagues, that if any one in our group wished to depart from the pattern set for the delegation and desired to drop out of the delegation to pursue some individual interest—even in cities hundreds of miles away—we were accommodated. We were not followed on our individual trips in the various cities. I was entirely on my own several times in departures from the official visit, sometimes embarrassingly so, because I have never felt as deficient linguistically as in the Soviet Union. My joy would be to find a Russian professor who knew French or German—and, in the professorial generation, German is known a little more frequently than any other Western language. With the discovery of a common language, all other barriers seemed to disappear simultaneously. So much can be said in direct communication that somehow fails to "come through" when you have to pass through an interpreter's mind. Also, the interpreters sometimes "edit" remarks.

I was reminded a number of times by our own interpreter that my remarks in our professional exchanges were a little more frequently "edited" than those of my colleagues. That didn't surprise me too much, first of all, because of my own professional contacts in public education. After all, I was with a delegation that included the president of Cornell University, the chancellor of the University of Pittsburgh, and the president of the University of Pennsylvania—a rather heavy representation of our large, so-called private universities. As we discussed Russian and American higher education, my experience in public education would sometimes be more directly relevant to Russian conditions. Brooklyn College is a part of the College of the City of New York, which has been tuition-free for more than a hundred years, and Russian universities have only recently become tuition-free. Some of the challenge in my remarks was "edited out." This was one small warning of the dangers in communication which a linguistically illiterate America will face in the future when it competes for the world's attention with the *present* younger generation in the Soviet Union which will be proficient in our language, while we will continue to depend on Russian interpreters if we wish to reach their minds.

Now let me return to the eighteen institutions which we visited and to the eight thousand miles which we "covered." Let me first give you the traject: From Stockholm to Moscow, from Moscow to Leningrad, from Leningrad to below the Caucasus to Tiflis in Georgia, then to Baku, and Samarkand—for sentimental and romantic reasons; there is no big university there. Then to Tashkent and the big University of Uzbekistan, and to Alma-Ata, the University of Kazakhstan. If your geography skips a bit—mine did before I made the trip—the University of Uzbekistan at Tashkent is north of Afghanistan, and the University of Kazakhstan at Alma-Ata is directly north of New Delhi. From the university at Alma-Ata you can see the mountain range, snow-capped like the Alps in Switzerland, that separates you from Mongolia and China.

Incidentally, that reference to China touches on one of the important facts in the Soviet Union's academic and industrial development of that part of Central Asia. I couldn't document this, and this is just intuition, but it is hard to escape the impression that a very large part of the feverish urgency in the development of Kazakhstan and Uzbekistan is based on the desire to fill that area with population before overcrowded China gets ideas about it. Kazakhstan is five times as large as France and has a population of eight million. These simple facts give you the picture: Kazakhstan is just the other side of the Chinese borderline and it is virginal territory with untouched and rich geological resources. Now with modern power development and our new technical knowledge of irrigation, it has a potential for development that matches the old American "West."

SOVIET EDUCATIONAL STANDARDS

There is a great deal of diversity in higher education in the Soviet Union, more than I had expected to find. There are very high standards of academic and research work at the top. My physics colleagues—and there were two in our group who were professional physicists—tell me that the equipment in the best institutions is at least comparable to the best in the United States. In some cases they said—I don't quite appreciate what that would mean—that it was perhaps a little "over-designed." Perhaps they mean by that that the Russians, like Americans, are rather gadget-minded, that is to say, that they like gadgets for the gadgets' sake as distinguished from the function which the gadget is supposed to serve.

Incidentally, it would be a very interesting subject to philosophize on the extent to which Americans and Russians are alike, because this has astonishing ramifications. When I say alike, I mean good, bad, and indifferent qualities, not just the good ones or just the bad ones. There are astonishing resemblances in many respects in the material and technical values and attitudes of the people you meet in both countries. There are also, of course, profound differences but they receive sufficient attention elsewhere. Perhaps we do not stress enough the differences among the various peoples in the Soviet Union. After all, only forty-eight percent of the people in the Soviet Union speak Russian as their native language, and a Russian in the "national" sense does not speak Georgian or Uzbek any more than a citizen of Chicago. With the development of the national cultures of the constituent Soviet republics, the dominant language of the universities in the various republics tends to become Georgian, or Uzbek, or Kazakh—with corresponding difficulties in the transfer and exchange of academic personnel. There are interesting perspectives for the future here, especially in view of the tendency to decentralize the Soviet Union's economic development.

If the level of academic achievement is high in the strong institutions, we received the distinct impression that Soviet standards are higher than ours in the lowest grade of school or university. They are higher because the central pattern is imposed by Moscow, and certain minima are achieved because of this central pattern. By contrast, of course, our "bottom category," which is a large part of the American educational system, has standards which are set locally in accordance with our dogma of local control in education. In the Soviet Union there is no "local control" and the minimum standards—set and determined in Moscow—are constantly checked by competitive and comparative examinations which are centrally administered.

Central control is exercised through the Ministry of Higher Education in Moscow. This Ministry is to be distinguished from the Ministry of Education, which controls elementary and secondary education through a structure of separate ministries in the constituent republics. University textbooks are centrally chosen and determined. Syllabi are centrally selected and determined, and changes have to clear with the Ministry. These things govern examinations for admissions. Quotas for admissions are set from year to year by the Ministry for all the institutions, and only about twenty-five to thirty percent of the applicants are given the opportunity for further study.

But offsetting that—and in Russia you constantly have to say "offsetting that"—the Ministry of Higher Education controls only two hundred out of over seven hundred institutions working in higher education because many institutions of higher education are assigned to cabinet officers in accordance with their specialized function. Medical schools are, for instance, operated under the Minister of Health. Agricultural colleges are run by the Ministry of Agriculture. Many schools are run by ministries that are charged with the industry involved—metallurgy, for instance—and they are not related directly to educational administration. Sometimes they are financed by the industry and they do not even appear in the education budget. There is in consequence an enormous diversity within the centralized structure of Soviet higher education.

Thereby hangs a tale, by the way, of a possible future weakness in the Soviet system that is perhaps not as apparent now as it will be in the future. They are now concerned with immediate acceleration of achievements—with crash programs in the training of medical men, for instance—and they have certainly achieved some impressive results. The future weakness lies in the fact that the staffs are all decentralized. There is little of what we call cross-fertilization.

Medical schools, for example, operate apart from the universities and are under a different ministry, as I pointed out. The research work in medicine is under yet another set of institutions, under academies of research. The result is that there is not the constant fruitful interaction of the professors of chemistry, biology, physiology, and psychology with the professors of medicine. We know from our experience with medical schools that, in general, medical schools tend to degenerate when the professors of medicine, the M.D.'s, run the institution, that is, when the biologists, the chemists, and the psychologists are under the orders of the doctors. We know that medical progress depends on a built-in professional challenge of received ways of thinking in medical practice by independent professors of the various sciences that are directly related to medical practice and medical research. Administrative organization which insures closeness of contact is as important as the autonomy of the professional position of the supporting scientists, and both are missing in the Soviet administrative organization.

In the United States we sometimes suffer from the excessive size of our huge administrative units, but in the Soviet Union these specialists work in different institutions, and sometimes under separate ministries. The byproducts over time do not look too good if our experience has any predictive value. This holds, incidentally, in a wide range of other kinds of professional training too. They have an enormous and exaggerated faith in specialization.

Basically all the educational and scientific objectives are formulated as a part of national economic planning. The crucial principle is "from the top down," and not "from the bottom up." We know the unfortunate byproducts in inertia and lethargy in overcentralized bureaucratic organization in the United States, and it is hard to believe that similar results will not follow in the Soviet Union.

While educational objectives are frequently formulated by professors, by universities, and by the Ministry of Higher Education, their basic approval takes place in the making of the economic plan for the country for the next five or seven years. There it is decided that these resources are going to be developed; that this industry is going to be enlarged; that these areas will need so many more doctors, so many more engineers, and so many more interpreters. These quotas are referred to the Ministry of Higher Education, which then percolates them down to the institutions, and the corresponding quotas for student admissions and staff appointments are then digested in terms of several ministries and hundreds of institutions.

The whole is a little like prescription filling in a drug store. It is not an operation in which the momentum is generated in the course of the pursuit of professional objectives by scholars and teachers on a university campus. It is an operation that consists of doing what the quota said had to be done for the next five or seven years, and then training people to fit that particular set of specifications. The dominant value is service to the state as contrasted with our conception that service to the community is best realized through the maximum development of the potential of the individual.

There is one other major weakness from our standpoint, and that lies in the very fargoing separation of research and teaching. Theoretically, our higher education insists on the fruitfulness of a process of togetherness of teaching and research. We often fail in that, of course. The City of New York, for instance, makes no money available in the New York City municipal colleges for research at all. With strong faculties we succeed in financing research from a variety of outside sources: private foundations, government departments, and private industry.

We believe that teaching suffers if we do not have a good percentage of people engaged in research and the students with them, and we believe that research workers are stimulated by continuous exposure to the compelling discipline of a teaching relationship with advanced students. In wide ranges of the present American college and university system we may fail to live up to our ideal view of the fruitfulness of combining research and instructional functions, but there is hardly any difference of opinion as to the theoretical objective.

In the Soviet Union there is a firmly held belief that the best results in teaching and in research are achieved by separating those groups. This is a logical consequence of their faith in specialization and in a very fargoing division of labor. Our experience would seem to indicate that in the long run this will not pay off.

Now let us look at some of the strong qualities of the Soviet structure in higher education. In every one of the republics there is a structure of universities and professional schools. In every one of the republics there exists a corresponding structure of research organization, all of them grouped under the general administrative organization of the Moscow Academy of Science. Science is here used in the general European sense of knowledge, including not merely the pure sciences, but also the humanistic disciplines, such as literature and archaeology. The Academy of Science budget, we found as we went from one Soviet Republic to another, varies a good deal from one republic to another, but the lowest figure we discovered was six times as large as the university budget. The highest we found was sixteen times as large—sixteen times as much money spent for research as for the university teaching budget. These are proportions that dwarf anything we have in the United States in that respect and they are probably sinister in their implications for the future, unless we manage in some way or other to catch up dramatically relative to the position in which we are now.

There is a surprising amount of autonomy in many areas in the individual universities. The staffs have preserved a good deal of freedom of a sort, as, for instance, in the selections of people for the lower ranks for academic appointment and in the right to nominate people for the highest rank. Nominations for the rank of full professor have to be approved centrally, but the record seems to be, from what we were told in a variety of places, that typically the nominations are accepted—except, of course, in the case of people who go flagrantly against the party line in one way or another.

Academic life seemed to be in the main rather indifferent and casual as far as the party line was concerned. Large numbers of the faculty personnel—a large majority—did not appear to be members of the party. Take, for instance, the atmosphere with regard to the required courses in party indoctrination that every student in any academic program has to take: a course in philosophy, which is really a history of dialectic materialism, and a course in economics, sometimes called the "history of the working class." But the attitudes with regard to these courses have become attitudes of rather stereotyped compliance, a bored kind of acquiescence. Nowhere did we encounter any enthusiastic defense of these requirements, which is very interesting. They were just described, nothing more. When we asked questions about the materials, we encountered an attitude of rather passive indifference with regard to what was being taught in them. Perhaps this accounts for some of the scepticism concerning "community attitudes" which is reflected in some of Mr. Khrushchev's statements.

In general we must visualize the Russian university and the research world as a world of exceptional privilege. This is very difficult to do from an American standpoint when we think of the downtrodden academic proletariat that carries the responsibility for the role of trained intelligence in this country's survival. The Russian full professor gets about the highest salary paid in the Soviet Union; if he has the rank of Academician he receives the salary of the grade one, top industrial plant manager. The only salaries that are higher are open-market earnings, so to speak, of ballerinas and popular artists, and here and there some popular authors.

In addition to his salary, the Russian full professor "Academician" gets the big black car that is the symbol of the highest status and prestige. There are three types of cars in Russia, and their assignments carry prestige connotations. The "Academician" gets the big black car and chauffeur, in addition to salary, and a summer home maintained also in addition to salary. He has three times the normal housing allowance. That also is the maximum housing allowance given to any privileged class, including ministers. One can see that the motives for getting into academic and scientific life are overwhelmingly strong. The motives are strengthened by the methods of recruiting students. Students are paid for competitive academic achievement, that is to say, they are paid for being students. They call it the stipend system. We could call it the scholarship system, except that scholarships have connotations that are different from their stipends.

More than eighty percent of the Soviet Union's students receive stipends. The stipend is roughly about four hundred roubles a month during the first year, and as the recipients demonstrate their ability to pass the grade and do well, the stipend may increase to about six hundred roubles a month. In other words, the pay goes up as the grades go up. There is, therefore, competitive motivation in the student years backed by substantial material motivation in the choice of the subsequent academic career. If we compare this with our own picture of almost total indifference with regard to academic achievement, we have a measure, again, of a very important differential in the atmosphere of the Russian university. The twenty percent or less that do not receive stipends are partly people on their own who get incomes sufficiently high to remove the need for stipends, and partly people on their way out.

Incidentally, while I am on that point, let me push it just a bit further. This combination of paying students for the quality of their academic work, paying them better if it improves in academic achievement, accompanied by the prospect of a career (if you are good enough to get into it), of scholarship and research that is the most highly paid career in the country, insures that Russia gets the full potential in science and in scholarship, and in teaching ability, which may be available in a given age group—and that, of course, is very different from what we get.

In the United States it is still true that roughly about one-third of the ablest quarter of our students in high school do not go on to college. The reason for this great waste is not so much a question of economic means as of motivation. The reason is deeply embedded in our culture, in "motivation" as it is reflected in our attitudes toward scholarship, and in "motivation" as it is reflected in the choice of postgraduate careers, in salary expectations, family attitudes toward the choice of a career, and so forth.

From the standpoint of the retention of intellectual ability for academic purposes, we must add to the facts that the Russians are getting a larger share of the potential ability in the age group trained and developed, and that they retain them in scholarly and research work, the fact that if their students graduate with the equivalent of our Ph.D. degree, industry can hire them only at a lower salary rate than they could obtain in academic life. This is a matter of law. It is set for the Soviet Union so there is no seepage or loss to industrial occupations from the training and the research apparatus.

There is one other aspect that is probably overwhelmingly

important, although one would want to have more time to study it in all of its ramifying detail, and that is the use of women. They make very much more use of women in scholarly research and academic work. The figures on that are very impressive. One-third of their university faculties are women. I do not need to tell you that is very far from the fact in the United States. There are no teacher shortages, on any level, in the Soviet Union. Fifty-one percent of the university students are women. That is also very far from the American fact. In agricultural schools the student body is about fifty percent women. In an area like medicine, feminine enrollment is sixty-nine percent of the total. Medicine is a woman's profession in Russia. Incidentally, that is not wholly a Soviet idea. I am told by colleagues that in European universities before 1917 feminine students of medicine from Russia were very common under the Czarist regime.

The full use of female "manpower" is, of course, a general characteristic of the Soviet economy. There are very unpleasant aspects of this too. Women do physical labor of the crudest sort in Russia, including street cleaning and bricklaying, as well as some of the roughest physical labor in the fields of agriculture and construction. In Moscow all you had to do is to turn into a construction job—and no one stopped you if you wanted to do that—and you could see that the overwhelming majority of the people working on the big new skyscraper were women. Many of them, I am told, are married women. The educational system is adjusted to take care of children after they have reached the age of six months, and the children are therefore removed from the mother's care during the hours she is on the job, doing a job which, by our standards, would be altogether too demanding for a woman of almost any kind of physical stamina.

To an outsider the general role played by women—the crude one in industry and in agriculture, the more specialized and qualitative one in academic and research work—is one of the most characteristic traits of the Soviet social system. It could all by itself be a determining factor in a struggle for survival between two social systems, if the difference in that respect remained as striking as it is now.

Another vitally significant factor is the teaching of foreign languages. The older generation Russians, my age group, the ones who are now the full professors and the rectors, are, I would say, linguistically as illiterate as their American equivalents. It is amazing how few of them can understand or speak English, German, or French. We found one university rector, the one in Leningrad, who spoke admirable English. We found several who were reputed to have training in one or more languages, but I couldn't find a single one of these who could respond to any conversational efforts on my part.

With the younger generation it is stunningly different. The twenty-year-olds are getting five years of a foreign language in their secondary school and, no matter what they specialize in, four more years on what we would call the university, college, and fifth-year level. Much of that, however, is reading knowledge. They do not have acquaintance with people who speak these languages. They are not allowed to travel, nor are foreigners allowed to enter the country in sufficiently large numbers to share linguistic skills with them.

But the figures are impressive. For instance, in Moscow a huge Foreign Language Institute of university grade shows a forty-eight percent English specialization, with thirty percent in German, and twenty-two percent in French, and in the Pedagogical Institute in Moscow there was an eighty percent enrollment in English. The future is predictably going to be a situation in which, when Americans and Russians meet one another and meet the rest of the world, Americans are going to be dependent on interpreters, while the Russians will be "on their own" in direct linguistic communication with us, and with the rest of the world. There is no more debilitating weakness than to be dependent on the other fellow's linguistic skills in cultural exchanges, in political negotiations, or in competitive propaganda. He can dance circles around you and your objectives, unless you have the ability to meet him on his own ground. It strikes me as one of the most dramatic and one of the dangerous potentials in the present differentials between our system on the one hand and the Soviet system on the other.

Before I attempt to summarize these rambling remarks, I should say something about the quality and adequacy of Soviet secondary school preparation. Wherever we went, we were very much concerned about ascertaining the attitude of the Russian university professor toward the products of the secondary school because we had heard so much in the U.S.A.—from the Admiral

Rickovers, from the editors of *Life* magazine, and from other comparable education experts—about the superiority of the Russian secondary school. In that respect, we are not nearly as disturbed as some of our amateur critics of American education.

Attitudes in the Russian university with regard to the quality of pre-university preparation are amazingly like American attitudes, perhaps because of comparable problems in dealing with huge enrollment increases. They think ten years is not enough for academic preparation, and everywhere they are experimenting with eleven years for the secondary school, and the twelfth year is in sight. They complain about textbooks, about the parrot-like instruction. One Russian professor when asked the question, "Are you satisfied with the preparation of the secondary school graduate as he comes to you?" said, "Satisfied? They know no mathematics, their physics is parrot-like repetition of a secondary school textbook, and their Russian is abominable!" This was said in the presence of the rector and other high academic officials, and he was apparently expressing a generally shared attitude. He was very surprised when we all laughed, and he did not think it was funny. We had to explain that we laughed because we had heard this in the United States again and again, too. That was news to him.

Let me try to summarize. There have been astonishing achievements in the Soviet Union in a short period of years. There are weaknesses in their form of academic organization, weaknesses in their excessive faith in specialization, and in their neglect of what we call general or liberal education. I also see weaknesses in their stereotyped ideological formula of always wanting one book, one course, one syllabus—in fact, their ideological inability to understand that truth can sometimes be plural. They want one solution for every problem. They do not understand that we sometimes feel that provision for the presence of choice is a desirable method of seeking and teaching the truth. They do not understand choice. They always want the argument narrowed down to one formula and one solution.

Even when we were talking to them about American problems, they did not understand why we didn't have one solution rather than say, as we did, that we favored a policy of advising students in accordance with their respective individual abilities. They always wanted to know why we didn't focus on one formula just

as they themselves seemed to operate under the compulsive necessity of seeking the one solution for everyone in every Soviet
Republic rather than a variety of formulas to fit different circumstances.

I have spoken of the strengths of their system in the fields of
student motivation and in the choice of academic careers. They
are to be found particularly in the field of physical science.
Geology is overwhelmingly much more important with them
than it is with us, in addition to the fields I mentioned. We
found more interest in humanistic disciplines than we were led
to believe. The academies of science pursue historical and
archaeological research. Expeditions are digging out the past.
At Samarkand some of them were digging out the Moslem past
and reconstructing, with Soviet public money, big Moslem tem-
ples with the political objective of making Arabs turn to Samarkand rather than to Mecca or Medina, sometime in the future
when they have been rebuilt. The humanistic interest in religion
was pleasantly merged with political objectives in that particular
connection.

Our impression is not that they have superiority over our
results now. There may clearly be equality in some fields, not
superiority. But the impression of almost everyone in the delegation was that if you measured the dynamic, the direction of
change, if you looked at the overwhelmingly big capital outlay
budgets for new buildings now going up and projected for the
future, if you looked at the qualitative emphasis on achievement,
and if you compared all these things with our complacency and
inertia, there were vital weaknesses in our corresponding institutions and procedures which called for a major breakthrough
in our effort if we were to avoid losing out merely by staying
where we are.

The Soviet dynamic, the direction of change is very impressive.
If you think of the role that trained intelligence plays in national
survival—and I think it is true in that respect to say that no
modern community in the world in which we live can survive
unless it respects trained intelligence—then a comparison of the
direction of change in the Soviet and in the American systems of
higher education could make you very gloomy about the American comparative picture ten years from now and twenty years

from now, unless we have what I called *a major breakthrough* in moral as well as material support.

As an economist, I constantly asked questions about the percentage of the national income that is going to education and research. It is hard enough to get reliable American data in answer to that question. It is even more difficult to secure reliable data in Russia because in their system all these things are buried in a wide variety of ministerial and production budgets. In the United States we know that it is approximately three and one-half percent of gross national product, and we know that it has roughly remained at that level for the last thirty years. In other words, it has not increased with the increasing burdens, with the increasing numbers of pupils and students, and with the increasing costs of diversifying programs.

My rough impression would be that in Russia it is more than double that percentage of the national income. In the United States—allowing for the depreciation of the dollar and increasing enrollments—this would mean not a doubling, but *more* than a tripling of the actual number of dollars spent for education. You will remember the shock in Washington when we talked about doubling budgets for education beyond the high school level, in spite of the fact that everyone should know that the doubled budgets by 1970 were supposed to provide for doubled college and university enrollments. Under those circumstances doubled budgets would simply mean that we were merely keeping up with ourselves, and not getting better at all. If we desire to improve our dynamic, that is to say, if we wish to improve our achievement, we will have to provide for more than double our present budgets. This will be mandatory in order to counteract the present deterioration in our standards, but a comparison with the direction of change in the Russian system seems to indicate that we must do a good deal better than this if our provision for trained intelligence is to be adequate to insure our national survival.

There is one danger against which I would like to warn, in closing. It is rather easy to understand the weaknesses of an excessively specialized system of education. We can see the weaknesses of our present programs in foreign language instruction, too. The danger is that, as we try to overcome these weaknesses, we shall begin to teach subjects, and languages included, as tools with which to acquire direct power in the achievement of national purposes. If we do that we will be selling our own birthright down the river because we should not be concerned with languages as a tool for the successful achievement of state power objectives. If we are true to our own values in a free society, we should be interested in language and cultural education as a method of understanding the diversified richness of human cultural potentials in all these fields.

The Russians themselves have experienced weaknesses with that. While their interpreters are linguistically skilled, they find they do not have the general liberal education background to understand fully the thing they are technically capable of translating. This is a characteristic weakness of an overspecialized kind of educational training.

If we merely emphasize the financial and the technical side of the Russian challenge, we might eventually end up by being as good as they are in the achievement of *their*, and *not of our* purposes. This is a qualitative challenge and it is, first of all, a challenge to the values of American life. Even in the limited field of technology, it is not a question of more engineers, but of better engineers. We can restore the cutting edge of our values only by stressing the moral and the value aspects of our cultural life. If we do that, the budgets will take care of themselves.

12

*On the Educational Statesmanship of a Free Society**

EDUCATION IS NOT JUST A MATTER OF "RUNNING" A SCHOOL OR A college. It is—as Plato and Aristotle already understood and taught—the method by which a state or community insures its own stability and continuity. A country's education can therefore only be understood in relation to the values of its own culture, and education itself is—as Woodrow Wilson insisted throughout his life—"a branch of statesmanship." If Americans never cease to quarrel among themselves about what our education is—or should be—and if our educational opinions swing more widely from hysteria to complacency than American public discussion of any other issue, this may be ascribed to a vague but sure instinct for the vital relationship between the quality of national life, including its capacity for survival, and the quantitative as well as qualitative achievements of our educational programs.

A country's educational system is always an expression of its culture in general. American education has plenty of strengths and weaknesses, and they are the strengths and weaknesses of American culture in general. If our criticism of education gets below the surface level of a heated argument about a school bond issue or "the numbers that should go to college," and if we begin to inquire into the nature of a free society, and into the character of educational programs that would be likely to give us men and women fit for the intellectual and moral responsibilities of such a society, we are at once involved in a discussion of the most basic issues of statesmanship. Such a critical rethinking of our educational fundamentals will be in the deepest sense of the term a critique of the values of free

---

* New York: Woodrow Wilson Foundation [1959] (Education in the Nation's Service, No. 5).

men, it will lead into problems of motivation and the sources of responsibility, and it will ultimately be concerned with the question whether in the modern world a free society can survive if its public priorities are not anchored in a deep respect for trained intelligence.

These are searching questions, and they deserve to be studied before we engage in a discussion of secondary questions of man-power needs and budgetary availabilities. Before we reach this vital core of the argument, we must, however, clear up some of the underbrush of misinformation and irrelevancy that has cluttered up the landscape. In the hysterical panic of public discussion that accompanied America's first response to Russian rocket experimentation, we plunged into a series of comparisons with foreign educational systems which almost wholly overlooked the cultural context of American education as well as of its Western European and Soviet Russian counterparts.

It is possible to borrow educational features from other national cultures if care is taken to "translate" them into the appropriate cultural context. American elementary schools were originally deeply influenced by German models, American colleges borrowed heavily from their English counterparts, and the debt of our graduate schools to German universities is still visible to any observer. Professor I. L. Kandel, one of our best informed students of comparative education, has observed that some of the most serious maladjustments in American education can still be traced to the lack of articulation in the assimilation of these varied foreign stages in our own system. In our recent comparisons with the Soviet Union we completely overlooked the social and historic context, and advocated the adoption— on very spurious evidence—of features in the Russian educational system which derived their motivation as well as their discipline from Soviet culture, in which it is the educational system's primary assignment to strengthen the Soviet state. From a Russian standpoint it may be quite legitimate to conceal the conscription of Soviet youth for industrial or agricultural employment as a program of "polytechnical education," but it would be folly to regard such a program as an answer to the glaring and growing weaknesses of our American educational system which is a part of American culture and which must draw its support from American values and American motivation.

Now that the new cultural exchange agreement with the Soviet Union has given us the benefit of the informed comments of a few dozen American educational visitors to the Soviet Union, some of the sharp edge of the comparisons with the Soviet Union has been dulled. Selecting from a thick file of publications we find that the discussion is characterized by the denunciation of our "lack of standards," due to the fact that "the American educational system was not a national system at all but a ramshackle structure with varying standards and different methods, depending on state and local administrations"; there is alarm concerning "the spectacular educational advances of Soviet Russia"; selective evidence of American parents stationed at Western European posts who because of their experience with European schools were persuaded that "most American schools came off a poor second"; and *Life* magazine"s demand that "we must stop kowtowing to the mediocre," and "close our carnival."

"Relaxed studies in the United States" were compared unfavorably with "the rough haul all the way" in the Soviet Union, and admiration for foreign "standards" and "discipline" was curiously interwoven with a rejection of any "Federal" interference with education, which was regarded as inextricably interwoven with the imposition of "political control."

It may well be admitted from the beginning that there are many crucial weaknesses in the standards of American education —and especially in its high schools and colleges—and that there are admirable educational achievements in many Western European countries and in Soviet Russia. Nothing but chaos will result, however, if we insist on discussing educational programs apart from the culture as a whole of which they are a characteristic expression. Russian education is—as Stalin said—"a weapon for strengthening the Soviet state," and European education is in all its varying forms a reflection of the European social system as it has historically developed.

Nothing is more "international" than sharp controversy about the quality and nature of postelementary or secondary education on either the "free" or the Soviet side of the Iron Curtain. Both in Russia and in Western Europe there is a wealth of data to suggest that all is not well with the educational programs that are now in operation. The Russian system of education is centrally controlled, and in this as well as other characteristic features it is typically European. There is much rigor in the controls that are exercised in Soviet Russia, and at the other end of the spectrum there is considerable opportunity for local and philosophic variations in the Netherlands or in Switzerland; but on the whole the generalization will stand that the educational standards are directly related to the administrative and legal sanctions that are vested in the central government in all continental countries. By contrast we have the political and legal principle in the United States that education is a matter of local control, that it is a state function, and as a consequence we have fifty state systems in which varying mixtures of private and public control compete with one another in rigor and laxity.

It is a direct and unavoidable consequence of our political principle that almost anything is true somewhere in the American educational system, and this fact makes it almost impossible to engage in rigorous comparisons of achievements at home or abroad. It also follows that a concern for standards can only be implemented if we are prepared to reexamine the principle of local control. Local control of education is a part of the general "grass roots" ideology of American democracy. The legacy of the autonomous local community—validated by the enthusiastic support of Thomas Jefferson and the subsequent admiration of de Tocqueville—has persisted in the face of the establishment of innumerable and overlapping local authorities in a wide variety of fields and in the almost unbelievable maze of man-made obstacles to efficient metropolitan government which the urban "sprawl" of the past generation has added to our inheritance of obsolete local government in rural areas. For centuries we have tried manfully to make the stubborn facts of land use, law enforcement, public utilities, transportation, fiscal policy, and educational necessity fit into our traditional beliefs, but in the face of the current criticism of the laxity of standards, which is now painfully obvious as the consequence of our "local control" in education, it remains an unavoidable part of any report or public address on the subject to endorse "the sanctity of the precious tradition of local control."

In the United States, if a local school board—or a local college administration—feels that the basketball coach or the training of the local high school band or cheerleaders is more important than the mathematics teacher or foreign language teacher, this local decision determines where the money goes, and this is why so many of our high schools have inadequate science, mathematics, and foreign language programs. In the area of educational policy the sum of the parts does not equal the whole. The sum of all the local educational policies does not equal a comprehensive and statesmanlike educational policy for the country as a whole. In a sense the real threat to desirable features of local control—such as the local authority to choose superintendents and principals—does not come from Washington or the state capitals. It springs unavoidably from the fiscal and educational weaknesses of the principle of local control itself.

Dr. Conant's finding that more than half of the country's high schools are too small to offer effective and defensible programs, and his recommendation that their number be reduced from 21,000 to 9,000 in order to insure minimum graduating classes of at least one hundred students, points in the direction of merged or consolidated control which may be one of the many channels through which a remedy can be found in accordance with American experience. The weaknesses in our system which are due to local control do not necessarily call for a Federal ministry of education with the European and Russian powers of administrative control. It may be possible to work out characteristic American patterns of voluntary self-regulation, but in the present financial emergency of public as well as private education there will almost certainly be a call for a larger measure of Federal fiscal support.

An examination of some of the criticism that is at present directed at Western European and Russian educational programs, by the educators who are themselves involved in their administration, may help us to become aware of the pitfalls involved in copying traits from another culture. The growth of an educational program is in direct response to the needs of a society in a given state of economic and social development. Education is designed to meet the needs of a community, and the needs include vocational objectives as well as cultural deficiencies. In many European countries—including Russia—industrial employment is still on a six-day-a-week basis, and so are the schools. In a country where the five-day week is normal it may legitimately be argued that a more intensive use should be made of the time that is available; but a six-day week for pupils and teachers is practically impossible as long as parents have a say in the matter and as long as teachers have a free choice of alternative employment.

Western Europe and Soviet Russia today are merely beginning to face the almost insatiable demand of a modern industrial society for an unlimited variety of trained and partly trained technical and administrative personnel, whereas we in the United States have, since the days of Benjamin Franklin, sought to prepare our youth for practical affairs as well as for the academic requirements of further intellectual development.

Some of the struggle for the establishment of public elementary and secondary schools, for compulsory attendance, and for the diversification of educational programs to match the variety of interests and aptitudes of pupils which is now taking place in many European countries, took place in the United States several generations ago. On the other hand, some of the educational needs for "Americanization" and "citizenship" that were imposed on this country's schools by the existence of a huge flow of immigration in the nineteenth and early twentieth century are now modified by the presence of a more homogeneous student body. In the rethinking of our programs, the qualitative as well as the quantitative factors appear in completely different proportions in the United States from those appearing in the European systems.

There is no European equivalent of what is sometimes called our "catchall" high school; it is a peculiar byproduct of American social and ideological democracy. Even at its best—and its best can be very good as illustrated, for instance, in those public high schools in New York City which clearly distinguish vocational, general, and academic (Regents) diplomas—it is not as responsive to the rapidly changing needs of advanced study as many college faculties would desire. Standards could undoubtedly be raised in fields such as mathematics or foreign languages, but the presidents of some of our Ivy League colleges might reflect on the share of the responsibility for relaxation which they themselves will have to shoulder as a result of the discretionary admission policies that were initiated in the thirties when applicants were scarce. The increasing percentage of successful candidates for admission from public high schools to colleges and universities that have previously drawn more heavily from "independent schools" is another valid comment on the chorus of denunciation of high school standards which comes with ill grace from institutional representatives who have never competed as eagerly for the graduates of these despised public high schools.

Dr. Conant's careful and discriminating endorsement of the "widely comprehensive high school," his advice to "avoid generalizations," and his emphasis on the wide diversity of practice point in the same direction. The questions here are: *How* can we generalize the best existing practice wherever it may be found under public or private auspices, and *who* should impose the standards or norms for minimum achievement? As things stand, however, comparative statements concerning average achievements in American and European school systems should be scrutinized with great care.

It is rather obvious that *average* standards of performance in secondary schools are going to be different—and inevitably lower —in a country where ninety percent of the age group are expected to go to secondary schools from standards established in a system where only seven to fifteen percent of the age group are admitted to such schools. Average standards of achievement are not a valid basis of comparison under such different circumstances. If the top ten or fifteen percent of the graduates of American high schools were to be compared with the entire enrollment in the European secondary schools, the comparison would be more valid and it would reflect great qualitative strength in the American system. Even then it would be necessary to consider such variables as the average length of the school year and the school week and the fact that the average European secondary school extends its program into the sophomore year of the American college.

On the higher levels of education, American schools could benefit greatly from earlier discrimination between children who have an aptitude for academic achievement, and those who should continue in general or vocational studies. We should not confuse the American ideal that all children should have "equality of opportunity" with the egalitarian notion that all children have equal endowments, and we should not permit our able students to use the excesses of our elective system to evade the full development of their intellectual potential. European experience underlines the warning, however, that some methods of eliminating the existing variety of standards in American local school systems might expose us to the great danger of closing the doors of educational opportunity to large numbers of pupils with great potential ability, and no matter how careful our testing and examination procedures, there is always the question concerning the so-called "late bloomer."

In the European system the age at which the final selection for advanced study is made is usually somewhere between ten and twelve years. Under the circumstances the so-called *Sexta* examinations—that is to say, the tests which determine who should be permitted to continue in advanced academic education —become a major psychological and career hazard. Teaching is directed at the passing of the tests administered by outsiders— with educational consequences in the restriction of initiative and the limitation of creative impulses that are obvious to any teacher. A general fever spreads through both the educational system and the families of candidates, which leads to the hiring of examination coaches and the hectic participation of the parents and older brothers and sisters in the homework of the children. This has led one distinguished German observer to say that the examinations administered during this crucial three-month period are not so much a test of the children as of the capacity of their parents to hire or to supply intensive supplementary instruction.[1] This criticism of the European schools is perhaps the greatest single common denominator of educational concern in Europe. Pupils do not seek knowledge for its own sake but solely to pass examinations that block the road to a career.

This criticism includes the Russian schools where coaching to meet the outside examinations extends to all levels (including the admission to the universities) and where teachers and schools tend to be evaluated in terms of the percentages of their students' success in passing the centrally administered tests. "Socialist competition" leads to a bureaucratic sin described as "percentomania," officially defined as "the intolerable practice of chasing after bloated percentages of success."[2] But the practice prevails in spite of official criticism because the standards of achievement are centrally defined, because applicants for higher education may apply in only one institution, and because bureaucratic refinements are continuously concerned with increasingly numerical standards of evaluation.

Estimates by European educators concerning the number of

"late bloomers" who are disqualified in these early tests for twelve-year-olds vary from twenty to forty per cent of the age groups. American educators, who are accustomed to an atmosphere in which readjustment of programs can be arranged in terms of individual interests and aptitudes up to and including graduate education, will find it hard to imagine the variety of frustrations and educational malpractice that can be built into a system of premature selection. Helmut Becker describes the pressures as "diabolical," denounces them as the chief cause of the decline in the prestige of the teaching profession, which has lost its freedom as well as its creative initiative, and sums it up as a system which was designed to achieve creative polarity of tension between centrally defined standards and local teaching talent, and in fact results only in reciprocal frustration.

There is some warning in Alfred North Whitehead's disagreement with his Harvard colleagues who were disposed to favor only the "A"-man in their selection of candidates for academic advancement. Few will wish to question the standards of this observer, who was speaking of selection among candidates for advanced graduate work and not about twelve-year-old children, when he said that the student who rates as an "A"-man may merely be good in answering "what you want to hear," and that "B"-men may actually include a significant percentage of those capable of creative thought. "When my colleagues chaff me for giving more A's than they are willing to do and tax me with tenderheartedness, I reflect that I would rather not have it on my head that I was the one who discouraged an incipient talent."[3]

Excessive reliance on early tests and examinations administered by central authority overrates not only the validity of such tests, but it also might destroy one of the great strengths of the American system in which individual colleges may accept the guidance of centrally administered college entrance examinations yet retain the individual institution's authority to interpret such examinations in accordance with its own professional experience. We should continue to beware of standardized minima which might compel us to refuse admission to promising students of literature or creative writing simply because of low mathematics aptitude tests, and vice versa. There is great qualitative virtue in some aspects of our pluralism, and in the search for standards there is considerable danger that the baby might be thrown out with the bathwater.

Misinterpretation of the significance of examinations also plays a role in some of the currently fashionable comparisons with European and Russian experience. Translations of examinations are compared with American equivalents and invidious comparisons are widely publicized. Korol has drawn attention to an article by a distinguished American journalist who, on the basis of one of these examinations, draws the conclusion that "Russian boys *know* [*sic!*] about as much physics by the end of their last year in high school as the physics majors [*sic!*] at the Massachusetts Institute of Technology have learned by the end of their sophomore year."[4]

This journalistic observer had overlooked the fact that Russian examinations are published months in advance of their administration, and that many of the questions are repeated year after year in the same or slightly varying combinations. Under the circumstances it is easily understood that a very different level of examination readiness can be anticipated without implying any corresponding qualitative difference in the educational achievement. It was probably this same newspaper story that led a great industrial leader to make a widely publicized address in which he announced that:

> The physics examination given to Soviet high school graduates was given without gimmicks or identification to the freshmen at M.I.T. Not a single one of them passed. Only the highest of the sophomores achieved an acceptable score. Not until the junior level was reached was a creditable showing made.

When I asked one of my colleagues to check on this story with the Massachusetts Institute of Technology, we were informed that no Soviet examinations were ever given to M.I.T. students. No retraction or correction was ever published; we were obviously dealing with a determined "will to believe." Even after the high tide of hysteria regarding U.S.S.R.–U.S.A. educational comparisons had passed, an article in the *New York Times*[5] could still compare the "thirty-two hours" of chemistry required of chemistry teachers in the United States with "three hundred and forty hours" of chemistry required in the Russian ten-year school without pointing out that in the first case these "hours" were "registrar's credits" required for graduation—in which three hours would represent a typical full-term course—while in the second case the "hours" represented actual instructional time.[6]

Admiring comment on European and Russian schools usually includes endorsement of the discipline inherent in a single required curriculum in which all students are compelled to go "the rough haul all the way." The Russian ten-year school includes as many as eight to twelve subjects in some of its years, and European equivalents are sometimes even more ambitious. These overcrowded programs are generally criticized by European educators as a cause of superficiality, which stifles initiative and creative impulse. American experience also leads us to question the qualitative superiority of such overloaded programs, and the University of Chicago's experience with a three- or five-course program is suggestive. As the percentage of the age group that reaches the secondary school grows, the qualitative questions increase in their urgency. Required subjects that are taught to groups of ever-increasing diversity of aptitude and interest may simply lower the average level of achievement, or may lead to ruthless elimination of the majority from any further education, as is the case in Russia where only a third of the students entering the ten-year school complete it.

European educational criticism of these requirements is plentiful, and everywhere—including the Soviet Union—there is a pattern of experimental concern with diversified patterns designed to match the differing individual students. Nothing is more characteristic of a comprehensive survey of Western European schools than the active concern with diversified programs of secondary education, with provisions for optional and elective courses, and with the corresponding difficulties in articulation of such studies with the requirements of the universities and professional schools.[7] Here—with increasing numbers of pupils of varying initial ability—the course is clearly set in a direction that parallels American development. And we often find in European literature a somewhat idealized discussion of the achievements of the American comprehensive or multilateral high schools, as well as alert interest in the elective features and in the counseling and guidance programs that have developed in American colleges.[8]

At a recent educational conference in France,[9] these views were reflected in the observations of the French hosts. I select two representative passages, the first from an address by Louis François, the Secretary General of the French Commission for UNESCO:

We have come to an almost catastrophic situation in France. During the *baccalaureat* examination in June, parents, grand-parents, great-grandparents and children all go into a fever. It's worse than a national election. The number of students sitting for the *baccalaureat* has trebled in ten years. Subjects are crammed, and then forgotten three weeks later. What we need is an examination system that takes into account the aptitudes and ability of the student to solve problems, not the testing of encyclopedic knowledge.

and the second from remarks by Roger Gal, education advisor of the French Ministry of Education:

. . . The ideal falls somewhere between the U.S. system and the present French system. We do not wish to destroy what is worthwhile in our culture; but, on the other hand, I hope that the pendulum in American education does not swing back too hard towards traditionalism.

It is clear that we who have already experienced the "defects of our qualities" will have to profit from our own experience with some of the qualitative deficiencies of mass education rather than follow a pattern which is historically in an earlier phase than our own.

Before Mr. Khrushchev's most recent "reform" of education in the Soviet Union, the Russian ten-year school was graduating more than five times as many students as could be admitted to the universities. In discussion of Russian education, interest focuses on whether the educational process should not be adjusted to the careers in industry and administration to which the surplus students are now destined to be directed. The revival of the principle of "polytechnization" of the schools—that is to say their "practicalization"—is directly related to these pressures. In Western Europe this has led to a proliferation of secondary schools with classical, with modern language, with scientific and mathematical, and with a variety of technical and "extended elementary" emphases. The trend is clear, and, with the progressive response of school systems to democratic goals and to individual needs, European schools are more likely to learn from American strengths and weaknesses than the other way around.

Inability to read and write the native language seems to be a source of international complaint. In the United States we discuss it as a failure of our high schools and we are inclined to hold teachers responsible for being unable to teach composition in the large classes that are the lot of the average English instructor. Complaints about the inability to write Dutch or French are as commonplace among Dutch and French educators, and Sir Cyril Norwood's report, *Curriculum and Examinations in Secondary Schools,* stated that "from all quarters" in Britain "we have received strong evidence of the poor quality of the English of Secondary School pupils." The language is so similar to the terms in which we habitually describe American experience that it suggests a shared weakness in all forms of modern industrial society, irrespective of social ideology, political institutions, selective or comprehensive educational practices:

> The evidence is such as to leave no doubt in our minds that we are here confronted with a serious failure of the Secondary Schools. The complaint briefly is that too many pupils show marked inability to present ideas clearly to themselves, to arrange them and to express them clearly on paper or in speech, they read without a sure grasp of what they read, and they are too often at a loss in communicating what they wish to communicate in expressive and audible tone. If this complaint is true—and we are left no option but to believe it true—it deserves the most earnest attention of the schools.[10]

There is evidence of the same complaint in Russian schools where the People's Commissar of Education is quoted as critical of the pupils' inability to put their thoughts on paper or in speech. The teachers, too, are warned "to look to their Russian." Here, too, as in Britain and in the United States the responsibility is partly sought in the tendency of the teachers in other academic disciplines to leave the instruction in the native language entirely to the teachers especially assigned to this subject. It is probably also true that in a modern society of mass communication the models of excellence in language instruction are undermined by the low standards of language use that are present in all modern mass media ranging from the daily press to radio and television, from advertising copy to political propaganda. It is increasingly difficult to set standards of excellence in daily competition with levels of communication that are aimed at the mental "twelve-year-old"—the conventional objective that governs efforts to reach a mass audience in our type of modern social order.

At the very best, more widely diffused social and economic opportunity will tend to depress talent and genius to less exalted levels. The identification and the development of talent will be increasingly difficult as democratic and egalitarian aims are more widely shared. There is little to suggest that European or Russian experience will have much to teach America in this field; we have already passed through phases of this development that are still on the horizon elsewhere. If we are to avoid some of the sources of possible qualitative disaster that are clearly evident in our current experience—such as, for instance, evidence concerning the consequences of "equal" salary scales for elementary and secondary school teachers in the face of widely divergent standards of professional preparation and of intensity of effort in active service—we shall have to seek remedies in the wide range of good and bad experience that is available in our own educational system.

European education which is an expression of a social organization that is now rapidly fading away, and Russian experience which is based upon the direction of human talent to the achievement of Soviet political goals—"the will of the party is the law for youth"—can hardly be a guide for the education of citizens who are to be made fit for the responsibilities of a free society. If we are to upgrade the standards in areas of our educational system that are now below par, and if we are to make more effective provision for the education of the gifted, we can safely do so only if we are clear in the formulation of the American social goals which our educational enterprise is to achieve. If we are to produce men and women who know how to think, and knowing how, do it, and who having done it, will have the courage and the responsibility to voice their opinions, we are likely to find little inspiration in models of standardized and bureaucratized education abroad.

The present concern for standards in basic requirements regarding such academic fields as foreign languages and mathematics can only lead to effective action if we are prepared to establish limitations upon the sacrosanct dogma of local control. European and Russian models of centralized bureaucratic control, including reliance upon "percentomania" and impersonal examinations, promise to throw us back into a pattern in which we may lose all the advantages of the present in exchange for the weaknesses and frustrations of European and Russian education. The pattern of American achievement clearly indicates the alternative which calls for an imaginative use of the techniques of self-regulation, which can be stimulated by the judicious use of Federal fiscal subsidies. In this connection American experience is rich in constructive examples in the accrediting procedures of our colleges and universities, in the development of College Board examinations, and in the ranging record of the American Council on Education's tests. In our fear of governmental control we have overlooked some of the perils that are inherent in the protection of various vested interests through our private "accrediting" agencies. Dean Dayton D. McKean has recently drawn attention to some of these negative byproducts of academic or professional organizations in an article entitled "Who's in Charge Here [The Universities or the Professional Organizations]?"[11] Here, too, the "countervailing power" of public educational authority might strengthen the articulation of a national educational policy.

There is no need for panic or for hasty improvisation. Sputnik was not evidence of irremediable weakness in the intellectual achievements of free society. It merely proved that a dictatorship can make advantageous use of crash programs, and that our political leadership did not have the imagination to understand the appeal which such an achievement might have to the world's political opinion. The Russian success has, however, had the great merit of challenging our smug complacency in educational and intellectual matters, and specifically of dramatizing our great vulnerability to possible qualitative weakness *in the future*. When the Russians need mathematics and science teachers, they simply *assign* a larger percentage of their qualified graduates to this task. Korol reports the "assignment" of sixty per cent of the physics and mathematics graduates to secondary school education in 1955. This is, of course, strictly in accord with the basic assumptions of Soviet society.

It is also in accordance with the basic assumptions of American society that we in the New York City municipal colleges saw only five per cent of our science majors and twenty per cent of our mathematics graduates enter secondary school education in the past two years because the salary incentives were inadequate. There are about one thousand of these graduates every year. This is not a weakness of education but a failure of American society to act according to its own basic assumptions. If we wish to draw these graduates into the field of education, the salary scales to warrant such an individual redirection of their vocational choice will have to reflect a corresponding rearrangement of national priorities. Much of the present criticism of American education originates in a schizophrenic desire to maintain private economic incentives in industry and commerce in accordance with the best American tradition, while it is assumed that intellectual manpower will be assigned to its stated conditions of economic servitude in accordance with basically Russian assumptions.

If we would simply act on the basic values of free society in our desire to redirect the career judgments of American youth, we would soon find our American educational problem reduced to manageable proportions. For those who were shocked at the recent statement that America needed a major breakthrough in educational finance which might call for a doubling of educational budgets, it should be sobering to reflect that doubling educational budgets will be thoroughly inadequate in the light of the predicted doubling of enrollments by 1970. Twice the budget for twice the number of students would merely provide for the same quality of service which is now given—we would merely be marking time in the same place—whereas we need to recover lost ground and to move forward to higher quality of service.

It is crucial to remember that our American problem is one of *quality*, and not of quantity. Russia and China have a population base of 800 million, more than four times as large as the United States. If we rely on quantity, we will be licked from the beginning. Many of the Russian engineers and technicians included in these comparative statistics are no more than vocational high school or community college graduates. We do not need *more* engineers. We need *better* engineers, and above all more and better scientists to give our technical programs an adequate theoretical foundation. Our program must aim at quality—the maximum qualitative and diversified use of our limited quantity on all levels of potential ability.

The situation does not call for standardized and bureaucratic mass processing of our youth. It calls for an honest effort to apply characteristic American values concerning individual aptitude and motivation to the field of education. If we wish to go a step further in this direction—profiting from an undeniably strong feature of Russian education— we might consider the implications for the United States of a procedure in which rigorous examinations in the high schools and colleges would establish priority in the admissions to universities, and in which such university students would be paid a salary for their services to the national community. There is excellent American precedent for such a policy in Thomas Jefferson's proposal in his *Notes on the State of Virginia* for the strengthening of our "natural aristocracy" of "virtues and talents" by the establishment of rigorously selective tests in free public education in which "the best geniuses" would "be raked from the rubbish annually," and in which the cream of the crop would be sent to William and Mary College at public expense, including tuition, room and board. By this means "we hope to avail the State of those talents which nature has sown as liberally among the poor as the rich, but which perish without use, if not sought for and cultivated."

It is sad to recall that President Eisenhower's Commission on Education beyond the High School concluded—even *before* Sputnik—that colleges and universities would "require something like a *trebling* of the current level of expenditures." Meanwhile there is some consolation in the thought that when the editor of the *Economist* (London) devoted an editorial to the proposition that the 84,000 students in British colleges should be increased to 160,000 by 1970, the stress was placed on the need for diversity of programs adjusted to the varying aptitudes and interests of the new levels of academic ability that would be involved. Without denying the need for the stimulation of programs for training the highest caliber of academic and scholarly talent, the argument stressed the hope that on the secondary levels of management, technical training, and administration the new British generation would be "at least as educated as their counterparts in America."

It is easy to imagine what the tone of the editorial would have been if the British proposals had involved multiplying the percentage of the appropriate age groups going to college by *ten,* which would have made the situation roughly comparable to the *present* figures in the United States.

A comparison of educational achievement and criticism in European and American educational systems prompts the warning that the transplanting of educational features from one culture to another may intensify rather than alleviate critical conditions of which the American public has now become aware.

Some of our current criticism of American education is merely a contemporary version of the old attack upon the democratic assumption that all children should have the benefit of an education designed to maximize each individual's achievement in accordance with his potential ability or, as Thomas Jefferson said, "in accordance with the capacity and the condition of every one"—and the case against our traditional American assumptions should be argued in those terms. If the criticism is really based on a desire for comparative "standards," it should be directed at the deep-rooted political tradition of local control, and in full awareness of the qualitative weaknesses that are amply evident in European experience with centralized and bureaucratic control.

On the other hand, if the criticism is anchored in a concern about the philosophical foundations of American education—or their absence—it is relevant to recall that Russian education is designed to achieve Russian philosophical objectives and that in precisely the same sense American education should be a democratic community's method of preparing men and women for the responsibilities of a free society. If egalitarian drift has threatened to undermine some of the qualitative objectives that are essential to the achievement of our social goals, the *clarification of our American values* is more likely to lead to constructive educational consequences than the copying of educational patterns deliberately designed to achieve political goals that are alien to American experience or tradition.

To "clarify our American values" is an easy phrase with rather stupendous implications if we give some thought to them. Woodrow Wilson's struggle at Princeton University was an effort to clarify our American values in higher education, and his endeavors in his first term in the White House to bring a dynamic, competitive economy under social control were another. There are some to whom clarifying American values means primarily the establishment of a wholly competitive society with the apparent exception of the employment conditions of teachers and scholars. There are others who see in the *total* individualism ("What's in it for me?") of so many Americans today, including scholars and engineers, the greatest single weakness in the pattern of formative influences to which American society exposes its youth.

The greatest single cause of our confusion in the discussion of a national philosophy of education for citizenship in a free society lies in the fact that we no longer understand our own tradition. Our "liberals" and "progressives" talk of freedom as if individual rights can be separated from the common disciplines which free men must accept if a free society is to be sufficiently strong to make its guaranty of rights meaningful. Our conservatives talk of "fads and frills" in education and call for the removal of programs that do not contribute directly to the development of intellectual power as if education of the "whole man" were a Marxist invention rather than a basic conception shared by Benjamin Franklin, Ralph Waldo Emerson, and Woodrow Wilson. I hasten to add that confusion—and even chaos—about these issues is as prevalent in educational circles as it is in American society in general. Our relaxed grip on the fundamental principles of free society is perhaps the greatest single cause of our weakness as we confront an ideological alternative in which every social and cultural activity is directly related to a dogmatic faith.

The average teacher—like the average critic of education— is inclined by tradition to stress reason, intellect, analysis. He may not define the "3 R's" in the same narrow spirit, but he comes up with a conception that emphasizes an essentially intellectualist manner of interpreting the function of education. He is reinforced in this by the dominant influence of our economic life, which is rooted in specialization and in division of labor. Modern life—in all its ramifications—teaches the compelling necessity of specialization in trade, in industry, in science, and in scholarship. Freedom, however, is rooted in the responsibility of men *as men,* and not merely as specialized splinters of men. In our specialized pursuit of the development of free society we may easily drift into so intense a splintering of the total personality, in which free society is anchored and rooted, that the quality of individual responsibility may vanish as the fruits of our specialization increase.

This is true not only of our educational activity and of our economic life, but it is also true of the picture we manage to convey to the rest of the world about ourselves.

Some years ago I was in India under the auspices of the State Department, speaking to a very large audience in Madras, all Indian students. The topic of the day was "What is freedom?" Preceding my remarks, an Indian gentleman who was a leading political figure and an old friend of Gandhi's made a long address the purpose of which was to make it very clear that India certainly was not going the Communist way. But it interested me that, as he was standing there, he found it necessary to take a crack first at the United States, then at Soviet Russia, before he spent the greater part of his time in developing what he presented as the Indian position on the subject of the day.

The crack at the United States was that he, like all other Indians, rejected "totally unregulated selfishness." That was America. And sometimes he said "totally unregulated capitalism." That also was America. Then he described the Russian alternative as "total control by the state" and after he had rejected both the American and the Russian extremes (and in India it takes courage to reject Russia), he plunged into an explanation of what to him was the Indian conception of freedom. This Indian conception of freedom turned out to be "self-control." He backed this ideal with quotations from the Indian Holy Books, the Vedas, the Upanishads, and so on.

But when it was all over, I caught this particular gentleman in the Governor's palace at lunch when I had him to myself, so to speak, and I asked him, "Did you really think that you were talking about something uniquely Indian when you were talking about *self-control* as the Indian conception of freedom? Don't you know, don't you really know that that is what Abraham Lincoln, that is what Ralph Waldo Emerson, that is what pretty much every responsible American who has done any thinking or writing about freedom has always said the American conception of freedom was?"

He just gave me a wink and quoted Emerson to me, showing that he knew very well, but these were the ways, he intimated, in which you had to package things in India today. You had to package them first of all by rejecting a caricature of the United States, then by rejecting not quite so much of a caricature of Russia, and then you explained that India stood pretty much where the United States stands, only you had to avoid making it appear that way.

We ourselves are, of course, partly responsible for the caricature of America that has come to plague us all over the world. We have talked so much of our individualism in an extreme atomistic and economic sense that we have forgotten our own past, including Alexander Hamilton's "Report on Manufactures" with its program of Federal measures for the economic development of our continent, as well as Woodrow Wilson's establishment of Federal controls over the monetary and banking system fully a generation before a British Labor Government took over the Bank of England. And we have forgotten Emerson's stress on the development of the *whole* man so completely that we can pretend to detect collectivist propaganda in so-called "fads and frills" programs in public education, which are related to John Dewey's restatement for contemporary America of classical and historical American cultural objectives.

Such misrepresentation of our history and such ignorance of our own cultural strength in the past is dangerous for a free society. It is essentially a most "un-American activity" in a new and historically more valid sense of the term. The American conception of freedom is not merely the selfish expression of whim. It is not merely self-expression. Freedom is self-control as contrasted with control by others. The cultivation of inner-directedness is therefore the core of the educational problem of a free society. The sources of responsibility are not cultivated by drift, nor by the pervasive advertising in press, radio, and television that promotes an ever-increasing diversity of material wants, nor by a journalistic overemphasis on "news" which is defined as the unusual, the pathic, or the exceptional, nor by a sport page's systematic confusion of the reading public's ability to distinguish among commercial sports, spectator values, and an educational interest in students who play rather than in athletes who register. Neither are they clarified by a view of freedom that stresses the removal of inhibitions, because the very essence of civilized society is defined by the presence of an appropriate selection of inhibitions, and this is merely another way of saying that freedom is self-control.

The sense of responsibility from which this self-control is to spring is rooted in a disciplined life of mind as well as of emotion, a balanced grasp of frequently conflicting values; it is rooted in a sensible, realistic picture (to which reason and intellect can contribute) of the nature of man. The nature of man is not just intellect. Some of the biggest swine in human history have been great intellects. Some of the weakest spots in Western free society are due to excessive preoccupation with intellect, with analysis, and it is healthy to recognize this in the face of the fact that the great achievements of Western society also are rooted in the cultivation of intellect and reason.

The hazard is in lopsidedness. The hazard is in doing only one thing and letting the rest go by drift. For if the rest goes by drift, the man on horseback may come along to exploit this drift. Whether he is a demagogue from the right or one from the left makes no difference— the consequences to freedom are just as serious in the one case as in the other. Typically, he is an expert in exploiting undisciplined emotion. And when it comes to that kind of challenge in a period in which national survival is at stake, you can trust the expert in the exploitation of emotion, whose only rationality consists in his rational exploitation of the irrational in man, to win—unless there is a systematic strengthening of the subjective factor in free society by the use of education in all of its broad ramifications.

Now this is nothing new, and whatever we may hear today in the storms that are being promoted throughout the United States with regard to progressive education, it is well to remember that this emphasis on man at his best being far more than cultivated mind is a classical American emphasis. In this connection it is refreshing to have a new look at Ralph Waldo Emerson's famous Phi Beta Kappa address on the American scholar. Emerson was not influenced by John Dewey, by William James, or by any of the smaller fry of the so-called progressive education movement. This is classical American cultural doctrine, of which William James and John Dewey are simply more recent expressions.

"The American Scholar" was an address given to a Phi Beta Kappa audience at Harvard. In my own summary, and to sharpen a long passage, Emerson's thesis was: "Man is not a professor, an engineer, a farmer, a garment worker. Man is whole. He is priest and scholar and statesman, and parent, and lover, and soldier."

It is essential to observe the emphasis on what we might call "the altogetherness of things." How many present-day Phi Beta Kappa speakers would think of combining priest, scholar, parent, lover, soldier—all as *objectives of scholarship?*

Let us recall that Lincoln almost never mentioned freedom without linking to it in almost the same sentence or paragraph the word "responsibility." Carl Sandburg, who knows Lincoln's life perhaps as well as any of our contemporaries, once counted the frequency of reference and concluded that Lincoln used the word "responsibility" just a bit more frequently than the word "freedom." Or take Woodrow Wilson's articles and addresses on American education in which the object of education is described as "not learning but discipline," in which a plea for "intellectual" training is interwoven with a concern for the awakening of the "whole man," in which the perfect law of liberty is defined in the language of the *Epistle to James,* with explicit reference to "the deep foundations of Christian teaching" in their relation to our "conception of duty," and in which all abstract rights are stated in the framework of a realistic theory of the nature of man in "the gardens of the mind where grows the tree of the knowledge of good and evil." All of this is *classical* American doctrine, and derived from our Jewish and Christian heritage which was recently summarized by Pope John XXIII in the statement that "priests, teachers and doctors belong to the same ministry—a ministry whose object is the *whole of man,* soul and body, intellect, will and sentiment."

In other words, it is American doctrine to think of freedom as fundamentally *governed by the sources of responsibility.* And the sources of responsibility are not primarily analytically intellectual. They are, in first analysis, anchored in conscience, and they are strengthened by the shared values of the American community. They are *rooted in experience,* and they are based on faith and related to a cultivated grasp of mind as well as emotion.

This is one of the things that desperately need stress in America today, particularly for America's liberals. At the height of the McCarthy hysteria a distinguished Harvard professor made a Phi Beta Kappa address. This was a 1953 equivalent of the Emerson address. It made a deep impression, and it was widely reprinted. For a while, in the East at least, no speech on any campus was complete without some reference to this Phi Beta Kappa address. The address dealt with the "problem of freedom" and how we were having, all of us—to put it in my language —more or less of a "moral bellyache" about freedom, how every man who was independent enough to think a thought of his own was identified with subversive elements of a conspiratorial sort. Then the speaker went on to say that there was a problem of freedom in America today because—unlike the generation of Thomas Jefferson—we had lost our faith in man and "faith in freedom rests necessarily upon faith in man."[12] We had historically a faith in freedom because we had a faith in man. Today we no longer have this faith in man, and therefore our faith in freedom is destroyed.

When I read this speech, I hardly believed my eyes. The author had clearly not read his Thomas Jefferson in the original for a long time. And in that sense, he is representative of many Americans who quote Thomas Jefferson today. If you go to the Jefferson monument in Washington, you will find quotations on the wall that are all selected to prove that Thomas Jefferson was some sort of modern liberal. The classical liberal citations aren't on the wall anywhere. Yet Thomas Jefferson said some very severe things about the indefinite extension of majority control, including among other things the idea that any town over thirty thousand was a cancer on the body politic. His writings also show a very vigorous insistence on not trusting majority rule in a large number of areas in which he described the extension of majoritarian control as "democratic despotism." This is true Jeffersonian language, and this is the philosophical ground for his insistence that a Bill of Rights should be added to the constitution to safeguard the areas in which the majority would not be allowed to press for legislative controls. If we will look it up in a copy of the *Kentucky Resolutions*, we will find that Thomas Jefferson said just exactly the opposite of our

Harvard author's thesis. He said, "Free government is founded in jealousy, and not in confidence."[13]

Now, in the matter of free government we can look the whole world in the face. Whatever they may say abroad about immature, young America, our written constitution is the oldest one by a wide margin now operating in the world, and it was not written on the basis of a philosophy of faith in man. It was written on the basis of a realistic conception of the nature of man, wholly aware of the fact that man is potentially good—that's why we trusted ourselves with free government institutions—but also deeply aware of the fact that man who is potentially good is also potentially a beast. *Therefore,* we would not trust the government we set up with unqualified power. *Therefore,* we established governmental institutions that separated power and dispersed control. We saw man not just as mind, but we saw him as *potentially* evil in character; we saw even the potentially angelic element in man as, under the trust of complete power, most vulnerable indeed to the temptations and the lusts for power that bring out the bestial. This Phi Beta Kappa address supplies a striking and a representative example of a crucial weakness of modern liberalism: its illusion about the nature of man, its illusion that the evil in man is all due to unfavorable circumstances for which he is personally not responsible.

We tend to think that when man is evil, it is due to his poverty, to his inadequate diet, to his poor health, or to his substandard housing. And we tend to think that the evil will disappear if we have high standards of living, better housing, and good medical care. But all of human experience with man is to the contrary. It is not true—to put it very mildly—that men are virtuous in proportion to the extent to which they are healthy and wealthy.

If we look at the nature of man realistically, and that includes a full allowance for his emotional potentialities for good as well as for evil, we run straight into the major intellectual and moral confusion that is brought about by the wishful character of modern democratic thought. And this holds whether we catch man in his thinking about God or religion, or whether we catch him thinking about politics and war. Whatever phase of modern experience we take, we will find this naïveté, this simple-mindedness about the nature of man as the chief cause of our irresponsibility in the presence of choice. This misconception of the nature of man vitiates much of our contemporary reasoning about world politics as well as about education. When we speak of freedom as self-control and of freedom as rooted in the responsibilities of man, we postulate an historically valid theory of the nature of man. A sound theory of education calls for prudence in avoiding the fallacies of excessive intellectualism as well as the pitfalls of a perfectibilist optimism concerning the nature of man, or the equally hazardous implications of a theory of human nature that is based upon experiments with dogs, rats, and cats. This theory assumes the unlimited plasticity of human psychology under various types of "conditioning," and in it, it becomes as easy to move from perfectibilism to control in one step as it later becomes to go from "conditioning" to "brainwashing."

The Greeks had, as they often did, a word for it. The word *idiot* as we use it today describes, technically, a type of feeble-minded person and, popularly, a person who is very stupid and incapable of intellectual effort, one who has an *idiotic* way of doing things. The Greek word, of course, meant something very different, although it is the word from which we drew ours. The Greeks used the word *idiot* for a man who might have very keen analytical capacity, who might be a scholar, but who had no interest in the whole of things. The Greek idiot was an altogether private man. He had no public spirit, as we might express it. He had no awareness of his being part of a larger whole. In that sense, we can say that the American college and university, with all of its specialists who know only one thing and are very little interested in the total impact of all these separate things on the whole of the young personality for which they are responsible, contains—in the original Greek use of the term—a larger percentage of idiots than the population of the country as a whole.

And the whole of public life is full of *idiocy* in the Greek sense of the term, because all of public life is rooted in the assumption that the determining fact of all public policy is its bearing on the pursuit of higher standards of material living. This is taken for granted on the right as well as on the left. Presidential candidates differ in the United States not in their acceptance of this objective, but in methods of achieving that objective. Some Democrats will say that we can achieve it with a little more public action, some Republicans with a little less public action, but they will all agree that the purpose should be the increase of material standards of living. But increasing material standards of living implies more specialization, more division of labor, more conveyor-belt, doing-just-one-thing-all-the-time action, because that's the way in which analytical man has demonstrated that he can increase material returns per individual involved in production.

If there is anything to the picture I have presented here, it will be observed that the implications of the public drive toward increased productivity, toward applied science and technology, toward specialized, conveyor-belt production, is a sharper drive toward increasingly specialized use of only a small part of man's whole personal endowment. The danger of increasing unawareness of the need for cultivating the whole of a balanced human personality is implicit in the temptation to increase vocational and specialized pressures directly related to economic as well as to defense needs.

Historically and morally we know that freedom is anchored in a realistic view of the nature of responsible man, and in his nature *as a whole*. And this has challenging educational implications especially in a time in which family, church, and community have in varying ways lost a good deal of their effectiveness as educational agencies. Man has a body as well as a mind, man has glands as well as a brain, and free man has a need for disciplined emotions as well as for a disciplined mind. It may be a fatal gap in our total defense of free society to overlook the role of disciplined emotion, trained imagination, the significance of rhythm, tradition and ceremony, the cultivation of the subjective and the valuational in our exclusive pursuit of intellectually and economically productive byproducts of specialized competence.

These things are not developed or safeguarded by another academic "course" in which they are verbally covered; they are only preserved as a vital part of the total educational experience if they are carefully and thoughtfully interwoven with the student's experience *as a whole*. And if there is any truth in these observations, they should be the basis of a genuinely radical (and not merely verbal) reorientation in our educational philosophy. Since the need for specialized competence in science, in technology, and in administration is undeniable in the present struggle for survival in world politics, this way of thinking seems to suggest the need for a *compensatory* conception of education in which the nation's formative agencies deliberately develop an educational program designed to *offset* some of the lopsided educational consequences of other agencies of the national community as a whole.

There is great peril in a blind continuation of present educational tendencies to serve existing vocational needs in our rapidly shifting economic order. Automation and modern scientific developments have given a special urgency to Woodrow Wilson's warning more than fifty years ago that "the man of special skill can be changed into an unskilled laborer overnight." If public education is to be genuinely "in the nation's service" it should be deeply concerned with the erosion of community values and all the other unplanned and unintended cultural byproducts of the proliferating variety of economic and technical "interests" which are part of the mainstream of our economic life. We should increasingly think of education as concerned with the total of the formative influences that are brought to bear on our youth by the American community. The content of formal education should be modified in accordance with observable shifts in the formative impact of other social activities such as those of the church, the family, and the increasingly more significant influence of competitive advertising in the press, in the movies, in radio, and in television.

No one with even elementary acquaintance with our teenagers—and they will increase by forty per cent in the next five years—can deny that this is a major educational challenge. Some of the cultural byproducts of our economic institutions could easily be more destructive of the stability of our free society than a complete breakdown in the material productivity of our economy, and these cultural byproducts are today a major formative—that is to say, educational—force in American society. It is not a rejection of the principle of the free enterprise or competitive economy to believe that "profit and loss" may be admirable governors of material productivity but questionable guides in areas of national cultural life in which they are simply irrelevant to qualitative achievement. When "profit" governs the choice of cultural or formative (that is to say, educational) programs in television, it is being used in a context in which it is as unfit to discharge its social function as it would be in the selection of appropriate curricular materials in the elementary schools. For some incomprehensible reason Americans who are understandably insistent on the maintenance of professional educational standards in the construction of formal educational programs in schools abdicate their parental responsibility after school hours to the naked pursuit of material profit in the commercial exploitation of government-granted channels without appreciation of the obvious fact that a formative educational influence is exercised in both cases.

A "compensatory" conception of education would be strictly in accord with some of the healthiest and most enduring features of our society. Offsetting or compensatory institutional controls were anchored in our constitutional order in the form of the separation of powers. "Dispersed controls" in the form of "checks and balances," the relations of Federal, state, and municipal governments, and in the modern conceptions of the compensatory economic and fiscal responsibility of the Federal government in the nation's business activity, are all well-established features of the American landscape. "Built-in" stabilizers in economic life, in which public activity expands as private activity is curtailed, are now recognized as essential safeguards of the health of the economic order as a whole.

These compensatory or "offsetting" ideas may have a constructive vitality in our educational future as well. If education in all its ramifications restricts itself to analytical and intellectualist concerns, it will intensify the centrifugal forces that are now at work, but if its conception of the nation's service is broadened to include major preoccupation with offsetting some of the unplanned and unintended cultural byproducts of increasingly specialized pursuit of private interest, it may help to furnish the social setting in which young men and young women might become fit for the responsibilities of free society.

There is no room for complacency in such a philosophy, and, to put it very mildly, the millennium does not appear to be imminent. There will be plenty of room for "controversy," but we can pride ourselves as free men with a true professional spirit that freedom has never been a gift to the complacent who sought peace of mind.

There is a sense in which freedom will ultimately be preserved or lost in this nation's educational establishments. No amount of technological productivity and no increase of professional military proficiency can overcome the vital fact that the effectiveness of a nation's total performance in the world community will be finally determined by the *disciplined will* and *purpose* of its youth, and by their *commitment* to and their *experience* with the values of free men and women. These qualities are *not* by-products of specialized or vocational scholarship, and they are not supplied by a program of supplementary verbal indoctrination as if they could be finally added to the program of instruction much in the manner in which a fudge sauce is poured over a dish of ice cream.

Inertia and complacency are as dangerous in education as they are in rocket experimentation. "We are not put into this world to sit still and know; we are put into it to act." If we are to summon up the moral and material energy to restore our dynamic, and to match and surpass the dynamic of our ideological and political adversaries, we must be mindful of Woodrow Wilson's emphasis on liberal education as *power* in the understanding of the values and objectives of a free society in all its cultural ramifications, and not as mere ornament, nor as a tool to achieve political purposes. We should avoid like the plague the temptation to camouflage the protection of cherished routine and vulgar vested interests as the preservation of academic standards.

We should be as effective in the achievement of the aims of a free society as the Russians are in the achievement of Soviet purposes. This unavoidably means that we need to think of the restoration of the cutting edge of our own values, to achieve an understanding of these values not as tired words to be used rhetorically in conventional political speeches but as the living spring of human behavior in the context of a changing world. It means that we need to understand, for instance, that love as a Christian ideal is not just something soft, sweet, and sentimental, but that love can be understood as the cutting edge on a surgeon's knife because that, too, is love, if it is properly motivated and supported by trained intelligence. If we stress only the financial and technical side of the present challenge, we may end up by achieving their, and not our, purposes. This is a moral challenge, and we can restore the cutting edge of our values only by emphasizing the moral and the value side in our cultural life.

The target of education in a free society is the cultivation of the *sources of responsibility* of the whole man. The basic question in all its ramifications is: How can education prepare men and women to be fit for the intellectual and moral responsibilities of free society? At this stage of radical reorientation we can only ask for a sense of direction. We cannot expect to be presented with a blueprint and detailed specifications, but we can be quite certain that our marksmanship will be improved if we reject the notion that we will reach the mark by indirection or by drift rather than by a deliberate and concerted search for the target itself. And while the storms of sharp and essentially irrelevant controversy rage over our weary and overburdened heads, we might recall that Ralph Waldo Emerson—speaking in 1837, a year of acute depression and widespread demoralization —knew of similar misguided panic in high places and counseled his young Harvard audience, "not to quit [their] belief that a popgun is a popgun, though the ancient and the honorable of the earth affirm it to be the crack of doom."

13

*Plato and Eisenhower's America**

ROBERT M. HUTCHINS, MY FORMER CHIEF AT THE UNIVERSITY OF Chicago, used to say that it was a college president's principal duty in life to "afflict the comfortable." This might well serve as my text for these remarks to an honors assembly. And let me say at once that my choice of the topic "Plato and Eisenhower's America" does not indicate any intention to direct these remarks specifically or exclusively to one partisan group rather than another. The qualities in America that I shall discuss are shared by Americans irrespective of political identification. It would be as easy to cite Democratic as well as Republican examples. In fact, I could find my best single representative source in a statement made by Carl Sandburg on a recent television program. Having just returned from a visit to the Soviet Union, he was asked for a one-sentence summary of his principal concern about America. The old poet—who is something of an actor as well —looked very wise for a moment, and then said, "Well, the country is just dripping with fat."

We live in a time of historically unparalleled material prosperity, of smug complacency, and of deep-rooted anxiety. We live in a time of slogan-thinking—not only among the untutored but amongst the intellectually most privileged. I have a strong liking for plain speech and a healthy distrust of folks who live verbally beyond their intellectual means.

In intellectual circles it is fashionable to decry the "conformity" of our time, and it is usually suggested that this "conformity" is a special characteristic of America in the present

---

* Address delivered at the Annual Scholastic Achievement Convocation, Syracuse University, on April 18, 1960 [Syracuse, N. Y.: Syracuse University, 1960].

decade—a byproduct of McCarthy-ism and of a large-scale corporate industrial civilization. Anyone who knows his de Tocqueville or John Stuart Mill knows that this is a parochial and a provincial view. The trend towards a discipline of likemindedness came with the earliest phases of a large market economy. It is a deep-seated cultural byproduct of our commitment to the attractions of an industrial society. "Conformity" was the great hazard of the new economically oriented society, and it would be easy to document this statement with scores of citations from classical sources, all more than a century old. I do not say this to deny the hazard but rather to restore our perspective. To think of "conformity" as a peculiar characteristic of a Madison Avenue culture is to underestimate the depth of its materialist roots. It is as silly as the characteristic tendency to praise "nonconformity" as the opposite of "conformity." There is no special virtue in nonconformity for its own sake. I need only to remind you of an especially repulsive type of conformity which can be found in the conventual form of beatnik nonconformity. Clearly the opposite of conformity is not nonconformity. The opposite to being a conformist is to *"Be Yourself."*

To be yourself is first of all a question of integrity and truthfulness about yourself. It is a question of knowing where to find evidence, and how to test it. It is a question of honesty and courage in facing that evidence. These are rare virtues—even among scholars and professional intellectuals, and among liberals as well as conservatives.

Take, as an example, a quotation from a recent speech of one of America's most conscientious scholarly liberals. I refer to Professor Adolph A. Berle's recent address to the fifteenth National Conference on Higher Education. He was speaking on the subject "The Irrepressible Issues of the Sixties," and he declared that American colleges and universities would play a leading role in determining whether the nation would experience a "renaissance or a regression."[1]

Then he went on to say: "We are fortunate in having a country and a system technically and physically able to produce material goods enough for everyone." The big question, he said, is whether the nation has the spiritual and intellectual resources "capable of mobilizing this enormous heritage."

He said this mobilization "cannot and will not be decently done by Madison Avenue, or smart sales campaigns, or political quackery," and declared:

We know that the rat race for status symbols is a pathetic humbug propagated by hucksters for personal gain. From our education we are entitled to have a product of graduates who know this, and who cannot be fooled into false values by the monkey business of public relations counsel.[2]

Here we have a choice collection of conformist slogans in what appears to be a nonconformist sermon. It is easy to define sin in others—in this case in "Madison Avenue," in "the monkey business of public relations." It is even easier to cherish illusions about yourself—in this case about our colleges and universities. Ask yourself one leading question. What—honestly now!—is the truth about higher education in relation to "the rat race of status symbols"? Are not the colleges and universities deeply involved in this "rat race"? Do American students typically choose their colleges on the basis of their concern for learning, or do they choose them on the basis of the enhanced social status that is deemed to be attached to their baccalaureate diplomas? If we are—and rightly so—critical of the spiritually empty "rat race for status symbols," would it not be more relevant to look to ourselves rather than to that much flogged horse on Madison Avenue?

Professor Berle's definition of a sin on "Madison Avenue" that can be easily found on almost any campus in the United States reminds me of John Cotton's distrust of "man's perverse subtlety in inventing new ways of backsliding." If we are honest with ourselves, is it not true that the American "image" of college education is an image of social status—differentiated social status —and not an image of "learning?" Do American students or parents select their colleges of "first choice" because of reasoned convictions about the quality of learning to be pursued in these institutions, or do they choose these colleges because of a reasoned conviction about the social status to be derived from their diplomas? Is this false perspective due to "Madison Avenue," or is it due to weaknesses in our own colleges and universities, and in the goals which we set for ourselves? There are indeed large impersonal forces in any historic period which none of us as

individuals can budge or deflect. But do not the value commitments of a scholar require—as Albert Camus so convincingly
insisted throughout his short life—that we face the facts about
ourselves rather than hide behind comfortable slogans that give
a pleasantly nonconformist flavor to essentially conformist ideas?

In American education we live in a period characterized by
a weird mixture of anxiety and complacency that is reflected in
the battle of the slogans which have become a form of contemporary dogma. After a decade of shrill warnings from all
our educational leaders, we developed a sudden panic at the news
of "Sputnik and all that," and in a binge of self-criticism we
disregarded all the warnings of American teachers, and painted
ourselves an idealized picture of Russian education, only to discover that Russia itself has chosen this very moment for a major
overhauling of its own educational system. Our mass media have
mouthed so many stereotypes about American education that it
has become almost impossible to use certain words—such as "adjustment" and "needs," especially "felt needs"—which have become verbal tools of confusion although many of these terms
have a definite and constructive meaning.

A nation's educational system is a reflection of its culture.
Education in the United States has many strengths and weaknesses, which are those of our culture as a whole. Our national
weaknesses today are real: in foreign policy we are, as Carl Sandburg said, "dripping with fat" in our concern for consumer
spending rather than national needs, and we have neglected our
capacity for strength in defense so flagrantly that we would be
unable to carry out an airlift in Berlin or to fight a Korean
war if the aggressor chose to test our national determination in
that manner. These weaknesses are terrifying, but they can be
remedied in short order by crash programs if the will and the
purpose can be found to impose discipline on ourselves. It is
crucial to recognize that our weakness does not arise from the
strength of the Russians and their associates. Their relative
strength lies in our deficiencies, and these deficiencies are inherent in our own pattern of motivation and values. Specifically,
in the schools and colleges, our weaknesses are only educational
in a superficial sense. A country's educational values are derived
from the country's value pattern as a whole. American schools
cannot be better than America itself. Plato knew this long ago

when he said that nothing is *cultivated* in a country except what is *honored* in that country. If we are today deficient in the achievement of intellectual standards of the highest order in mathematics, in science or in foreign languages, in history or in philosophy, let us ask whether *adult* America *honors* such achievement. If it did, our educational institutions would reflect these educational values. If it does not honor such achievement, our schools will continue to buck the tide with indifferent success, and our schools will continue to reflect the values of adult American life. In this basic sense the remedy for our deficiencies in intellectual achievement is not to be sought in education itself —it is rather a problem, a vital life-determining problem of American culture as a whole.

Let me remind you briefly of some of the things that have taken place in the past eighteen months. First, we had Sputnik and Lunik, and all the rest of it, and we saw American smug complacency and pride shaken as ten years of speeches by educators and college presidents had not managed to shake it; after all, they had been predicting that critical weaknesses were going to develop in American education, talking themselves hoarse, as a matter of fact, in the process, and not registering anywhere significantly with American public opinion.

But then came that mistake in the judgment not of educators or of scientists but of American public officials on the highest possible political level, who had not understood the dramatic implications of using funds in public budgets for one purpose rather than another. The weaknesses of the imagination with which we had contemplated the international geophysical year were suddenly revealed in the fact that the Russians beat us to it. It was not because we did not have the scientists—well-trained scientists were available in handsome numbers—but because we did not have the political imagination to see the implications in terms of world public opinion of our failure to use the trained manpower we had in a way which met the needs of the international rivalry in which we found ourselves involved.

Following the vested interests in the military services as well as in industry, we chose to subsidize obsolete forms of armament rather than the emerging new ones, and then we blamed the results of this very sad disappointment on education, and on science, rather than on the poor political judgment that had not known how to use the available economic resources and the available scientific resources. It is crucial to keep our eyes focused on this basic fact. There was no shortage of scientists or of ideas. The scientists were there. The ideas were there. General James M. Gavin has told the whole sad story in his volume entitled, *War and Peace in the Space Age.*[3] There was never a reply to the basic thesis of this book. The storm broke over the heads of the educators rather than over the heads of the political leaders who had not used the ideas and the scientific resources that were available, and that were in fact itching to be used.

THE PRESENT THAT IS

How often do we hear as we discuss educational problems: "Now, when I was young . . .," and then comes a good speech on what one should do about it in terms of a romantically nostalgic picture of a past that never was. We are not dealing with a past that never was. We are dealing with a present that *is*—even if some people are trying very hard not to see it.

In American education we are not dealing with people who *once were* young. We are responsible for the education of boys and girls who are young *now*. And in the total picture of the formative, that is to say, educational, influences that are brought to bear on the young now, and the 40 per cent increase in the number of teen-agers that lies ahead in the next five years, we are dealing with an educational process in which the formative influences are much wider than the school.

We all know it; we are all deeply aware of it. Education is not just what goes on in the school. Much more than in the past, education is what goes on in American culture as a whole, in competitive advertising: competitive advertising in the press and magazines and radio and television—with its sadistic and violent dramatic sketches for six- and eight-year old children— all of it pitched on the appropriate intellectual level, all of it financed very well, all of it designed to create a materialistic discontent with what is and what you now have, a design to create a premature obsolescence in the things that you can now consume, to make you reach out for more than you can immediately hope to attain.

It is very naive indeed to assume that this is not a major
educational formative influence on the young today. And if you
add to that all of the other forces that come out of a commercial,
competitive society; if you keep in mind that it is quite possible
to be an admirer of a market society, a competitive society in
terms of the impact it has on productivity, on material standards of living, and at the same time to believe that competitive
and market controls may be a very poor test indeed of cultural
achievement and of educational standards, you can readily see
that you cannot safely depend upon a nostalgic reliance on the
achievements of the past. We must deal with the present, and
the boys and girls who are enrolled in our schools and colleges
today are, if the Lord is merciful and the life expectancy tables
retain their validity, going to live well on into the twenty-first
century, under conditions of ever-increasing speed of social
change and rapidity of social and economic transition, of a type
that we now see before us and of which there is only one thing
certain: the speed of transition is going to intensify unless we
in some way or another once again take control of ourselves
through the one educational agency that is subject to social control, that is to say, through the agencies of formal education
today. But there is no enthusiasm for this deeper type of social
criticism of our educational pattern.

This is not just a question of money; this is a question of
motivation in the broadest possible sense of the term. It is a
matter of the values by which you intend to live the rest of
your life. And it is not just a matter of getting at the boys.
Directly—and indirectly—it involves the girls. In American life
as it is today—as anyone can tell you who has taught graduate
students, and I have done my share of it—when you have sold
a boy on a career of commitment to scholarship for the rest of
his life, you have merely taken the first steps in a long, continuous
struggle with the prevailing values in our society. After you have
recruited him, he goes into graduate school and after he has
been there for some time he runs into *the* girl, *and* he runs into
the girl's parents. They want to know, "Are you a complete and
total fool to marry a future college professor? Haven't you heard
what that means in terms of the cars you can't buy and the home
you can't furnish, and so on?"

TRAINED INTELLIGENCE

This is a broader problem than budget. This is a problem of the culture of America, the basic core of the cultural motivation of the country in which we live. Book VIII of Plato's *Republic* should be required reading for all adult Americans. Unless we cope with its central thesis, and cope with it reasonably soon —I would say within a period which is dramatically short, of about five years—we are likely to find that the loss of that cultural battle will risk the survival of the free society which we all cherish. If there is one thing certain in the world in which we now live, it is that a country is not going to survive unless it builds into its culture—and then into its private and public budgets—a respect for trained intelligence, trained intelligence in *all* of its ramifications.

The most hopeful thing about contemporary America is the increasing recognition of the cultural challenge to our inertia and complacency. Let me cite two paragraphs from a remarkable book *The Waist-High Culture* by Thomas Griffith, one of Mr. Luce's editors.

. . . It is sometimes said that all we need is leadership, and while it is true that we have lately lacked it, I believe that what men generally mean by that complaint pays too little heed to the immensity of the difficulties we face. Rather, we need a revolution of goals, a change in what we value, what we preserve and what we pursue. It may be that our discontent is what most justifies optimism. It may also be that when the younger generation is accused of lacking ambition what is really meant is that it is no longer inspired by the old standards, and it may be that this is what the "silent generation" is being silent about (page 271).

Whether today's rustle of discontent will tomorrow become a breeze, I do not know, but I suspect that it would not take gale force to recapture the center of our society. It is not stoutly defended: "Troy in our weakness lives, not in her strength." The center is not well commanded: it is minded by men protecting their own interests but incapable of seeing even them clearly; they are uncertain of purpose and divided in counsel; they are listening at the door, and it is we who are still. *The news about our times is that the center is empty.*[4]

This—I repeat—is *not* a question of budgets, except indirectly. The crucial weakness of free society does not lie in its economic aspect; it lies rather in the diminished effectiveness of the sources of responsibility upon which we rely for our social discipline and the determination of our priorities in the use of our talent and of our wealth.

THE OLD AND THE NEW

We live in a time of danger and a time of great hope. Whatsoever offers us complacency blinds us to the danger and denies us the hope. The most positive thing in America today is the reorientation of its youth. The adult generations talk of the changing goals of America, and a generation bankrupt in leadership looks to the President of the United States for the appointment of a national commission to give us a report on the long-range goals of America. Even a child should know that in a free society the goals come from individual men and women. We are in a stage of our national development in which the conflict between the achievement of the goals of an earlier generation—goals of an individualist type reflected in our concern with the technical control of natural forces—and the rearrangement of our priorities in our individual lives is reflected in a younger generation which in a quiet and determined way is seeking within itself for some principles of order in the chaos of conflicting claims on our national and on our individual energy. An older generation of parents and teachers speaks with concern of a "silent generation," a "generation characterized by apathy and complacency"—because it does not understand that the present student generation does not attach the highest priority to the broad social and economic issues that led students in the twenties and thirties to mass participation in organized causes. The preceding generation does not understand the searching quest for order within itself that is illustrated by the concern for commitment, the search for a tradition that can be embraced in self-respect and in the light of reason, and—as Camus put it—"without shame."

In fact, the sudden discovery of the undergraduate's interest in Camus is a significant watershed between the generations. The zest for ideas has not disappeared as some older observers are inclined to say. It has shifted its focus, and the concern— it is as widespread among American undergraduates as it is among German and Scandinavian students—with the intellectual and moral pilgrimage of Albert Camus is a healthy and positive sign of the new light that is appearing on the horizon. Camus was an essentially lonely figure—rejecting the old commitments on the traditional right and left—deeply involved in and reflecting the disintegration of the old values, but in the darkest depths of his generation's essential nihilism always committed to a search for the means of *transcending it.* He was preoccupied with the search for that "truth without shame," in a lonely search for the convictions which could restore the dignity of man for a generation which was quietly determined, as he said, "to remain honorable in the midst of a history which is not honorable." Sartre, Camus' old ideological enemy, was speaking for American students as well when he said at the time of Camus' death in a silly accident that "rarely have the nature of a man's work and the conditions of the historical moment so clearly demanded that a writer go on living."

Americans today are not living up to their potential capacity, and I am not speaking of industrial productivity and the standard measurement of capacity in our conventional use of the term. We must indeed *stretch* ourselves but we must stretch ourselves in our own conception of the range of our intellectual and moral powers. This is nothing new in human or in American history. Every achievement of a human goal simply sets new limits and new horizons for other types of achievements. A period of smug complacency with the achievement of national goals is traditionally a time in which the seeds are sown for a new generation with new aims and new discontents. The beginning of all growth is a clear view of the truth about ourselves, including a balanced view of the role of reason in understanding the rational as well as the irrational elements in human experience.

William James had a favorite quotation from the Bible that is directly relevant. It is from the Book of Ezekiel. Ezekiel was having his trouble with the Israelites of his time, who were, as the Bible says, "a rebellious house," "impudent children and stiffhearted." They *were not* interested in spiritual warnings. And Ezekiel sought counsel from his God, and as he prayed he "fell on his face."

And then, it says in the second chapter of the Book of Ezekiel that the Lord said to Ezekiel, "Son of Man, stand on thy feet, and I will speak to thee."

In other words: The truth will be revealed only if you have the courage to seek it—and to face it.

We must stretch ourselves—morally, philosophically, intellectually, and this means education and effort on *all* levels. To this group of Syracuse students who have shown their ability to profit by the highest intellectual opportunities made available by the American university, I add that specialized intellectual effort is only the beginning, the essential beginning. Specialized learning is not the faith men live by. If we are to commit ourselves to the faith of free men—and without such commitment we shall perish —that faith must be nourished by the devoted cultivation of the general philosophical and moral framework from which the specialized learning draws its meaning, and without which it can be a tool to serve totalitarian ends.

We must stretch ourselves—and if we do, we shall find new meaning for our time and for ourselves in our own moral tradition and in the spiritual insights of that tradition.

"Son of Man, stand on thy feet, and I will speak to thee.'"

14

*The Literature of Freedom and Liberal Education**

CONTROVERSY ABOUT FREEDOM IS TOO OFTEN, IN THE LANGUAGE of Ecclesiastes, "vanity and a striving after wind." There is quite a breeze now as our academic specialists focus their scholarship on ever-narrowing aspects of the broad ideal of freedom and free society, and as the ideal of freedom becomes a football in the arena of world politics.

There is nothing new in semantic confusion about freedom. It is often defined in terms of the removal of the type of constraint that has been most recently experienced, just as order tends to be defined in terms of the type of insecurity that is currently remembered. Freedom was defined differently by the Greeks in Pericles' time, by the merchants of Adam Smith's time, by Karl Marx in the early stages of the Industrial Revolution, and by the peasants in contemporary Russia. A continuous sifting of the literature is therefore necessary if we are to select the universal as against the contemporary and parochial elements in the tradition.

"A WIDE FIELD OF DEBATE"

Thomas Paine, who thought that "hereditary" monarchy was the "one general principle" that distinguished freedom from slavery, argued in *The Rights of Man* that "when nations fall out about freedom, a wide field of debate is opened." With his basic commitment to the view that "the more perfect civilization is, the less occasion has it for government," and his charac-

* From *Measurement and Research in Today's Schools,* a Report of the Twenty-fifth Educational Conference, New York City, October 27 and 28, 1960 (Washington, D.C.: American Council on Education [©1961]), pp. 133-73.

223

teristic secular contempt for religion, history, and rights based "on the authority of a mouldy parchment," he would hardly recognize the nature of modern "issues of freedom," although he is still quoted out of context in the contemporary controversy.

Abraham Lincoln, speaking in a context that would still be valid today, stressed in his Baltimore address on April 18, 1864 that "the world has never had a good definition of the word liberty, and the American people, just now, are much in want of one." Montesquieu—to take one additional classical example from a rich literature—stressed the same point in *The Spirit of the Laws* when he said, "There is no word that admits of more various meanings and has made more varied impressions on the human mind, than that of liberty."[1]

While there is nothing new, therefore, in the conflict of interpretation, it is more disturbing to recognize that freedom as the core of our society's public values and pronouncements has during the past generation received, on the part of scholars as well as political leaders, an enormous amount of attention which has not diminished but rather deepened the confusion that surrounds the subject. Political leaders abroad as well as at home continue to use the word "freedom" as if it were a simple and self-explanatory ideal. Our Secretary of State is described in the mass communications media as "a salesman of freedom"; our national anthem complacently describes America as "the land of the free"; the Statue of Liberty is accepted as a national symbol; and in the conflict with the Soviet-controlled part of the world we are generally and uncritically described as "the leaders of the free world." Freedom has become our national trademark during the same generation in which scholarly enterprise, operating in a tradition of specialized scholarship which concentrates on splinters of the subject rather than the historic tradition as a whole, has revealed a veritable swamp of semantic confusion and conflict in the interpretation of the core values of our society.

In a volume designed and edited to "clarify" the meaning of freedom, a distinguished anthropologist tells us that "freedom is a concept that has meaning only in a subjective sense. A person who is in complete harmony with his culture feels free. He accepts voluntarily the demands made upon him."[2] In other words, the completely brain-washed Nazi or Stalinist is the perfect example of a free man. Pushing relativism to its ultimate extreme, a distinguished historian tells us that "the word liberty means nothing until it is given a specific content, and with a little massage will take any content you like."[3]

Pushing this confusion even further, an equally distinguished sociologist tells us that freedom "cannot be analyzed into component parts or reduced to simple statements":

The child knows it who is forced to work when he wants to play. The savage knows it who is prevented from following his tribal customs. The criminal knows it who is put behind prison bars. The property-owner knows it who is not allowed to use his property as he pleases.[4]

A distinguished scientist, developing an American version of Friedrich Engels' classical statement that "freedom is the recognition of necessity," informs us that "freedom is almost the reverse of unrestraint."[5] A philosopher,[6] reporting on the findings of a team of scholars subsidized by a large foundation grant, declares that "true freedom" consists in doing one's duty, being virtuous and wise, being one's "true self," without further clarification on the crucial concepts of duty, or wisdom, or on the role of "conscience" when it calls for the rejection of "duty" or conventional wisdom.

Socrates, Giordano Bruno, Martin Luther, Thoreau, and Matteotti were all individuals who came to a point in their experience at which they refused to obey. Were they exercising a crucial "freedom"?[7]

A psychologist contributes to the chaotic swamp a volume in which a commendable concern for maximizing the ability of every man "to resist manipulation, whether institutional or deliberate, insofar as the manipulation serves other interests at the expense of his own," and a fresh and vigorous plea that "a society is free only to the extent that its least privileged and its least tolerated members are free" are combined with the pervasive view that property rights are not human rights but social privileges, and that an indefinite expansion of the state's powers over the economy is somehow compatible with the reduction of manipulation and the widening of freedom.[8] He does not even discuss the questions whether the public monopoly of manipulation is likely to be more restrictive of freedom—even for the least privileged elements in a society—and whether dispersed and competitive control is not essential for the emergence of freedom, although it is, of course, crucial in the historic life of free society as it has been hammered out on the anvil of experience.[9]

Perhaps these few samples from the growing literature will suffice to prove the statement that in the discussion of freedom we are living in a swamp of semantic confusion. It is, of course, true that there are occasional additions to the growing shelf of literature which make a substantial contribution towards sifting the relevant and the irrelevant, distinguishing between "feeling" free and "being" free, and aware of the inevitable cultural togetherness of historic, spiritual, social, and economic elements in the tradition. The recent publication of F. A. Hayek's *The Constitution of Liberty*[10] is not only a tribute to the vitality of the classical tradition, but a rich source of cogent and exciting discussion of the whole range of relevant literature during the past fifty years. Frank H. Knight has fought a lifelong battle against the rising tide of obfuscation, and in the European literature the work of W. Röpke and A. Rüstow has kept a clear focus on the social framework of the free market.[11] I would also single out Bronislaw Malinowski's *Freedom and Civilization*,[12] and Herbert J. Muller's *Issues of Freedom*.[13]

It is also true that most of the writings which I have discussed critically include a wealth of material that can be put to good use by careful scholars. Adler's *The Idea of Freedom* contains valuable keys to relevant literature, and it allows the individuality of the authors who are discussed to shine through in spite of the rigorous taxonomic treatment. It is clear, however, that we can no longer assume that there is a Western consensus regarding "freedom" which could be compared with the earlier writings of John Stuart Mill, Lord Acton, and de Tocqueville.

The crucial problem does not lie in the totalitarian countries which have used our vocabulary in the best Orwell tradition to convey the opposite of the traditional meaning. We can all understand Lenin's motives when he described freedom as a "conventional phrase which, like a nickname, becomes legitimized by custom," and when he denounces revisionists who have become impressed with the free and democratic traits of Western European society as impressed by "the dusty pages of bourgeois

books, permeated through and through by bourgeois democratic prejudices, and thereby becoming, objectively speaking,
the lackeys of the bourgeois."[14] We can even smile when Lenin
tells us that "freedom is a precious commodity, so precious that
it must be rationed," or when *Time* magazine reports a discussion between a British Labor Prime Minister and two leading
Soviet representatives in which the meaning of the word "freedom" was explored with the help of a bewildered interpreter,
with the final agreement that in the West it meant "freedom
to choose," while in the Communist East it meant freedom
"from having to choose."[15]

Few of us are disturbed when Harold J. Laski tells us, in the
article on "Liberty" in the *Encyclopedia of the Social Sciences,*
that "liberty is unattainable until the passion for equality has
been satisfied"—too many of us recall Acton's and de Tocqueville's explicit warnings.[16] None of us is disturbed by the Nazi
effort to define "freedom" in terms of a critical attack on the
Versailles Treaty *(Freiheit und Brot),* or when it is reduced in
Rosenberg's ideological manual for the Nazi party to the "eternal
racial soul substance" with the explicit nonsense that "freedom
means to be bound by the ties of race."[17]

These efforts to define freedom as its opposite are in the last
analysis a tribute to the compelling challenge of the idea of
freedom itself. The confusion in our own ranks is more serious.
If "liberal education" has freedom as its core value, what *are*
we—or what *should* we be—teaching about freedom? If freedom
is the ideological center of our position in world political rivalry,
where and how can our statesmen find the philosophical, the
historical, and the cultural support for their position?

THE SPECIALISTS AND THE WORM'S EYE VIEW

The semantic confusion that prevails in our discussions of
freedom arises primarily from our specialization in scholarship
and secondarily from the identification in some quarters of freedom with total laissez faire in economic policy ("freedom from
the state is freedom from law"), which is particularly common
in the United States today but which had already led de Tocque-

ville to tell his French materialistic contemporaries that "the man who asks of freedom anything other than itself is born to be a slave."[18]

In our academic division of labor, issues of freedom—in their inevitable togetherness of historic, religious, cultural, and economic aspects—are deemed to be "political" or "popular"; they are, as the saying goes, "out of my field." The result is either a dangerous and artificial singling out of narrow special aspects, which do not fit together into a meaningful and socially realistic whole, or the occupation of the field by people with various special vested interests, or leaving the battleground, by sheer drift, in the exclusive possession of those who are interested in "feeling free" rather than in "being free" and who will be primarily drawn by their interest in subjective aspiration rather than their concern with observed, realistic human behavior. The field is left to artists, poets, philosophers, psychologists, and writers who draw their inspiration from imagination and who substitute armchair mental processes for the empirical study of historic and cultural processes which have in fact defined our various freedoms.

A physicist does not define his basic concepts by poetic imagination, by a dictionary definition, or by a Gallup poll. He defines his terms by reference to observed reality. Similarly, our discussions of freedom should be rooted in a realistic theory of human nature, social and historic experience, and a study of the social, political, and economic conditions under which human beings define their purposes, pursue them effectively, and reap the fruit of their labor. The concept of freedom should be defined in terms of the social context in which man as he *is*—and not as he *might* be—has achieved freedom and can extend his achievement by augmenting the freedoms that have historically been realized.

The primary cause of confusion lies in the varied types of freedom that together constitute our freedom as a whole. Our specialized scholars in their pursuit of separate splinters of the log are like the six blind men in the classical Indian story who describe an elephant in terms of his tail, his tusks, or his trunk. Liberty was not created by a philosopher's definition. It can be defined in a manner that will make it impossible to achieve, but we know that in varying degrees it *has* been achieved.

EMPIRICAL AND RATIONALIST TRADITIONS

Liberty is not created by reflection—it is always rooted in historic reality, and it typically appears as a byproduct of a struggle for power. It is almost always interstitial, and not deliberately planned. The English tradition from precedent to precedent, as it is reflected in the writings of John Milton, John Locke, David Hume, Adam Smith, Edmund Burke, John Stuart Mill, and Lord Acton, stresses these historic and crescive factors, and this empirical factor is obscured in the French literature where a rationalist absolutism was concerned with "redesigning the whole of free society" rather than with the piecemeal process in which liberties have in fact been established. In its final outcome, one of these traditions led to "freedom" and the other became, through Rousseau, and the Jacobin tradition, one of the ancestors of populist democracy and of modern totalitarianism.[19]

In the French tradition Montesquieu and de Tocqueville place themselves on British or "empirical" foundations, while Bentham, Paine, Jefferson, and even Mill show the influence of French rationalism in the English and American literature. Political freedom in the sense of the participation of men in the choice of their own government, and freedom as national independence, illustrate many of the possible "issues." The conflicts between democracy as majority rule and the idea that freedom calls for limits imposed on the state (think of federalism, civil liberties, and the Bill of Rights) furnish another example. The consideration of "inner" or "subjective" freedom raises more issues, and the historic fact that the state or the "king" had to establish a monopoly of physical coercion in order to protect freedom against arbitrary constraint by others supplies another source of broad confusion.

The confusion of freedom and power is a final source of philosophical conflict, and the shelves of philosophical literature concerned with the problem of "freedom of the will" serve as a final reminder of the perils of metaphysical reflection detached from the empirical record of historic achievement. Some of the more extreme determinists in psychology and in philosophy argue that the word "will" has no meaning, and they question whether there is such a thing as voluntary action. This type of

semantic confusion is probably a comment on the present state
of philosophy rather than on liberty. As Hayek argues: All that
matters is that there are kinds of action that can be influenced
by rational considerations as well as those that cannot. Does
a person believe, or does he not believe in his capacity to form
and to carry out a plan and to make a choice? If he does, there
is freedom in the only sense that matters historically.[20]

The process through which a slave in various countries was
"liberated" is a strong empirical reminder of the essential elements, and many of these factors do not even appear in the
systematic "philosophical" treatises that attempt to "define" freedom. A slave became "free" if he was made subject only to the
same laws as his fellow citizens, if he became immune from
arbitrary confinement and free to choose his own work, and
if he was able to own and to acquire property.[21] There is nothing
here about freedom of the will, about "inner" freedom, or even
about the right to vote, and a review of these basic historic
tests of freedom throws a strange light upon some of the "new
freedoms" that receive so much attention in contemporary intellectual and political discussion.

A NEW REALIST VIEW OF MAN

Considering that many of our academic "specialists" have
virtually abdicated their responsibilities to free society, the continuous rise in the intellectual influence of Reinhold Niebuhr
is one of the most cheerful factors in the national scene. It is
not necessary to accept Calvinist—or even Christian—conceptions
of human nature to recognize that wherever significant freedoms
have in fact been achieved, the framework of free society was
constructed on the assumption that human nature had elements
of determinate evil in it as well as potentialities for transcending it. Ideas such as our separation of powers, the limitations
placed on the power of the state and of the majority (the Bill
of Rights), and the concept of "checks and balances" are all
rooted in a realistic theory of the nature of man, while the most
revolting forms of cruelty and abuse of power have coincided
with perfectibilist illusions. These ideas are not confined to our
culture; they are universal in their human validity, and it may

well be that the professional clerical tendency to overemphasize sexual and simian factors in the catalogue of sins, in contrast with the theological inheritance which placed "spiritual pride" at the head of the list of mortal sins, has made it incumbent on our secular thinkers to rediscover the political and the cultural significance of the moral experience of the race.[22]

Order may be imposed by power, and such order may be incompatible with any conception of freedom. It is quite possible to have discipline without freedom, but it is impossible to have freedom without discipline, as the classical cycle of government expounded in Aristotle's *Politics* made clear more than two thousand years ago. The common linguistic root of the words "disciple" and "discipline" is meaningful, and the type of order that is compatible with freedom is not, as Ortega y Gasset has emphasized, a pressure which is imposed on society from without but it is an equilibrium which must be set up from within. Freedom is not the absence of discipline; rather, it calls for discipline by internal constraint in contrast with control by others. When you throw a man in the water, his freedom does not express itself by merely splashing around. He can be free in the water because he has learned to swim, that is to say, only because he subjects himself to a form of discipline, and a blend of self-suppression and self-assertion. The discipline of free men is not submission of one person's will to that of another, but it is anchored in a strategy of learning to balance the tensions within yourself. The ideas of freedom, self-control, and balance are inextricably interwoven.

The undisciplined mobs of commoners with "rights" and no sense of responsibility for being anything other than "a buoy that floats on the waves," the men who are characterized by "root ignorance of the very principles" underlying free society, and "who are scarcely conscious to themselves of any obligations," the men who enter upon life "to do jolly well what they like," the irresponsible scientist who as "a learned ignoramus" still evinces all the petulance of one who is learned in his own special line—all these folks who believe that, wholly apart from their own responsibility, civilized free society is there "in just the same way as the earth's crust," all these beneficiaries of the struggle and responsibility of their predecessors will before long be surprised when "there will be heard throughout the planet a

formidable cry, rising like the howling of innumerable dogs
to the stars, asking for someone or something to take command,
to impose an occupation, a duty."[23]

THE SOURCES OF RESPONSIBILITY

The quest for the source of responsibility is crucial. As Lord
Bryce said in *The American Commonwealth,* "The wisest statesman is he who best holds the balance between freedom and
order."

Freedom is not "doing as you please," for a society in which
men recognize no check on their freedom soon becomes a society
in which freedom is only the privilege of a savage few. Freedom
is not, as John Locke stressed in his *Second Treatise on Civil
Government,* "a liberty for every man to do what he lists,"
because freedom is the presence of responsible choice, and it
calls for the removal of restraint by others and the establishment
of opportunities for self-control. *The refreshing of the sources of
responsibility is therefore the core of the problem.* Liberty in
the classical tradition—"ye shall know the truth, and the truth
shall make you free" (John 8:32)—meant the acceptance of a
shared moral tradition. Paul's *locus classicus* in Corinthians II
(3:17), "Where the spirit of the Lord is, there is freedom,"
stressed the same insight. It is neither a justification for "doing
as you please," nor an argument for the parochial view that
freedom is only compatible with one particular religious tradition. It is obviously compatible with the voluntary acceptance
of the authority of any source of moral responsibility, in the
same sense as Reinhold Niebuhr's views of the "nature of man"
are compatible with a secular or an other-than-Christian religious commitment.

FREEDOM FROM LAW AND FREEDOM THROUGH LAW

Freedom clearly calls for the removal or the restriction of
arbitrary restraint by others, and it therefore calls for the establishment of impersonal rules or laws which apply equally to
all "under the law." The conception of freedom as "the absence

of restraint" is one of the principal causes of our present confusion. John Stuart Mill's insistence on the minimized control of the individual, which was related to his stress on freedom of thought where it is valid, is frequently pushed to the extreme form of "more liberty, less law,"[24] where it flies in the face of the obvious fact that restraint by others can only be removed if restraint by law or restraint by self-control is available as an alternative method of establishing social order.

Freedom *from* law and freedom *through* law are only apparently contradictory.[25] If with Hegel, and all his impact on Marxist ideology, we hold that positive freedom is characterized by total obedience or complete abnegation of one's own opinions, we are simply indulging ourselves in a familiar trick of rhetoric in which through freedom *from* freedom the emotional appeal of one value is used to sell another. If we mean by freedom a condition in which the individual may decide for himself between good and evil, if we include, as did Dostoyevsky with his Russian Orthodox background and Lord Acton in a Roman Catholic setting, freedom of conscience, that is to say, "the assurance that every man shall be protected in doing what he believes to be his duty against the influence of authority and majorities, custom and opinion," then it is clear that new types of freedom may be found not only in the removal of legal constraint but through the establishment of new law which may clearly call for the imposition of corresponding restraints on freedoms that have previously been enjoyed. It is quite possible that the constraint of one type of activity may open up wider opportunities of choice in other directions. This is a question of practical wisdom in assessing public policy; it is not a matter of dogma.

There is a pervasive temptation, as was made evident in my review of recent literature, to confuse subjective personal experience with objective cultural and historic reality by making the claim for freedom total, absolute, and ubiquitous. It is a total confusion of human aspiration and cultural reality to speak of freedom as "a child knows it who is forced to work when he wants to play," or as "a criminal knows it who is put behind prison bars," or as "a property owner knows it who is not allowed to use his property as he pleases." Real freedom, as it is observed in historic forms of human culture, is never absolute or total. Education, including education for responsible citizenship in a free society and the "discipline" of liberal education, is always a gradual curtailment of the recipient's subjective experience of "freedom." It inevitably involves the discipline of a child's moods, whims, and drives. The machinery of the criminal law is the foundation of social order, and it inevitably implies the curtailment of a criminal's aspiration to be "free" to commit crime.

If freedom is the presence of responsible choice, the nature of the process through which the sources of responsibility are refreshed is crucial, and it is certainly not necessary to remind educators that choice implies commitment, and not "free-floating freedom" to follow whims or subjective aspiration. As Malinowski says:

Follow up the life history of yourself or of anyone you know well and you will see that the human career consists in making one choice or the other and sticking to it. The more successful the career, the less "changes of mind" are necessary in it—or possible.[26]

There is no education without punishment or reward. There is no game without rules and penalties. It is not necessary to keep choice permanently open to pursue freedom. It is necessary to preserve and to extend the availability of several alternatives in choice, while it remains clearly recognized that the fact of choice implies a commitment to the rules that govern in the area of the option that is exercised.

There is no such thing as total freedom, and liberty, as Edmund Burke said, must be limited to be possessed. If freedom is the presence of choice—and the cultural opportunity to pursue a purpose—there is always a possibility of increments of freedom in one area in comparison with the possibility of losses in another. Just as one can never be a Christian in the sense of complete acceptance of and compliance with the teachings of the Sermon on the Mount and it is only possible at best to be forever "becoming" a Christian, so a state of total freedom is culturally inconceivable although a continuous *process of liberation* is a historically and socially defensible goal.[27] In Wordsworth's words in *The Prelude*: "Man free, man working for himself, with choice/Of time, and place, and object," with the understanding that redefinition in terms of changes in time, place, and object is the core of the challenge.

FREEDOM AND ITS MORAL CONTEXT

Freedom is in its very nature always relative and never absolute. The nonconformist is never "on his own." He always draws his spiritual strength from a moral or philosophical tradition. In this sense a prisoner may be more free than the guardian at the gate of his cell. In an American setting we can think of Thoreau. In a Russian cultural context—and the Russian tradition of freedom is exceptionally rich in this respect for obvious historical reasons—we can recall Dostoyevsky's rediscovery of the Biblical tradition during his period of Siberian exile; or Dudintsev's character, Lopatkin, who as a product of Soviet education had inevitably cultivated the questioning mind that was essential for good scientific and technical work and who tells about his prison experience in these sentences: "The words 'deprivation of liberty' are inaccurate. Whoever has learned to think cannot be completely deprived of liberty";[28] or, most recently, Boris Pasternak, who had "paid little attention to religious practice" until nonconformity made him seek for sources of moral support, which are described in the nineteenth poem attached to *Doctor Zhivago* as Biblical teachings which restored his "consciousness" and turned his "impotence into life."[29]

A man who must choose between submission to tyranny and "total" cultural isolation is likely to conform or to go insane, unless he follows the pattern which Dostoyevsky established in his novels and to which Durkheim gave the classical sociological expression, and solves his problem by suicide. This is the weakness at the core of "total freedom": no society could endure as a society if it were composed of individuals detached from all cultural constraint and, more cogently perhaps from the standpoint of an advocate of free society, no individual can endure under such conditions.

My reference to religion in relation to freedom and my citation of Russian experience draw attention to another weakness in our current Western picture of free society, and that is our tendency to establish a narrow, almost a parochial picture of its foundations. It is not necessary, as I have already stressed, to draw parochial religious conclusions from the dependence of free society upon a source of responsibility that lies beyond the state, or majority control. It is not necessary either, as I shall develop further on, to assume that the Indian, and more broadly the Eastern, identification of freedom with detachment from material wants is contrary to our own conception of freedom. It is least of all necessary to restrict our discussion of freedom to Western, that is to say, to French, German, English, or American, sources. There is a rich mine of relevant literature and experience in Central Europe and in Russia which strengthens our tradition not only because of its content, but also because it widens the range of the appeal of the tradition of free society.

FREEDOM AND CENTRAL EUROPEAN TRADITION

Thomas Garrigue Masaryk, founder and first president of Czechoslovakia, would be an admirable representative of Central Europe's tradition of free society. Let us recall Sir Richard Livingstone's concern about the weaknesses of specialized scholarship and the need for education "in the presence of greatness." "I should like," he said, "to see every child carry away from school portraits of a few great men . . . as standards for judging, and touchstones for testing, human character." And then he proposed as five names for such a list: Christ, Socrates, St. Francis, Abraham Lincoln, and "certainly" President Masaryk, who "is on a different level, and yet among the statesmen of the modern world perhaps no figure is so instructive as this coachman's son who became head of a state."[30]

It is no accident that Lenin described Masaryk as "my most serious ideological antagonist in Europe." It is no accident, either, that the name of Masaryk is still today the most active Central European symbol of loyalty to free society, as we know from responses to broadcasts.[31] His unflinching support of truth as a scholar even when it was unacceptable to his students and unpalatable to his political supporters, and his constant stress in an age of materialism on the moral basis of a free society; his emphasis on the independence of freedom from any particular legal document or within a wide range from any form of economic organization, and his insistence that freedom was primarily anchored in the value commitments of free men, including particularly a respect for truthfulness in the search for and in the use of evidence—all of these together make Masaryk a fresh and a continuing source of inspiration in contemporary free society. He knew that freedom can never be "doing as you please," but that it called for the establishment of the opportunity for self-control to replace the constraint by others. He knew, as only the author of *The Spirit of Russia*[32] could know, that a blind reaction against czarist autocracy and ecclesiastical abuse turning into unlimited freedom would merely lead to a new swing of the pendulum to unlimited despotism—and he was aware that this was an insight as old as Aristotle's *Politics*.

RUSSIAN LITERATURE: THE REDISCOVERY OF THE WHOLE MAN

The response to unlimited freedom may seem to be a strange introduction to the available Russian literature, but this will be so only because we have allowed the present Russian regime's need to justify itself and the revolution of October 1917 to color our own thought. Following the historical procedures which have been so convincingly portrayed in George Orwell's *Nineteen Eighty-Four*, everything in the Russian past has to be presented in black or white, in a picture of czarist autocracy and ecclesiastical abuse on the one hand, and the triumph of the Communist revolution on the other.[33] If possible the revolution of March 1917 must be forgotten, and the contingencies and potentialities which ranged throughout the nineteenth century, from Belinsky's acceptance of the most extreme form of Western "atomistic individualism" through the nihilist and anarchist period to Dostoyevsky's religious and moral concern with the problem of freedom, are more or less obscured.

A distinguished American historian tells us—following the pattern—that "communism has been efficient enough, it has made Russia a great power in a single generation." If America became a great power in the same generation, does it prove that "capitalism" was equally "efficient"? Was the Russia that played a major role in Napoleon's final defeat a "minor" power, and what role did Russia play in the origin and formulation of "our" Monroe

Doctrine? Similarly, we have allowed our discussion of Russian education to follow the Russian pattern. It is possible to have a high opinion of quantitative achievements in Soviet higher education in the last twenty years and still to recall that Russian universities played a major role in the nineteenth century and that they were in certain periods and in some respects more "free" than contemporary Russian *and* American institutions (in the appointment of new professors, for instance). Have we forgotten the relatively "liberal" treatment of political prisoners in the nineteenth century which permitted a Bakunin or a Lenin to study and to write during their Siberian exile, and which permitted courtship and marriage to political prisoners? All of these things are omitted—or underemphasized—in the present official history, but is there any reason why free scholars should not continue to be mindful of them?

Unlike the West where the fragmenting of intellectual and literary experience followed the economic and technical example of the division of labor, Russian literature continued to treat politics, religion, and philosophy in their inextricable human togetherness, and when the Western intellectual fashions penetrated, it was Dostoyevsky's great contribution to have insisted in a masterly manner—as no Western literary figure did with comparable effect—on the "incompleteness" of the ideas that were placed into circulation. Through the embodiment of ideas in vital literary characters Russian literature has shown an astonishing capacity to impose the personalities created by its authors on the national imagination. Where abstract ideas dominate in Western intellectual life, Turgenev's Rudin (based on Bakunin's life), and the nihilist Bazarov in his *Fathers and Sons;* Goncharov's Oblomov; Dostoyevsky's Raskolnikov, and his whole family of Karamazov characters, but especially Ivan and Alyosha, together with Stavrogin, Shatov, and Shigalev in *The Devils,* have become "types" in national political as well as literary discussion, in the same sense in which, more exceptionally, Sinclair Lewis succeeded in doing this in American literature with his character Babbitt. An evaluation of Russian contributions to the literature of freedom, therefore, turns quite naturally to these authors instead of to the political philosophers, the historians, and the economists who play so prominent a role in the West.[34]

In Dostoyevsky's reaction against the fragmented ideas—that

is to say, ideas detached from their social and historical context—
which were becoming fashionable imports from the West, and
especially against the secularist and nihilist implications of these
ideas, he was pursuing a lifelong campaign initiated with the
radical reorientation in his philosophy that began in the early
years of his penal servitude. In the final pages of *The House of the
Dead*, which described his Siberian exile, Dostoyevsky develops
the idea, which was full of insight into Russian philosophical and
political developments, that the dreams of the convicts and their
long divorce from reality had made them "think of freedom as
somehow more free than real freedom." "The convict had an
exaggerated idea of real freedom, and that is so natural, so characteristic of every convict."[35]

TOTAL FREEDOM VERSUS TOTAL DESPOTISM

This concern for "total" or "unlimited" freedom was reflected
not only in anarchists and nihilists but even appeared in a
realistic social observer like Chekhov, who could speak of "absolute" freedom when he was simply concerned with freedom from
coercion and untruth (in other words, with personal freedom).
It became a lifelong concern to Dostoyevsky, who was to his
Russian readers not only a novelist but, as Nicholas Berdyaev
phrased it, " a dialectician of genius and Russia's greatest metaphysician,"[36] who knew how to fuse thought and plot more
brilliantly than any other writer before or since.

It is impossible to understand an author like Dostoyevsky
without some study of the background of Russian history, which
is a great hurdle to Western readers educated in a setting in
which Russian history is underemphasized. The abiding memory
of peasant rebellion—highlighted by the revolt in 1670 led by the
Don Cossack Stenka Razin, and in the years from 1754 to 1766
by a peasant named Pugachev, who had fallen under the influence of the schismatic "Old Believers"—was kept fresh by the
abortive attempt at revolution by the Decembrists (December
1825), but also by literally hundreds of minor revolts in the
nineteenth century in which the proprietors of isolated rural
estates were murdered by their serfs, as Dostoyevsky's father was
assassinated in 1839. The unparalleled violence and destructive

enthusiasm of these outbursts has even endowed the Russian language with the word *Pugachevshchina* to describe the revolutionary potentialities of the peasantry, and it was clear that the real challenge to established order in Russia merely awaited the arrival of a "Pugachev of the university." This is the background against which Russian political thought in the nineteenth century began its opposition to the bureaucratic state of Nicholas I, and this political thought was inextricably interwoven with acceptance of the most extreme forms of Western rationalism and anticlericalism.

Belinsky, who as a literary critic played the leading role in the early recognition of Dostoyevsky's promise as a writer, came to reject the role of the "community" in the establishment of freedom and responsibility by asserting that individual personality is "more important than the fate of the whole world." Chernyshevsky, who took Feuerbach and Comte as his mentors, imported Bentham and Mill without stressing the implicit dependence upon the moral like-mindedness of the England of their time. Dostoyevsky's Ivan Karamazov, who "renounced the higher harmony—it is not worth the smallest tear of one tormented child," is a true product of a form of atomistic individualism which had been recognized by authors in the best Western tradition, such as Durkheim, Simmel, Weber, and in a brilliant American version in Robert A. Nisbet's *The Quest for Community*,[37] as the basic cancer that affects a free society if there is no continuing concern for replenishing the sources of responsibility.[38]

But the Russians had all the zeal of new converts in their "religion of humanity" and the influence of Rousseau and Voltaire predominated. Herzen, in his first trip to Paris, "entered it with reverence, as men used to enter Jerusalem and Rome," and Bakunin, the most extreme of Russia's nineteenth-century champions of liberty, insisted upon "absolute" freedom, unlimited faith in human nature, the rejection of bourgeois culture, the acceptance of the purity of the revolutionary force of the peasantry, and complete rejection of religion in any form. "If God exists, man is a slave—if man is free there can be no God" would be a good short summary of the Bakunin doctrine and of its anarchist and nihilist variations.[39]

This is the background of the Slavophile reaction for which Dostoyevsky became a spokesman in his later years. The authors who created and reflected this movement indulged in mystical and unhistorical idealization of the Russian past, they denounced rationalism as "the mortal sin of the West," and they idealized, in a reaction against the rational egoism of the bourgeoisie, the community-mindedness of the Russian peasant, using the ecclesiastical term *sobornost*, which, like the German word *Gemeinschaft*, is almost untranslatable but describes "altogetherness," stressing the dynamic life of the community and carrying overtones of religious sanction.

The ideological importance of Dostoyevsky can only be understood in this context. When Dostoyevsky is introduced in the American college curriculum, he is usually presented as a psychological novelist whose literary genius led him to anticipate many of the insights of Freud, Nietzsche, or Kierkegaard, and who described the phenomenon of "alienation" long before Karl Marx and without the benefit of historic materialism. If Dostoyevsky is, as Irving Howe says in a brilliant chapter on him in his *Politics and the Novel*, "the greatest of all ideological novelists," it is precisely as a philosopher of freedom.[40] His novels *The Devils* (sometimes translated as *The Possessed*) and *The Brothers Karamazov* (especially "The Legend of the Grand Inquisitor") are classics in the literature of free society, and they deal with the most acute problems of freedom *in America today*.

It is possible to read them, and this is commonly done, as a comment on Russian radicalism in the seventies and as a reflection of Dostoyevsky's characteristically Russian bias against the Roman Catholic Church. This was done by Gorky, who called *The Devils* "the most talented and the most vicious of the innumerable attempts to slander the revolutionary movement in the seventies."[41] It is possible to read the novel, as Ernest J. Simmons does, as a reflection of Dostoyevsky's "lack of understanding of the revolutionary movement of his own day" but "amazingly prophetic of the worst excesses of the Soviet Revolution some fifty years later."[42] It is possible also to read it as a caricature of the murder of a young student by a conspiratorial nihilist group led by Nechaiev, but a subsequent study of all the police records made available after the revolution of 1917 makes it clear that the truth was stranger than fiction—in the light of the actual factual situation, Dostoyevsky's version was not an exaggeration but an understatement.[43]

It is more plausible, however, to read *The Devils* as a penetrating and universally valid comment on the confusion of anarchy and freedom in which, with the dualism that is so characteristic of Dostoyevsky as a novelist, two of the characters, Shatov and Kirilov—at opposite poles ideologically—become the spokesmen for the polarity in Russian society between the religious God-is-God and the secular Man-is-God positions, while a third, Shigalev, elaborates the Man-as-God planning principle summarized in a single sentence: "Starting from unlimited freedom, I arrive at unlimited despotism."[44] The description of the corruption of systematic rationalism, the tendency to drive all dogmatic positions to extremes, and the unawareness of the need for limits in the exercise of freedom are all elaborated with profound insight into the nature of man and his political behavior, and with characteristic Dostoyevsky sympathy in the exposition of opposite points of view.[45]

If anything, Dostoyevsky, who is currently cast in the convenient image of a "pessimist" and a "reactionary," remains an optimist in his "honest" description of the depths of evil to which unmitigated rationalism might eventually lead—he did not anticipate, as Irving Howe points out, that a twentieth-century Shigalev would never have frankly stated that he would arrive at "unlimited despotism." In the disintegration of totalitarian morality which we have witnessed, unlimited despotism would have been described in Orwellian fashion as "a still higher conception of freedom," and for this perversion we could have found ample precedent in Hegel's respectable philosophy. *The Devils* is far from "pessimistic" or "reactionary" in any meaningful sense of the words because of the manner in which the book indicates how the classical liberal position, represented in a faintly ridiculous character, Stepan Trofimovitch, characteristically ground to dust between the two millstones of extremism, can recover its position by a rethinking of religious experience.

Dostoyevsky in *The Devils* says in book length that nihilism is the inevitable outcome of liberalism if liberalism ignores its responsibility for the cultivation of religious or moral limits, and this makes *The Devils* as relevant to contemporary intellectual and political experience in the West as it ever was, or has been, in Russia.

"The Legend of the Grand Inquisitor" is, in effect, a fifth

gospel. Its superficial appearance as an indictment of Roman Catholic history is easily understood in the context of its Russian setting or of the position of the Russian Orthodox Church in Dostoyevsky's time. Separation of church and state is a classical requirement of free society, and Dostoyevsky uses "The Legend" as his answer to those who misinterpreted his religious position as a plea for an "established" church, and it can also be read as a prophecy of the consequences of an imposed secular religion. George Steiner in a brilliant book, *Tolstoy or Dostoevsky, an Essay in Contrast,* has said that recent history has made it difficult to read "The Legend" with detachment:

It testifies to a gift of foresight bordering on the daemonic. It lays before us, in precise detail, a summation of the disasters peculiar to our times. Even as earlier generations opened the Bible or Vergil or Shakespeare to find epigraphs for experience, so ours may read from Dostoyevsky the lesson of the day.[46]

The Grand Inquisitor oppresses the ignorant in order to accomplish their salvation, and Steiner rightly stresses that the context is universal, and not only Russian. While the Soviet regime has tended to treat Dostoyevsky more or less as the Inquisitor did Christ, favoring *Poor Folk, The House of the Dead, Crime and Punishment,* and *The Gambler* as pictures of czarist autocracy and the disintegration of capitalist society, and fearful of Dostoyevsky's major works, *The Devils* and *The Brothers Karamazov,* as possibly subversive of contemporary Shigalevs and Inquisitors, the fact is that the writings of this supposed "mystic, pessimist and reactionary" reflect a prophetically acute insight into some of the most evil tendencies of a conformist, materialist culture dedicated to "full bellies" and "suffocated souls"—a critique that is no less relevant in the West than it is in the Soviet Union. Shigalev's system and the doctrine of the Grand Inquisitor are exposed together as a religion of higher standards of material living and the socialist antheap, and Dostoyevsky returns here to his prophetic thesis in *Notes from Underground*: "I wish to tell you, gentlemen, why I have never been able to be an insect."

Dostoyevsky saw "boredom" as the greatest evil that was implicit in the antheap collectivism he anticipated, and since man hardly knew himself well enough to plan a perfect society or to develop laws for its development, he anticipated the encouragement of war and of violent social destruction as a reaction to the frustration of free development.[47] The background is different but the conclusions are close to Thoreau's statement in *Walden* that "the mass of men lead lives of quiet desperation."

Dostoyevsky sees the choice in total freedom between nihilist liberalism on the one hand with the antheap and inevitable bestiality in its wake, and Christ on the other—and Christ must be an option in free choice, and not a religion imposed by an established church, by miracles and quackery, and by the tyranny of the state. The God of Jesus was not the "angry" and the "jealous" Jehovah of the Old Testament whose justice and wrath were to be "feared," and the religion of Jesus was not a discipline to be imposed by an ecclesiastical establishment. His disciples accepted by choice a teaching which would make them free: "If ye continue in my word, then are ye my disciples indeed; And ye shall know the truth, and the truth shall make you free" (John 8:31, 32).

Dostoyevsky was certainly close to heresy as it would be defined by some ecclesiastical authorities, but his views were completely in line with the classical doctrine of a free society. Here Dostoyevsky meets the final view of Masaryk, who at the height of his career wrote that "Jesus, not Caesar, is the meaning of history," and stressed the free choice in that option to a point which raised issues of blasphemy and atheism in some clerical circles.[48]

Although there is no evidence that Dostoyevsky was familiar with de Tocqueville's writings, he is in complete agreement with his views on the relation between freedom and religion which are summarized in his classical question: "How is it possible that a society should escape destruction if the moral tie be not strengthened in proportion as the political bonds are relaxed?" with the clear understanding by de Tocqueville, who like Acton was a Roman Catholic, that this could be true only of a "free" church.

From the standpoint of the future of free society the abiding interest in Dostoyevsky among educated Russian readers is one of the most hopeful signs of the times. After a generation in which Tolstoy, with his perfectibilist faith in man, his rational didacticism, and his identification of welfare with religion, was heavily favored even if his moral anarchism and negative attitude toward the state continued to present problems, and a generation in which Dostoyevsky was only infrequently reprinted, the rising black market prices of old editions of his books remained an embarrassing index of the Russian readers' continued interest. A few selected works by Dostoyevsky were reprinted in 1955, and large editions were sold.[49] On the occasion of the seventy-fifth anniversary of Dostoyevsky's death on February 9, 1956, a new ten-volume edition of Dostoyevsky's works, including all the novels but not the political writings, was opened for subscription, and the entire edition of 300,000 sets was sold out on the day of subscription.[50]

Even in a society in which education is deeply committed to a narrow technical, vocational interest, the developing of a questioning mind cannot be permanently deterred from the critical study of its own cultural heritage, especially in contemporary Russia where the study of nineteenth-century literature is widely cultivated. It is now more than ever a matter of urgent intellectual priority that we in the West should intelligently appreciate the relevance of Russian intellectual experience in that period to the understanding of the Soviet Union *and of our own society.* The day may still dawn when it will be seen that an understanding of Dostoyevsky is at least as significant for the comprehension of contemporary Russia as acquaintance with Stalin's or Khrushchev's interpretation of Karl Marx or Lenin. Ortega y Gasset has well said that contemporary Russia "is Marxist more or less as the Germans in the Holy Roman Empire were Romans."[51] Soviet communism is a Russian and therefore a human phenomenon in which the materialist and the pseudo-Marxist appearance is a surface varnish that covers human realities and dilemmas which are unlikely to disappear with increasing material and educational achievement.

FREEDOM AND CLASSICAL EDUCATION

While it is crucial to see freedom in the context of a culture as a whole, including its economic, its political, and its social institutions and "habits of thought," it is equally urgent not to confuse the "culture" of the sociologists and anthropologists with the "culture" of the "cultivated man." There is a clear tendency within all the Western countries as well as in the Soviet Union to divorce education from the task of forming character and tastes. Sometimes this is done quite frankly in programs of vocational or polytechnical education. Sometimes it creeps into our programs as the fruit of the "permissive" implications of the student's free choice among options. The result is inevitably the dwindling of the elite in any free society which shares the cultural heritage of which freedom was the choicest fruit.

It does not follow that the restoration of classical education as the core of the curriculum would be the remedy for the subversion of public morality in democratic nations. The phrase "public morality" sounds almost archaic, as Irving Kristol has recently argued in a cogent article in *Encounter*.[52] Most modern readers will think of censorship of the movies, or pornographical literature, or police regulations against necking on a beach. Such reflections are, of course, the natural fruit of excessive preoccupation with the identity of sin and sex. In the great century in which the fundamentals of free society were established for the English-speaking world, "anyone who had ever given thought to the matter would have asserted, as a matter of course, that the ultimate basis of popular government was what in America was called republican morals, and in England civic virtue."

As Edmund Burke phrased it in his "Letter to a Member of the National Assembly":

Men are qualified for civil liberty, in exact proportion to their disposition to put moral chains upon their own appetites; in proportion as their love for justice is above their rapacity; in proportion as their soundness and sobriety of understanding is above their vanity and presumption. . . .[53]

Similar ideas were expressed by James Madison, by Thomas Jefferson, by George Washington, and later in a classical form by Alexis de Tocqueville. In the last fifty years it has become fashionable to overlook, or to depreciate, the moral component of the political life of a free or democratic society, and to stress impersonal forces of a materialist type. In our discussion of the problems of free society and of the viability of freedom in newly established nations we rarely inquire whether the people display the specific dispositions of mind and character that make free and democratic government possible. In Irving Kristol's words:

What are these dispositions? This is a large question, and any short answer will be inadequate. But it is not too gross an oversimplification to say that included among them must be: a veneration for the rule of law as against the rule of men; a reliance on common reason as the dominant human motive, as against superstition or passion; a sense of community that transcends class divisions and the recognition of a common good beyond individual benefits; a scrupulous use of liberties towards these ends for which those liberties were granted; a distribution of wealth and inequalities according to principles generally accepted as legitimate; moderation in the temper of public debate and public demeanour; etc. In every historical case one can think of, these attributes have been prior and prerequisite to democratic government. When they did not exist, or where they did not exist sufficiently strongly, democratic government faltered. And if a democratic government fails to sustain and encourage them, it is undermining its own foundations.[54]

This is not an argument for the "restoration" of classical or religious education. On the supposed relationship of "character" and "discipline" to classical education, we can cite abundant American experience. One of the principal reasons for the abandonment of the classical curriculum was the difficulty of insuring student discipline as long as it remained a general requirement. We have forgotten about these problems today because our so-called elective system—with all its peculiar weaknesses—has at least given students sufficient challenge to their interests to remove the crudest grounds for campus discontent. The "Great Rebellion" at Princeton in 1816 might be selected as an example in which, in the language of one observer,

. . . all college exercises were suspended for several days, and half the country was given a new topic of discussion. The tutors were imprisoned in their rooms, the doors of Nassau Hall were nailed up; a bonfire was made of the college outbuildings; the bell was rung continuously; windows were smashed . . . and billets of firewood fell in all directions on the heads of officers who tried to break their way in.[55]

Andrew D. White's radical innovations at Cornell were based on the correct assumption that disciplinary reform would follow curricular modification. In his "Autobiography" he described his own undergraduate college with the words, "Of discipline there was none." Similar evidence could be cited in a dozen institutions. It is plain unvarnished poppycock to identify required classical education with discipline or character. Such arguments are typical of the nostalgic comments about the past that are so characteristic of a good deal of contemporary wishful thinking on the conservative side.[56]

Nor is this to be confused with a plea for religious education as it has been commonly understood, for religious education has not been typically concerned with the unifying force of a shared source of voluntarily accepted moral authority, but rather with sectarian, denominational, or dogmatic authority which has in its consequences typically been divisive. I am thinking of A. N. Whitehead's statement in *The Aims of Education* that "moral education is impossible without the habitual vision of greatness."[57] and Sir Richard Livingstone's elaboration of this thesis in his chapters on "Character and Its Training" and "The Training of Character through History and Literature" in *On Education*.[58]

FREEDOM AND DISCIPLINE

Character and discipline are indeed desirable qualities, and I, for one, would be disposed to agree with the thesis that they are areas of weakness in our current situation. Character and discipline are not, however, produced by imposing a curriculum. They are rooted in *purpose*. They are probably more closely related to the methods of teaching than to its content, and our present "spoon feeding" is unlikely to produce a self-reliant student with a respect for methods of finding and of testing evidence and with a sustained capacity for self-study. Character can only be defined in terms of purpose, and discipline is a matter of shared purpose, unless we are thinking of a certain type of military discipline which is indeed a matter of "theirs not to reason why" and which, as every student of military morale knows, fails to achieve its purpose unless it is based upon a preceding period of inculcation of national purpose. Any effort to produce either character or discipline by imposition results in explosions and bad morale.

The strength of the old classical curriculum was its preoccupation with authors who stressed the enduring values of human civilization. Its characteristic weakness was a typical specialist's tendency to deteriorate into "gerund grinding and reciting by rote" in which the "enduring values" were lost in the grammarian's shuffle. Most of us have heard equivalents of the story of the classicist who introduced his class to the "pleasures" of reading a piece by Sophocles because it was "a veritable treasure house of grammatical peculiarities." It is, moreover, a peculiar modern heresy to identify classical education with exclusive cultivation of intellectual virtues. The choice and order of Plato's statements about education may be pondered in which the "body" almost always precedes the "soul," and in which the heaviest possible stress is placed on rhythm, the "harmonies," and especially musical training.

Morals and citizenship command wide support as educational aims because most of the arguments in favor of moral education are general, and therefore remain as meaningless as a general argument in favor of planning. The authors of such statements usually see themselves as the model or the planner. The real argument begins when it is specified "who" plans for "what," when the values to be inculcated are chosen or enumerated, and the procedures to achieve the purpose are elaborated.

The purpose of a liberal education is, as of old, the education of free men and the development of "a mind not easily imposed upon." Ability to evaluate evidence, historical perspective, and a nice discrimination in the use of language are obvious criteria of our success. A mere glance at our own student publications casts more than a little doubt upon the efficacy of the means which we have chosen to achieve our ends. Perhaps a fresh focusing on our professional purposes will give us a new view of the procedures that are now followed. It is possible to have a college in which all academic departments win national prizes for excellence and in which the final product, the graduated student, does not correspond to any educational aim that the faculty may have had in mind at the outset, just as it is possible to have a factory in which every single production department is of unparalleled excellence but in which the final product may be disappointing because the coordination of these departments has been poorly planned in the control room.

We should ask some basic questions about the type of qualities that is required in the modern, urban world to preserve the species of free men and women, and about the extent to which education in its academic as well as in its guidance phases can contribute to their development. If it should be agreed that shared values and a capacity for teamwork are essentials for the survival of a free society, then the argument might usefully proceed with an examination of the nature of the values that must be shared, and of the character of the essential teamwork. We spend a good deal of time and energy upon our purposes in mathematics or composition, but the general aim of education, as distinguished from the aims in teaching specific academic subjects, is taken for granted or reserved for commencement rhetoric. The academic subjects are, however, merely subordinate means of achieving our general purpose, and it is not likely that our general aim will be improved by treating the target as if marksmanship were an unplanned byproduct of the quality of armament.

The "permissive" heresies of contemporary education fly in the face of the discipline inherent in any commitment, and free men are committed men. In a recent paper, a Harvard professor of history observed that "our students yawn over the classics" because they have "very little to do with their own lives." He implied that we might as well forget about the classics, but as Ernest van den Haag remarked in a recent article:

Students have always yawned over the classics—only, in times past, teachers were not so sensitive to their own popularity rating nor so eager to entertain their students as to be willing to drop the classics. They dropped some yawning students instead and kept the interested ones. An immature mind cannot understand the classics, and it matures, in part, by learning to understand them—or, at least, to know them so that they may be understood later.[59]

There is a "treason of the intellectuals" evident in this Gallup-poll consciousness of academic teachers that is as subversive of the intellectual discipline indispensable to a free society as is a form of intellectual "featherbedding" which is quite common among academic language teachers who insist that Plato's *Republic* should be taught by professors of Greek or Dostoyevsky's *The Grand Inquisitor* by professors of Russian—they haven't excluded the rest of us from using the New Testament largely because there is no entrenched vested interest of teachers of Aramaic. If we are concerned with the enduring values of free society which are embodied in these works, it is clear that a professor of philosophy or of political science may be better equipped to teach these books than a specialist in Greek grammar or Russian syntax. I hasten to add that I would not exclude the teachers of the original language if they had the required philosophical sophistication, which does not inevitably accompany the acquisition of the linguistic skill. Clearly, however, a teacher with a professional interest in political philosophy will be more highly qualified than a Greek grammarian to teach Plato's *Republic* or Aristotle's *Politics,* even if he does not know a word of the language in which these works were originally written.

FREEDOM AS AN INTERNATIONAL POLITICAL SYMBOL

Thus far I have discussed the definition of freedom in terms of our own experience and the proliferating literature on the subject. There is nothing new in the need for redefinition. Freedom is not "inherited" in the manner in which the property of parents is inherited by their children. Freedom has to be earned by every generation in its turn through its willingness to undertake commitments and to assume responsibilities. Freedom is, for every generation anew, a question of sorting out essentials and nonessentials, and therefore a question of clarifying the yardsticks with which we distinguish between them. This is essentially a moral or a philosophical challenge, and it is particularly vital to contemporary Americans.

We think of ourselves as a practical and a pragmatic people. We think of freedom in simple materialist terms as identified with economic opportunity and ever-increasing standards of living, and our interpretation of American life to ourselves and to the rest of the world emphasizes our technology and the widespread ownership of automobiles, refrigerators, and all the gadgetry of our economic culture. It should be clear, however, that our physics laboratories, our technology, and our conveyor-belt production can be transferred to a totalitarian country—think of Nazi Germany or contemporary Russia—without any disturbance in their cultural or their political orientation. The essential difference between a free society and a totalitarian one lies in the philosophic and moral field.

Detroit's production techniques and the research programs in our sciences can be transferred to a totalitarian culture without causing any major upset, but the political philosophy and the view of the nature of man held by Thomas Jefferson, John Adams, Abraham Lincoln, Walt Whitman, Henry David Thoreau, or Reinhold Niebuhr would have more explosive effects than a hydrogen bomb. This is why the vitality of free society is so dependent upon the clarity of our philosophical commitments. It is also the reason for the relative weakness of the moral image which we present to the rest of the world. It is true that our money and material aid are anxiously solicited throughout the world, but if necessary these can be found elsewhere. What is missing in the picture we present to the world—and to ourselves—is a coherent and reasoned view of the true nature of a free society, and convincing evidence in our practice that we understand the nature of our own moral commitments.

The absence of a firm grip on the basic principles of our own political philosophy is apparent in our domestic politics. How many Americans have a clear understanding of the polarity of "freedom" and "equality" as social ends? How many here understand that the Bill of Rights in our federal Constitution is essentially a limit imposed on majority rule, and therefore a limit imposed on democracy in the interest of freedom? How many have any clarity in their thought about the distinction between a federal and a central government? If we lack such rigor in our own thinking, how can we cope adequately and convincingly with foreign misunderstanding of our own social goals?

It has been a rich and rewarding experience for me in recent years to be drawn into close contact with educational programs designed to interpret America to foreign academic groups. Some years ago the State Department sent me to India for several months, and I remember still, with the freshness of a shock recently received, the experience in Calcutta with a large, well-educated Hindu group which had invited me to speak on "Changing American Conceptions of Freedom."

I have described this experience elsewhere[60] but it fits into this context. I spoke for forty-five minutes and there was an hour and a quarter of animated discussion. When the chairman was about to close the meeting, a Buddhist priest in the back of the hall rose to thank me in flowery and courteous language for the "erudite and elegant" address, ending with the words, "But we have been listening for two hours to a flood of Atlantica *without one word* on the announced subject." It hit me like a stone between the eyes, but, as I discovered later, he had in his mind the word *moksha* every time I used the word "freedom."

Moksha is a dictionary translation of "freedom," and it means some of the things of which we think when we use the word. Typically, however, it means something like freedom of the soul in the sense of renunciation, the achievement of absence of desire, the detachment of all desire for food, sex, even affection and esteem by others. Just think of the conflict with the common American assumption that freedom is the political aspect of a culture characterized by constantly increasing material standards of living based on an ever-expanding awareness of increasing consumer needs. Can we understand the confusion, and even indignation, in an Indian mind committed to the *moksha* view of freedom when he finds us illustrating our freedom with pictures of our crowded road traffic, our parking lots for the workers in our factories, and our general gadget worship? Are we hypocrites unaware of the conflict between such slavery to possessions and true freedom? Or are we unbelievably provincial in the interpretation of our own values, while we are pretending to teach others from the depths of our own parochialism?

There is, of course, no essential conflict here, if we know our own tradition.[61] In the first place, these are, of course, issues of *personal* freedom and not of political freedom. There is a strong Western tradition relating personal freedom to the curbing of desire, passion, or even impulse. Diogenes in his tub has long

been the ideal of some free men, including contemporary beat-
niks. The idea of self-control, as old as the Greek philosophers'
teachings about "virtue," called for control of passion, impulse,
and prejudice. The Mediterranean ideal has been celebrated by
MacLeish. The rejection of wealth and of the flesh has been a
significant part of Buddhist as well as Christian tradition up
to and including the saintly Origen, who achieved his freedom
by castration. It is to us significant, however, that this tradition
implies in its extreme form the rejection or denial of life itself. Freedom cannot be preserved or strengthened by collective
suicide. If freedom is to continue as a living ideal of human existence, we have to think of it with reference to decisions that
relate to the choices of living human beings. We do not wish to
end or to suspend human life—we wish to establish conditions
for ever-widening circles of free choice, including the choice to
curb or to deny human passion or greed.

An American thinks of Emerson or of Thoreau. Thoreau
would be appropriate enough in view of the influence which his
"Civil Disobedience" had on Gandhi. Thoreau taught that a
man is rich and free in proportion to the number of things he
could afford to leave alone, and the "economics" of the first
chapter of *Walden* is more subversive of the goals of the advertising profession than anything that Karl Marx ever advocated.[62] Horace in his *Satires* defined the free as "the wise who
can command his passions, who fears not want, nor death, nor
chains, firmly resisting his appetites and despising the honors
of the world"; and Epictetus in *The Discourses* taught the Stoic
doctrine that a man to be free should "eradicate desire utterly,
and should be willing to give up everything, his books, his
property, his reputation and his office."

Here, again, there is no distinction made between *feeling* free
and *being* free, and this is the core of the distinction between
our definition of freedom and the Indian conception of *moksha*.
The right to pursue freedom from appetite or passion is clearly
within the conception of freedom as the presence of choice, and
equally clearly a man governed by impulse or passion is limited
in his ability to choose amongst his purposes. Freedom ceases
to be free, however, if the pursuit of higher standards of material
living should be excluded. It would also be contrary to the historical facts to deny that the highest civilizations are charac-

terized by the fact that the largest number of luxuries are regarded as necessities.

There is substantial common-sense validity to the view that available cash may mean freedom and power, just as there is a sense in which it may merely enhance susceptibility to, and increase capacity for, conformity with a pattern of consumer tastes planned and promulgated in all the mass media by specialists in the art of creating consumer discontent. Indian advocates of renunciation as freedom, and other philosophers, poets, and mystics influenced by such ideas, need to be reminded that genuine freedom as a historic and social reality must, if we are to be objective and not determined to impose our own subjective preferences on others, include both options as valid alternatives of choice. It is their presence as alternatives that *defines* freedom, and the attempt to define freedom as either detachment from material wants—the *moksha* view—or as inevitably and causally related to increasing material satisfactions —the more common American heresy—is in and of itself a *limitation* of freedom to the extent to which it restricts the area of choice.

FREEDOM AND NATIONAL INDEPENDENCE

Throughout Asia and Africa today freedom is given another narrow interpretation. In India, or Indonesia, or Egypt, or Morocco, or the Congo, freedom is simply interpreted as "the absence of the British, or the Dutch, or the French, or the Belgians.[63] Now this confusion of national independence and freedom is understandable, and no American would care to argue that 1776 was not an important date in the history of American freedom. The removal of the most recently experienced foreign constraint does not establish a free society, however. Think for a moment of Russia or of Spain. They are ideologically far apart, but they have one thing in common. Neither has experienced control by foreigners for a long time, but neither of these countries is free in the sense in which John Stuart Mill or Thomas Jefferson or Alexis de Tocqueville used the word. They are independent nations but they are not free in the sense in which I have been discussing the subject in this paper. There is no freedom of choice in politics or in religion, there is no Bill of Rights, there are no enforceable limits on the power of the state or the dominant political party, there is no provision for dispersed controls in political or economic life, and there is no free associational life in the community.

I am not arguing that these Asiatic or African nations could be expected to establish free societies today. The required cultural discipline and shared values are absent,[64] and it may well be one of the most pernicious political illusions of the "liberal" in our time to believe that the mere act of abolishing the power of colonial control suffices to establish a free society. There may be considerable truth in the observation of a realistic journalist that "countries with per capita incomes under $200 a year and adult literacy rates under 50 per cent cannot be expected to govern themselves democratically."[65] Many forms of modern nationalism and collectivism are blind efforts to hold together a society that has disintegrated. The state is used as a tool to prevent further erosion, and although social objectives are always prominently discussed by the leaders in such nations, the collectivism that is practiced is not social in the sense that it is rooted in the community. These countries lack the moral heritage—whatever its origin—and the free individual initiative as well as the free associational activity that are the essential framework for the behavior of free men. The national independence of such new nations may be an asset to us in world political rivalry, even if their foreign policy is neutralist. But it is a tragic confusion of essentials to speak of such nations as free except in the limited aspect of national independence which would also apply to contemporary Spain and Russia.[66]

FREEDOM AND PRIVACY

During my recent experience as a visiting professor at the Free University in West Berlin, I encountered another rather characteristic modern heresy concerning freedom, typical not only of Germany but of the whole Western world. Germans, with their experience under Hitler and their current continuing subjection to Soviet control, have a tendency to interpret freedom as privacy. "I would like to be a private citizen" is one of the most commonly heard reasons for belief in freedom. It is humanly understandable after the experience with state and party interference with family life and the almost total loss of control of leisure time, but clearly a society of nonparticipants would soon lose its theoretical freedom as a response to almost any determined minority with deep conviction. American examples of the same drive for privacy abound, and the success of our pressure groups and the condition of our big-city politics are phenomena that are directly related. Here again we have evidence that political rights, no matter how firmly anchored in law or constitution, will be essentially meaningless in the absence of a moral framework in which the sources of responsibility are continuously refreshed.

This paper has traced in rough outline some of the confusion that surrounds our discussion at home and abroad of the ideal of freedom, which is the basic value of our culture. It is also theoretically the core value of our liberal education, and it is sobering to reflect that most of the authors of the semantic swamp of confusion in which we now find ourselves were educated in colleges which make a special feature of the liberal arts in their curriculum. A critical examination of such college programs reveals very little direct concern with the study of freedom. It reveals an unstated assumption that an understanding of freedom will inevitably emerge as a byproduct of the pursuit of other objectives, and it ignores the obvious objection that the education of men and women who can be trusted with freedom and will be fit for the responsibilities of free society may well be a sufficiently central objective of our education to place it quite explicitly at the core of our educational effort.

If we are honest in facing the facts we shall find that the enemies of liberal education are not restricted to the supporters of vocational or technical education, or to the Philistines in general who do not even share our philosophical interest in freedom. Many teachers in the humanities or in the social studies have no reasoned general conception of liberal education apart from their own vocational vested interest. They contribute nothing to the study of freedom or to the refreshing of the sources of responsibility which I have been discussing in this paper.

Several years ago in a paper entitled "On Rethinking Liberal

Education,"[67] I discussed some of these questions in general philosophical terms. The paper was received with interest, but I was told that I exaggerated the extent to which there was confusion in the minds of free men about the nature of their basic ideal. For this reason I have taken the trouble to spell that out in this paper, and I hope someone will succeed in demonstrating that I have been unfair to the present literature. I was also told that I did not make a specific suggestion to remedy the malady which I had diagnosed.

"A FREQUENT RECURRENCY TO FUNDAMENTAL PRINCIPLES"

It is not difficult to trace the outline of a proposal to place the study of freedom in a strategically central position in liberal education. Freedom must not be treated as a byproduct. It must, in and of its own right, be placed squarely in the core of the program, in the interest of both the students and the teachers, who will then be professionally justified in giving it a central place in their own professional concern.

The subject should not be treated as if it were a semantic exercise in philosophy or psychology. The basic issues and concepts should be clarified in a broad historical perspective, including Russia and Central Europe, as well as Asia and Africa. Too much of our thought and literature about freedom has been inexcusably parochial and ethnocentric, and it has weakened our own grip on our tradition and narrowed the range of its appeal elsewhere.

We should clarify the basic concepts of freedom, equality, democracy, the pursuit of happiness, and their relation to law, to economics, to work, and to leisure with direct reference to the basic documents of liberty, such as Magna Charta, the English Petition of Right (1628) and the Bill of Rights (1689), the American Declaration of Independence (1776), and the French Declaration of the Rights of Man and Citizen (1791). The central emphasis should be placed on de Tocqueville's thesis that liberty is generally established "in the midst of storms," and that it is "perfected by civil discords." Appropriate readings could be found in the writings of John Locke, and in John Milton's *Areopagitica*, Adam Smith's *Wealth of Nations*, Lord

Acton's *History of Freedom,* John Stuart Mill's *On Liberty,* Morley's *On Compromise.* There should be stress on the rule of law, and selected readings from significant Supreme Court decisions, and to illustrate specific types of freedom some selected academic freedom cases which are particularly useful to illuminate the gap between freedom and subjective aspiration and freedom as a realistic professional achievement.[68] The range of philosophical concern could include Aristotle's *Politics,* Mortimer Adler's *The Idea of Freedom,* and *Reinhold Niebuhr on Politics.* There should be readings from *The Federalist* and from de Tocqueville. Contemporary discussion would be drawn from Ortega y Gasset's *Revolt of the Masses,* Bronislaw Malinowski's *Freedom and Civilization,* Herbert J. Muller's *Issues of Freedom,* James T. Shotwell's *The Long Way to Freedom,* F. A. Hayek's *The Constitution of Liberty* (especially Part I and Part II on "rule of law"), and Frank H. Knight's *Intelligence and Democratic Action.* I would expect the students to read Dostoyevsky's *The Possessed* and *The Brothers Karamazov* (especially "The Legend of the Grand Inquisitor"), and generous selections from Learned Hand's *The Spirit of Liberty.* I would also include the sixth book in W. W. Rostow's *The United States in the World Arena,*[69] with its stress on the "higher orders of intellectual synthesis," and the need for "the cultivation of excellence" in relation to the new premium which these authors place on individuality.

The framework of the course of study would be concerned with an inquiry into the nature and the distinguishing characteristics of a civilized society, which is not only the source of freedom but in which freedom itself is a prerequisite for the exercise, the maintenance, and the advancement of cultural achievement, and these are simply another way of defining opportunities for self-realization and for the release of human individuality.

Freedom is not the fruit of academic scholarship but academic scholarship is one of the fruits of freedom. To underline the establishment of freedom as a concrete historical achievement, I would organize the course around two documents reflecting more than two thousand years of historic *experience.* The first would be the funeral oration which Thucydides, writing after the fall of Athens, puts into the mouth of Pericles to describe what Athens once was. The second would be Winston S. Churchill's "Tests of Freedom" which he drafted for the Italian people after the liberation in 1944 in reply to the question, "What is freedom?"[70]

Every line in Pericles' "Funeral Oration" and Churchill's "Tests" is charged with meaning and rooted deeply in historical fact. We could proceed line by line with the questions: What is this based on? What were the problems? What were the gains? Is the experience parochial and limited to one time and one people? Or is it universal and generally valid? Were there any significant elements omitted?

It is time for those of us who are committed to freedom to repair and even to reconstruct our philosophical barricades. The approach I have suggested would restore the cutting edge to words that have become, as Herbert J. Muller says, the "hurrah words" of our time. I would prefer to call them "tired words"— they have been worn thin by slogan use, by ceremonial repetition, and by academic pedantry until they have become useless in the communication of thought. If they are to serve us again in the struggles that lie ahead, we must, in our minds and in those of our students, relate these words again directly to the documented experience of the human struggle and achievement in which they came to embody the richest cultural fruit of our tradition.

"Truth will be Truth tho' it sometimes prove mortifying and distasteful," and if in the reestablishment of the clarity of "the fundamental principles necessary to preserve the blessings of liberty," we should be compelled to revise our opinions of some of the most impressive academic stuffed shirts of our time, we can reflect with Benjamin Franklin that "our Geese are but Geese tho' we may think 'em Swans."[71]

15

*Economic Growth and Educational Development**

THE ECONOMICS OF EDUCATION IS A NEW FIELD OF STUDY WHICH HAS hardly emerged from the scientific monographs and the scholarly journals in which its exciting new insights are recorded. There is an "egg of Columbus" quality to the challenge of received ways of thinking which is involved. In an increasingly more dogmatic commitment to the classical "factors of production," that is to say, to land (resources), labor, and capital, it had become customary to interpret the latter in a narrow sense which restricted it to physical (technical) equipment used as a saving from current consumption to promote future production. It had become financial and popular dogma to interpret the rise in productivity as directly related to the ratio of physical capital invested and the size of the labor force. Disturbing questions arose as the increasingly more competent analysis of productivity statistics in Europe under the Marshall Plan and in the United States by the National Bureau of Economic Research revealed a huge gap in the data.

Our present knowledge is still meager and the data are raw and unrefined. Professor Theodore W. Schultz of the University of Chicago is one of the pioneers in the study of the relations between educational investment and economic growth. He came to the problem with the background of his earlier work on *The Economic Organization of Agriculture*,[1] in which he presented the evidence concerning the astonishingly lucrative returns on American "investment" in agricultural research. He set the stage for the present debate in 1959 in an article entitled "Investment in Man: An Economist's View,"[2] and he has summarized the development of the quest in a subsequent article "Capital Formation by Education,"[3] and in his Presidential address before

---

*From *College and University*, XXXVIII (Summer 1963), 421-33.

the American Economic Association, entitled "Investment in Human Capital."[4]

The argument can be summarized quite succinctly, even if we do some injustice by the omission of careful qualifications. If we treat the annual increases in measured capital and labor as "inputs," the annual rate of increase was approximately 1.0 per cent for the period between 1919 and 1957. During the same period the annual increase in measured national income was 3.1 per cent. The search for an explanation of the "unexplained" gap has produced a mass of data suggesting that investment of capital in education—that is to say, investment in human capability, which had been treated as "consumption"—was in fact the factor in *production* which had been overlooked.

It is not easy to dig out the facts about our "investment in man" in the past. Our economic statistics are full of misleading "concreteness" because the ideas that govern the collection and interpretation of economical data are themselves obsolete. We try to study the contributions of "labor" and "capital" in watertight physical compartments because it is somehow considered indelicate to think of the changing value of human capability as similar to the changing value of physical equipment. The authority of Alfred Marshall's *Principles of Economics,* in which education is treated as a "national investment," was used against its calculation as a factor in production because it would not be realistic to treat human beings in terms of the market as capital in practical analysis. The slogan that "labor is not a commodity" made the mere thought of investment in human beings difficult to accept. Human beings are not capital goods, except in slavery, and we therefore refused to recognize the plain fact that a good deal of "consumption" is in fact investment in man's future productive capacity.

On the other hand, it is clear that the reorientation that is now in process is essentially concerned with ways of thinking about reality, and not with a change in the facts themselves. Conventional definitions of investment in studies of national income and economic growth have led to increasingly more narrow definitions of capital, but if investment is defined to include any use of resources which helps to increase our output in the future, a new light falls on the role of education in the promotion of economic productivity. Adam Smith, whose *Wealth of Nations* was essentially concerned with the conditions of economic growth and development, was deeply interested in education and included its efficacy amongst the factors that contributed to the capital of a country. His critical chapters on education at Oxford and Cambridge—in contrast with the national education of Scotland with its contributions to "the superior intelligence, and the providential orderly habits of her people" —are full of contemporary relevance. Alfred Marshall's observation that the professional classes, "while generally eager to save some capital for their children, are even more on the alert for opportunities of investing it in them" points in the direction of the emerging new insight.

Schultz's pioneer work has now reached a stage in which a quantitative basis has been laid for the validation of the view that the principal cause of American productivity in the past lies in the large and continuous rate of investment in education. We have a reliable basis for the reconstruction of our educational investment in the past in the statistics of high school and college enrollment which clearly differentiate the experience of the United States and of Western Europe. We can compile the "direct" costs of education, that is to say, the cost of salaries, buildings, and equipment. We can also make reasonably accurate estimates of the indirect or "opportunity" costs, that is to say, we can make reasonable guesses as to the "average" contributions to national output and income that were "foregone" by society because the individual pupil or student became a high school or a college student instead of entering the labor force. The results of all of this analytical and statistical work are impressive after a period of sharp and continuous discussion of the stages of its development. They are summarized in a recent report of the United States Office of Education.[5]

In a chapter of this report Schultz indicates that the accumulated capital investment or stock of education in the American labor force rose from eight and one-half to eleven times between 1900 and 1957 while the stock of nonhuman reproducible physical wealth rose only four and one-half times.[6] A careful study of direct and indirect costs of education by Rudolph C. Blitz concludes with the summary that in the years 1955-58 the American economy was investing about thirty per cent of the gross national product for future growth, and of this one third was invested on education. "This makes it probably the largest single component of all investment in the United States."[7]

The aggregative approach to the data concerning educational investment inevitably raises questions as to the inclusion of education related to "consumption" as well as "production," and as to the efficiency or efficacy of educational expenditures or programs.[8] Experience in Latin America, India, or Africa has clearly shown that large educational expenditures can be pure "waste" from the standpoint of production. The unemployed or unemployable "lawyers" and the "liberal arts" graduates who are useless even for elementary teaching assignments serve as a warning against the assumption that the traditional vocational choices and the productivity needs are necessarily related to one another. But there is plenty of waste and error in programs of physical investment, and there is no evidence available to prove that the factor of human error is quantitatively more significant in educational than in physical investment.

The radical implications of the new ways of thinking about the human edge of capital investments are gradually penetrating all levels of intellectual, administrative, and political concern. Much of the past discussion of economic growth—in developed as well as in underdeveloped countries—appears to be as obsolete as the abandoned and useless furniture in the attic of an old family homestead. We still talk of "development" as if it were a matter of "foreign aid" appropriation instead of a problem of finding the proper coordination of educational development or human investment with a specified rate of investment in physical equipment. Economists and editorial writers discuss economic growth as if it were a matter of more or less "balance" in the Federal budget instead of a question of a deliberate and reasoned strategy of educational development which is fitted into the properly timed stages of accelerated economic development as a whole.

If we ignore the fact that labor as a productive force derives its value from the investment of capital in the form of in-service training and formal education,[9] it is impossible to understand comparisons of economic growth in the U.S.A. and in the U.S.S.R., or to develop an intelligent understanding of our experience with the Marshall Plan in Western Europe when it is contrasted with the disappointing result of our billions of foreign aid in Asia or Latin America.[10] In Western Europe the "aid" produced increases in productivity that were more than proportional. In Korea or Indonesia there was no measurable enduring response in productivity.

In the European case our "dollars" literally "primed the pump"—a human pump consisting of trained and educated manpower with moral or customary attitudes that were compatible with development. In the Asian or Latin American cases the absence of the corresponding—or preceding—investment in the human factor doomed the venture from the beginning. In pilot studies conducted under the auspices of the Organization for Economic Cooperation and Development in Paris, the successor to the Marshall Plan machinery, the differentials in economic productivity between Norway and the German Federal Republic point in the same direction. The experience of Japan, which has shown an increase in productivity that is more than proportional to the flow of private capital assistance which it has received, is additional confirmation of the hypothesis that the rate of human investment is the crucial factor.

Now that labor is regarded as a "produced means of production, an item of capital equipment"[11]—matching the nineteenth century amendment of Ricardo's view of "land" as "the original and indestructible properties of the soil"—a radical review of the classical theory of distribution is in order with all the implications for the prevailing macro-economic and mathematical simplifications. Clearly, all the classical factors of production are becoming items of capital investment rendering current services to production, and a new concept of "capital"—and a new *political* economy—is in the process of formulation since the old concepts, which were limited to tangible property, are now manifestly inadequate. The main shift in the present development is characterized by the tendency to think of the cause of economic growth as the *capacity* to create wealth rather than the creation of wealth itself. The direction of the change in thought is suggested by the question: Can we formulate a theory of human capital which accounts for economic growth in terms of changes in the quality of human beings?

There is now a healthy stir about education in circles that have been primarily interested in the economic and financial aspects of productivity and development. Educational authorities throughout Europe are adjusting themselves to an unexpected change in the alignment of the traditional pressure group struggle. The Marshall Plan studies have shifted to a completely new set of questions.[12] The *old* questions which were addressed to the fiscal agencies by the educational authorities were based on the acceptance of existing limits as to ends and means. How much can we expect for the support of education? With the pool of talent available should we subsidize this or that type of education? Should parents or students pay for it themselves, or can we afford to subsidize, and if so, by how much?

The *new* questions are similar to those formerly asked about the investment of physical capital. Is our rate of investment in human capability—that is to say, in education—adequate if we wish to accelerate the rate of economic growth? Is it even high enough to preserve the status quo? Can the pool of talent be expanded by modern techniques of education, of selection and screening of potential talent, and how can talent of a second- and third-rate category be developed to optimal use? Is the present distribution of the types of human investment defensible from the standpoint of maximizing returns? Are we producing geologists, engineers, mathematicians, doctors, and teachers of all types and in the proportions that are most effective in promoting economic growth?[13]

The shift in perspective has its bearing on old as well as on new countries. In education some of Europe's "developed" economies are relatively underdeveloped. In secondary and higher education most of Western Europe shows a definite lag in comparison with the United States whereas Japan and the U.S.S.R., both starting from lower levels, have been moving ahead at a higher *rate* than the United States in recent years. In some countries the accumulated stock of human investment in the past is larger in the older age groups than in the younger ones. In Israel, for instance, the new immigrants have an inferior educational background in comparison with the highly educated people who entered the country in the early years, and here the maintenance of present standards of development will call for deliberate acceleration in human investment.

In the underdeveloped countries educational policy is more easily recognized as a part of overall economic policy. The difficulty here is the emotional resistance to the acceptance of a rank order of priorities that is compatible with a reasoned strategy of economic development. In the egalitarian passion for literacy, which was encouraged by some of the less fortunate activities of UNESCO, programs for "national literacy"—"the first six years for everyone"—were sometimes encouraged at the expense of all other educational and economic development. Literacy at the "sixth-year level" is not a reliable foundation for step-by-step articulation of a program that supplies essential human skills as they are needed in the acceleration of economic development. Here, too, we are beginning to witness the impact of the new thinking about education as human investment. In a report by the Commission on Post-School Certificates and Higher Education in Nigeria,[14] we find a systematic study of the needs for trained manpower used as the basis of a ten-year forecast for a synchronized approach to a strategy for accelerated economic development. It is interesting to observe that the core of the document was contributed by Professor Frederick Harbison of the Industrial Relations Section at Princeton University, who was invited by the Nigerian Government to work with the country's own educators. Every assumption with regard to the need for a specified skill calls for corresponding assumptions concerning the teachers of such skills, and all of them must be fitted into a whole that has a realistic relationship to the economy and the budget in its totality.

There are many unexpected economic costs in such programs. In view of the conflict between existing elites and the rising new student generations, it can be taken for granted that, for many years to come, it may well be more expensive for an African nation to educate its students in a native university than to send them to England or to France. The expatriate French and English professors who could only be induced to serve in Africa at salaries appreciably higher than the salaries "at home" cannot be replaced by native professors—as they become available—at salaries that correspond with the native scale, since a reduction of salary scales would be interpreted as a continuation of the old imperialist prejudice.

In the investment of capital in human capability, there are many difficult problems of joint costs and cost allocation. Instruction in geology and in techniques of extraction may change the known available physical reserves. Knowledge about river flows and meteorological interpretation of rainfall data may be the essential condition in the determination of the soundness of engineering calculations underlying the construction of a power dam. Knowledge of fertilization and irrigation may change the physical value of land, and the right type of educational system does not only train men—it also helps to discover and to select potential sources of talent. The dynamics of human investment places it right at the center of the problems of supplying the proper social framework for physical investment. This is the challenge of the period of "pre-investment" which is essential if the actual period of physical investment is to be fruitful. It also places educational development right in the center of political tension.

Meanwhile orthodox economic and fiscal opinion continues to ignore the drift of current development and the significance to public policy of the new insight which is emerging. We continue to build models of economic growth on strictly materialist assumptions which overlook the role of capital investment in human beings in our own experience. We classify a power dam, a school building, or a hospital as "investment," but if it is a question of education in irrigation techniques or training teachers or doctors, we call it "consumption," and we consider it "unsound." We disregard the role of the development of human skills and trained imagination in our own achievements, and as our planners continue to be concrete-minded in all the possible senses of the term, they tend to belittle the image of a free world which has built its strength on the development of human capability by presenting a picture of exclusive preoccupation with physical and material achievement.

This part of my argument can be summarized in a negative question: Does anyone doubt that our economic productivity in the United States would take a huge tumble if we turned this country with its *present* resources and its *present* capital equipment over to a population of the same size without job or school experience, and with a life span of forty years? We tend to take the past capital investment in education and in health for granted, but in determining the feasibility of development it is the critical factor—for the underdeveloped nations as well as for ourselves in the future.

II

My mention of the social framework for development brings me to another major subdivision of the topic which can only be noted here and which is treated in some detail in "Colonial Experience and the Social Context of Economic Development Programs."[15] In some countries, a transformation of the values by which the people live, resulting in a positive attitude to and moral approval of work, is the first prerequisite for economic development.

Adolf A. Berle has given a fresh and creative statement of the economic and cultural relevance of these factors in his recent volume entitled *The American Economic Republic*,[16] in which comparisons of the development of Utah and Nevada, of Israel and Iraq, and of the Netherlands and Bulgaria are used to prove that the vital currents in economic and cultural productivity are related to ethical motivation as it applies to economic growth. His concluding chapter on "The Value System and the Transcendental Margin" supplies an admirable statement—based on fresh observation of contemporary data and not on inherited sociological doctrine—of the direct relationship between an effective value system and the desires and behavior of the population of a given society. The word "transcendental" has no religious significance to Berle—it simply refers to the effectiveness of "values," irrespective of their secular or religious origin, and irrespective of the subjective evaluation of their sources as "good" or "bad."

It is characteristic of the modern form of materialist heresy in the study of the rich cultural heritage of free society that many of our social scientists, with their fashionable pursuit of "physical science" and "mathematical" models, and a corresponding contempt for "factors that cannot be measured," can speak of the "take-off" stages of economic development as if they were a mechanical series of phases in a materialistically predetermined pattern of evolution. The traditional societies of Asia, Africa, and Latin America show no inherent dynamic of development; their present state of development has sprung from varying historical origins and is culturally related to a different sequence

of "stages" of growth. We tend to overlook the creative relationship between the sources of human motivation and will, and
their expression in economic and material change.

If we refresh our awareness of the role of these moral factors
in the growth of our own society, we will recognize the strategically vital role of a conscious and intelligent concern with the
cultural prerequisites of a free society, which is another way of
saying that "production" and "consumption" in educational
investment should not be considered in separate compartments
but must be inextricably interwoven in an educational policy
that is designed to synchronize effectively with economic growth.
Free men will not make the sacrifices required for development
unless they see them as a method of realizing the picture of
themselves which is suggested by the values by which they live.[17]

Let me summarize some of the qualities that are essential
moral prerequisites for economic development. There must be
a willingness to control appetite, that is to say, a willingness to
produce more than is consumed. There must be a willingness to
invest the savings, either individually or collectively. There must
be an open attitude toward innovation and initiative. There
must be respect for the future and for children. There must
be respect for a promise and for property. There must be a sense
of responsibility and accountability, and a reasoned respect for
calculation in determining social and private objectives, and in
arranging the rank order of priorities.

These may seem to be academic and theoretical considerations,
and the traditional representative of the hard-boiled financial
and economic point of view may dismiss them as "mere sociology." They are, however, the core of the problem. It is the
presence of these qualities which made the Marshall Plan a historically unparalleled success. It is the absence of these qualities
that explains the sterility of many of our well-financed projects
in Latin America and in Asia. If we ignore this aspect of the
educational requirements of a sound development program,
the most effective and meticulous coordination of the vocational
and technical aspects of education with an articulated program
of physical development will fail to take root.

The moral prerequisites of development are not a subject for
sermons. They reflect the hard and tough experience of generations of colonial and postcolonial effort. I recall an incident

during a trip to Pakistan about two years ago. My trip was concerned with the relations of educational and economic development. I was fortunate enough to be in East Pakistan at a time when a huge conference of Pakistani scientists and economists was considering the problems of economic development. The opening speech at the conference was made by a leading Pakistani physicist, at the time a professor at Cambridge. Here he was—a physical scientist talking to physical scientists. What did he talk about? The Koran. Why did he tackle a religious, even a theological subject? Because he knew that the basic hurdle to any plan of action involving a deliberate and conscious program of social change was rooted in the pervasive religious conviction that "everything that is, is the will of Allah," and that therefore anything that is designed to change things as they are is by definition subversive of the will of God.

And so our physicist spent almost all of his time analyzing the teachings of the Koran about the problems of human suffering and poverty, and concluding that since Allah had defined the tolerance of poverty as sin (*kufr*), it was clearly the will of God to be doing what the conference was now proposing to do. He recognized the true rank order of priorities. If the ground was not morally cleared by a redefinition of prevailing theology, there would not even be an audience for the views of physicists and economists concerning the direction of social change. Comparable examples could be cited from all over the world, including the United States.

It is not merely a question of the removal of ancient moral hurdles to development. It is also a problem of moral reconstruction of a pattern of social cohesion that will be strong enough to contain the centrifugal forces that are released by economic and educational development. Transition and mobility alone do not make a society, and if we are to build a social context in which the ideals of a free society might be meaningful, the social and educational aim of economic productivity is clearly inadequate.

In this paper I have considered education as an activity that develops human capital and human capability in relation to economic productivity. I have dealt elsewhere with the cultural goals of education.[18] Education is vitally concerned with consumption as well as with production, and its commitment to the goal of the enrichment of personal and cultural satisfaction is inextricably interwoven with the need for a social context that will have the strength and the cohesion to permit the mobility that is an unavoidable condition of economic development.

Economic analysis can only interpret the search for economic productivity. It does not set social, cultural, or personal goals. All of these ends are interdependent. They are inseparable. The cultural achievement of a free society is historically and analytically related to the flow of wealth from which it draws its sustenance. Insofar as we are concerned with the optimum economic use of limited material and human resources, we are also concerned with the creation of the material circumstances in which cultural options remain or become a possibility. The investment in human capability is an economic means of achieving the more diversified cultural ends of free society. But we must not confuse the economic means with the cultural goals themselves.

16

*The Purpose of Higher Education: Reexamination**

THE STRIKING EVENTS OF THE PAST YEAR, RANGING ALL THE WAY from the Berkeley syndrome of frustrations to the phenomenal breakthrough in Federal fiscal support of education on all levels, make it clear that we are on the fringe of an age of unparalleled speed of change in education. I cite two statements as typical of the current climate. The first is the *New York Times'* summarizing caption over a recent report on our population statistics: "By 1966 one-half of the United States population will be under twenty-five." In other words: A twenty-five-year-old will be part of the older half of the American people. If we place that fact next to the Berkeley student slogan: Don't trust anyone over twenty-five (or thirty)! we have the setting for a dramatic survey of predictable social, cultural, political, and educational trends.

My second statement is President Johnson's frequently repeated warning that in our social and economic life "ceaseless change is the one constant." It is probably true that decline begins when people ask "What is going to happen?" rather than "What shall *we* do?" In other words: In the forthcoming *aggiornamento* of American higher education, shall we just *undergo* the change? Or shall we organize our efforts and try to channel the direction of the flow? Are we prepared for such leadership intellectually? organizationally?

THE EROSION OF SOCIAL COHESIVENESS

The speed of social change is the predictable outcome of trends that have been visible for some two centuries. These trends are

* From the Keynote Address at the Opening Session of the Forty-eighth Annual Meeting of the American Council on Education at the Mayflower Hotel, Washington, D.C., October 7, 1965. Published in *The College and the Student,* edited by Lawrence E. Dennis and Joseph F. Kauffman (Washington, D.C.: American Council on Education [©1966]), pp. 23-46.

all related to the development of the scientific outlook, not merely in the scientists who see themselves as objective students of "truth" but in the forces that support their work because it creates *wealth,* it affords *comfort,* or it enhances *power.* In the world of today—and even more clearly in the world of tomorrow —these social forces which have been strengthened by the progress of science raise searching questions about the continued viability of free institutions and even about the original commitment to the search for truth.

It is a commonplace that our enlarged physical power over the material environment has been accompanied by a continuous erosion of the traditional sources of moral authority which govern man's capacity for self-control. I do not have to remind educators of the historic movement which is characterized by Laplace's statement that there was no longer any need for "the hypothesis of God," by the Feuerbach phase in which God was redefined as man's projection of his own ideal self, and finally by the inevitable vulgarization that man himself is God. The movement is defined by the citation of Nietzsche's "God is dead," and Rilke's despairing words: "The world has fallen into the hands of men."

Today we are in the morally weary stages of completing the whole cycle of development: the free political and social institutions which are the matrix in which free science and free scholarship could develop depend for their viability upon the sources of moral responsibility which have run dry. Now it has become apparent that the social cohesion which is required if free institutions are to endure will have to be built by a consciously planned and rationally directed effort.

There are, of course, alternative methods of imposing cohesion: no one in this generation will overlook the totalitarian formula or the nostalgic efforts to impose order by a return to some romanticized picture of the past of which French and some phases of current American politics supply many colorful examples. There is an astonishing parallel—even in such incidentals as the preoccupation with sex, folk music, and the choice of musical instruments—between some of the beatnik phenomena in our youth culture and the dominant characteristics of the German middle class "youth movement" of the earlier part of this century. Walter Laqueur's *Young Germany: A History of the German Youth Movement*[1] makes it abundantly clear that the earlier apolitical phase of the movement, which was characterized by social criticism in the absence of clear definition of social goals, made the movement vulnerable to subsequent totalitarian exploitation.

Modern collectivism in its totalitarian and often in its nationalist form is a groping effort to hold together a society that has been ground to dust, to organize a community that has in the literal sense of the term been *dis*organized. In a remarkable recent book entitled *Insight and Responsibility*, Erik H. Erikson has drawn attention to man's tendency under the strain of indigestible change to restructure himself and the world by taking recourse to what we may call *totalism*:

Where historical and technological developments severely encroach upon deeply rooted or strongly emerging identities (i.e., agrarian, feudal, patrician) on a large scale, youth feels endangered, individually and collectively, whereupon it becomes ready to support doctrines offering a total immersion in a synthetic identity (extreme nationalism, racism, or class consciousness) and a collective condemnation of a totally stereotyped enemy of the new identity.[2]

It is as if we were trying to install a prefabricated "community" in the place of the organic cohesion that was allowed to erode away. Such forms of social organization are not "social" in the sense of being rooted in community or shared values. They are simply "atomism packed tight." In the fashionable Western forms of the heresy, these "contemporary ancestors" weep about our glorious past, they long for a simpler and more innocent age, they deplore the "immorality" and the crime of our urban centers—all of these things Thomas Wolfe described a generation ago in *You Can't Go Home Again*. In the words of his leading character:

You can't go back home to your family . . .
to a young man's dreams of glory and of fame, . . .
to the cottage in Bermuda, away from all the strife and conflict . . .

to the father you have lost . . .
to the old forms and systems of things which once seemed
   everlasting
but which are changing all the time.[3]

The prophets of the "new nostalgia" themselves are committed to accelerating the forces that make for intensified change. Their quarrel is not about the goal of material productivity; it is merely about the means of achieving it. They advocate increased productivity. The old stereotypes about "planning" and "free enterprise," about "socialism" and "capitalism" have become irrelevant in a period in which "conservatives" advocate collectivist fiscal and monetary controls as a method of achieving economic growth, while the same objective is sought by "collectivists" who now rely upon the price mechanism and market controls in Great Britain, Germany, and even the Soviet Union.

The symptoms of radical social unsettlement resulting from the indigestible pace of technical change are worldwide, and conservative preachment about the social byproducts is not "conservative" but simply irrelevant. Politically, there is no evidence that we understand the need for a therapy based on a realistic diagnosis, and this lack of understanding shows up most clearly in the behavior and the problems of the young.

THE SENSE OF USELESSNESS

I said that the problem is worldwide—and it is independent of geography, culture, or ideology. We can think of juvenile behavior in the New York subways or on the campus in Berkeley. We can think of Soviet concern over the noninvolvement or the apolitical attitude of their university youth. Or we can recall dramatic illustrations in old and culturally homogeneous countries such as Great Britain or the Netherlands.

One thing is certainly true of both contemporary America and the Soviet Union, of both the developed and the underdeveloped world, and that is that they will be radically different in 1970 and 1980. Productivity, scientific developments, and the related changes in the population structure have given us the population figures which indicate that in 1966 half of our people will be twenty-five years or younger. In 1964 there were one million more seventeen-year-olds in the United States than in 1963. The old are "retiring" in constantly increasing numbers, and the "productive" are able to protect their interests in job rights and seniority through legislation and organization.

The unacknowledged god of the modern world—in developed and in underdeveloped countries, in Communist as well as in so-called capitalist countries—is "productivity, higher standards of material living." This maximized rational exploitation of our productive potential gives us mobility, overly rapid growth of urban centers, and therefore urban slums. This is why we have automation and structural unemployment. It is better to have problems that result from progress rather than from stagnation, but at the same time the peculiar form of our American unemployment, which is disguised by a figure that includes relatively few adults but a large number of young people and members of racial minorities, is a red-light warning.

Accelerated economic dislocation is the reason for the youth in our urban slums without "a sense of belonging." Thomas Huxley said a long time ago that "the sense of uselessness is the severest shock the human system can endure," or in James Baldwin's more recent words in *The Fire Next Time*: ". . . the most dangerous creation of any society is the man who has nothing to lose."[4] This is also why public opinion everywhere shows a feverish concern with "education," although it seems to be true that the concern frequently focuses on the problems that used to exist rather than on problems that exist now or on problems that will exist in the near future.

There is nothing new about these facts or about their being inextricably interwoven with the progressive achievement of the central objective of increased productivity. More than twenty years ago the American Youth Commission—chaired by Owen D. Young and sponsored by the most respectable social and educational agencies in the nation—published its general report on *Youth and the Future*. Almost a year later Dorothy Canfield Fisher published *Our Young Folks,* an account of her personal response to her service of seven years on the Commission.[5] These are shocking documents to anyone who thinks our present problems are new, or that they are due to superficial causes such as automation or racial segregation. Owen D. Young and Dorothy

Canfield Fisher were not radicals. They spoke for a culturally conservative tradition which can be distinguished from present conservatism by its respect for facts. They called for the recognition of the "harsh realities of the present," for a program of public and private planning in relation to the comprehensive needs of our youth, and they made specific predictions concerning the "poisonous mental confusion" of social usefulness and the presence of usefulness in the sense of availability for paid jobs.

Today we can read these reports only with a sense of dismay at the intellectual sclerosis which has beset us in the past twenty years. Very little has been done about the problem itself. Mild and patchy proposals to deal with social symptoms are discussed as if they were a reflection of Karl Marx's nineteenth-century theories rather than a response to America's twentieth-century experience. A generation of Americans confronted with the accumulation of what James B. Conant called "social dynamite" in our cities praises an educationally illiterate admiral as its leading educational philosopher and calls for the "impeachment" of a Chief Justice of the United States Supreme Court whose opinions are as socially innocuous as his original service as a Republican Governor of California would lead one to expect.

Dorothy Canfield Fisher was a member of an American generation that had not yet been brainwashed. With a Vermont respect for Vermont wisdom she opens her book with a short program quotation from John Dewey:

What the best and wisest parent wants for his own child, that must the community want for all of its children. Any other ideal for our schools is narrow and unlovely; acted upon, it destroys democracy.

They are simple words, but the radical implications of their meaning in contemporary America are a measure of our failure to plan adequately for the place of youth.

In an unpublicized spontaneous outburst in one of the panels at the 1965 White House Conference on Education, this basic educational insight emerged in an eloquent statement from the floor which can be summarized in these words: Now that we have heard about the radical educational rediscovery of the basic fact that our culturally disadvantaged children need individual attention, that they need individual care, study and—yes—"love," can we perhaps draw the startling conclusion that this new insight should be applied to the overwhelming majority of our normal students? The warm and rousing endorsement in the applause of the rest of the panel was a comment on the quality of the discussion concerning "innovations," many of which are accelerating the trend toward impersonal handling and computerized treatment of essentially human needs. I do not know how many of the rest of my panel colleagues thought of it, but my mind saw the picture of the Berkeley student picket carrying the sign with the words: "I am a human being: do not fold, bend, or mutilate."

MAINTAINING EQUILIBRIUM

For historical perspective let me cite also the two-volume report on *Recent Social Trends*,[6] which was produced in 1933, as the result of the initiative of President Hoover, by a distinguished group of American social scientists. On pages xii and xiii of the Committee Findings (Volume I) one finds the following theme paragraph:

The outstanding problem might be stated as that of bringing about a realization of the interdependence of the factors of our complicated social structure. . . . It is the express purpose of this review of findings to unite such problems as those of economics, government, religion, education . . . to direct attention to the importance of balance among the factors of change. *A nation advances not only by dynamic power, but by and through the maintenance of some degree of equilibrium* among the moving forces. [Italics added]

For those who are concerned with the implications of Clark Kerr's statement that the "justification" of the modern American multiversity lies in its "consistency with the surrounding society," the key words in this summary are "the importance of *balance*" and "the maintenance of some degree of equilibrium." On page 122 of Volume I of this report it is stated that "science and technology are the most dynamic elements in our material culture," and a number of suggestive special studies of the social consequences of specified "inventions" are elaborated in great detail, with special emphasis on the cumulative character of modern inventions. The study of the social consequences of the automobile discusses the effects on cities, suburbs, railways, highway finance, hotels, on manners, morals, crime, on international trade (oil, rubber), and international politics (oil, rubber). The relationships between Ford's Model T and "communism" in the Malay States are traced as an example; European and Japanese readers might be distressed at the predictability from recorded American experience thirty years ago of their present experience with the automobile and the implication that cities and human life in general should be recast to fit the needs of a new means of transportation.

President Hoover's experts were not proposing a "moratorium on research." They were familiar with the most searching thought we can think—equally unfashionable in the Soviet Union, the United States, and Western Europe—which can be formulated quite simply in these words: Is it possible to reduce the impact of technical and scientific change to a pace more closely compatible with the psychological and moral tolerance of the average human being? They were not advising economic asceticism. They knew that poverty is tragically real and that productivity is the only source for its relief. In P. H. Wicksteed's words: "A man can be neither a saint, nor a lover, nor a poet, unless he has comparatively recently had something to eat." The report was quite clear about this:

Effective coordination of the factors of our evolving society [may] mean, where possible and desirable, *slowing up* the changes which come too rapidly and *speeding up* the changes which lag. The Committee does not believe in a moratorium upon research in physical science and invention, such as has sometimes been proposed. On the contrary, it holds that social invention has to be stimulated to keep pace with mechanical invention. What seems a welter of confusion may thus be brought more closely into relationship with the other parts of our national structure, with whatever implication that may hold for ideals and institutions.[7]

And, to bring the topic quite clearly back into focus today: the Committee Findings stressed that it is possible to exaggerate personal aspects of moral problems, but there is little question that moral perplexities multiply when old institutions decay rapidly. In their words:

> The spiritual values of life are among the most profound of those affected by developments in technology and organization. They are the slowest in changing to meet altered conditions. Moral guidance is peculiarly difficult, when the future is markedly different from the past.[8]

It is an insight as old as Seneca that if a man does not know to what port he is sailing, no wind is favorable. If we are to build our youth *for* the future, and if we are to build our future *with* our youth, we need first of all a set of dependable blueprints. Building is a purposeful activity. No architect builds just for the fun of building. You must tell him what you are building for—and this is where our problem of building a future for our youth begins. Nostalgic prescriptions based upon beautiful rhetoric which usually begins with the words, "when I was young," are simply irrelevant. We are not dealing with people who *once* were young. We are dealing with people who are young *now,* and who will be young in the next ten or twenty years. There is only one thing that is certainly predictable about the circumstances of their lives. The pace of social and technical change, which is already difficult to digest today, will speed up and intensify. The competitive and conflicting pressures which beat about our heads will not diminish: they will grow in number and intensity.

The basic facts are brutal. We live in a society which is generous with part of its youth—if its aptitudes and values are in conformity with adult needs and concerns for productivity. We also live in a society which *excludes* part of its youth—in fact, whether by design or by drift. We all know that "youth needs to be needed," and we are compelled to deal with the predictable consequences of the development of a generation which is deprived of a sense of belonging.

FREEDOM AT BERKELEY

No one can foresee the face of tomorrow, but it is easy to predict that an adult generation that is as unsure of its basic values as ours is will not be able to pass on to its youth an ability to rearrange its conflicting priorities, unless we manage to clarify our own judgment on these matters. The most significant thing about a society is its ruling beliefs and values. The characteristic of our contemporary world which most confuses our youth is the total chaos in the rank order of our priorities that prevails in our discussion of, say, education in all its ramifications, or taxation, or the conservation of national resources, or in the semantic confusion that mars contemporary discussion of the nature of a free society.[9] These are major problems to youth but they are adult responsibilities. Adults make the world in which youth grows up. Adults determine the formative pattern in which youth develops. Every generation of adults gets the type of youth it deserves.

It is difficult to hit a target if you do not know where it is. This generation of adults will have a hard time restoring—or placing—freedom in a central position in its educational programs.

Illiteracy concerning the meaning of freedom was glaringly illustrated in the Berkeley faculty resolution which stipulated that "the content of speech or advocacy should not be restricted by the university." The immediate and predictable consequence was the incident about the four-letter words which almost led to the resignation of the president and the chancellor of the university. How can a college or university confuse the question: "Is it legally actionable?"—which may be appealing to a commercial publisher interested in the exploration of the legal and moral ambivalence of recent court decisions—with the only question appropriate to an academic establishment, which is: "Is it educationally desirable, or even defensible?" How can a faculty—a distinguished faculty—take the position that "there is no such thing as more or less freedom," and that "limitation of the content of speech destroys freedom," if it should think for one moment (for instance and to stay near the range of its immediate experience) of a student who would say that his examination results were influenced by bribing his teacher? Is this within the content of free speech, or is this a definition of freedom which makes freedom synonymous with anarchy? Would anyone familiar with the classical cycle described in Aristotle's

Politics hesitate in classifying such a conception of "freedom" as the stage immediately preceding the resurgence of "despotism"?

REFORMING THE CURRICULUM: FACULTY RESPONSIBILITIES

While it is vitally important to see freedom in the total context of a culture, it would be a tragic misreading of the signs of our times to assume that the enormous expansion of enrollment in our baccalaureate colleges with the traditional stress on liberal and general education will automatically supply the essential balance and equilibrium. One of the most disturbing facts about current trends is that the sense of the relevance of liberal education is being lost precisely at the moment when, in the words of one of the White House Conference's documents, a college education is becoming "an accepted norm" of American society.

Two-thirds of American baccalaureate education today has little or nothing to do with "liberal education"; and in the third that remains, frequently an empty shell of courses that reflect the curricular thought of a preceding generation is taught by an increasing multitude of recent graduates of specialized doctoral programs who have no training and little interest in teaching what they call "secondhand" subjects. If, in addition to this, the graduate faculty dominates the staffing of the undergraduate program and compels the college to use unqualified and uninterested graduate students to teach from sixty to eighty percent of the instructional hours in the freshman and sophomore years, it is clear that demoralization and lack of a sense of relevance are not due to "the conflict of generations" but are, rather, a predictable outcome of questionable educational practice.

There is, of course, a great variety of practice in American colleges, and the stress on inadequate and impersonal teaching can be overdone, but Jacques Barzun's address at Hofstra in December of 1963,[10] with its deliberately selective stress on the critical aspects and its thesis that "the liberal arts tradition is dead or dying," was closer to the truth than is the euphoria induced by meditating on the free flow of Federal funds or the faith that all will be well since a college education is becoming the "accepted norm" of American society. The diploma is becoming the "norm" precisely at the moment when the unchecked trends toward specialization that govern the education of college teachers are destroying the educational significance of the traditional "degree."

The decline in the "relevance" of liberal education is intensified by the widening gap between the flexibility in institutional mechanism for change in elementary and secondary education on the one hand and in colleges on the other. While the graduate schools nibble away at the curricular autonomy of the colleges in the junior and senior years and erode the quality of college teaching in the freshman and sophomore years by imposing irrelevant methods of training on our teachers, a healthy and yeasty process of rethinking methods and content of instruction in the years below the college is increasingly promoting the obsolescence of the college curriculum. If an effective "innovation" in the methods of teaching mathematics, science, or foreign language can be plausibly presented to a superintendent of schools or an able high school principal, the innovation will be given an experimental chance; this was the case in the past in the creative periods in American higher education that are recalled by the citation of names such as Eliot, Harper, Gilman, and Butler.

Today in our representative institutions the responsibility for the curriculum has practically everywhere shifted to the faculty. In a suggestive and forthright recent paper by Professor W. H. Cowley of Stanford on "Critical Decisions in American Higher Education,"[11] the full implications of our present rigidity are presented quite undramatically in a mild historical context, but its message is just as clear as in the summarizing paragraphs in the seminal research report entitled *The American College: A Psychological and Social Interpretation of the Higher Learning*, edited by Nevitt Sanford. Sanford, whose volume should be read by every college teacher but in my experience is typically read by frustrated deans and college presidents, expects reform only when college teachers again assume "the professional identity of teachers of students rather than that of members of academic disciplines. . . ."[12] Sanford believes the faculty should have a major voice in determining educational policy and he stresses the inadequacy of the present method of implementing this professional objective. In a section on "Some Obstacles to Reform" one finds the following statements:

There is no denying . . . that when there is a movement toward reform in a college it is the collective faculty who usually seem to be dragging their feet. There have been few fundamental innovations in higher education in the past twenty-five or thirty years, and in even fewer cases have innovations been initiated by college or university faculties . . .
. . . college and university faculties, typically, have organized themselves in such a way as to make deliberate and concerted change of any kind exceedingly difficult.[13]

A perceptive student of the "multiversity" has recently summarized the trend in the following language:

It is surely time that someone, perhaps one of the ever beneficent foundations, calculated the true cost (in terms of time and money) of, for example, making a vital *educational* decision in our larger institutions of "higher learning." Flexibility, outwardly so apparent in the vast array of special interests, is in reality incredible rigidity when it comes to such crucial educational decisions as curriculum development, student guidance, and so on. While we may have learned to move with the ease of a leopard technologically, educationally our bulk has reduced us to the state of a wooly mammoth.[14]

There is no willingness in the average contemporary faculty to deputize responsibility to selected spokesmen for the faculty. There is no willingness to relate change to research and evaluation. It is probably no accident that in two of our largest "Federal grant universities"—one private, one public—recent proposals for curricular innovation in the *college* were defeated by an incoherent coalition of university and research professors —including what Clark Kerr calls "un-faculty"—in mass meetings composed of from one thousand to fourteen hundred "voting" colleagues.

Is the cloacal gathering of the staff of the multiversity, including a multitude of grant recipients chosen without any concern for their achievement as teachers, likely to result in educational wisdom in the formulation of a *college* curriculum? Would there be any loss in professional insight if the campus gardeners and the stenographers were also included? Shouldn't there be at least as much functional concern in the solicitation of relevant judgment in the determination of *educational objectives* as there normally is in the definition of a grant project?

Sanford correctly states that faculty-governed European universities have become extremely conservative institutions: "It has sometimes required acts of parliament to bring about changes in the curriculum."[15] Those of us who recall the juicy pages Adam Smith wrote in 1776 in *The Wealth of Nations* about Oxford will recognize hoary precedents for the professor whose status is measured by the disappearance of his "teaching schedule."

Today it is almost necessary to establish a new college with a hand-picked administration and faculty to insure a willingness to venture curricularly on the basis of insight and experience, and even here sclerosis sets in rapidly as the vested interests organize and cohere on the basis of the preservation of established perquisites.

It will be futile to seek remedies "consistent with the culture" in this area, but it should be possible to work out patterns of reform that preserve and enhance faculty responsibility, that limit faculty participation to those who are involved in the process, and that are rooted in the academic acceptance of change related to research and development which academic consultants are so eager to see established in any activity "off campus" in which they are invited to play a creative role. It is possible that the large foundations which have played a crucial role in awakening public imagination to the nation's educational and social needs in recent decades may find a new creative function in the stagnant areas which I have stressed.

My eye has been focused on liberal education on the baccalaureate level, on the study of the type of education that makes men and women fit for the intellectual and moral responsibilities of free society, and I have been deeply aware that this type of education has also been the principal baccalaureate source of our best scientific talent. Judging on the basis of the original competitive assumptions of rival teams engaged in nuclear fission research in the Manhattan project, we need from four to six independent baccalaureate establishments, focused on the basic value of "freedom" in liberal education, and organized in a manner that relates faculty responsibility for the program to continuous research and evaluation. One or two of these "models," which should be distributed widely on a geographical basis, might be especially concerned with the general education program of the junior or community college. Such a program would be "hard to sell" to Congress. It is a "natural" for the "venture capital" in American culture—and it will meet a crucial need in bolstering the qualitative needs of our higher education.

The type of research which is illustrated by Sanford's volume and the type of concern for the "identity" of our youth which is reflected in the final paragraphs of Max Lerner's background paper for this meeting, "The Revolutionary Frame of Our Time," will be directly relevant. The concepts of emergence, selfhood, commitment, and cohesion are basic to the problem. I do not know whether Commissioner Keppel's interest in national testing to evaluate educational achievement is intended to apply to colleges, but I am certain that a test of the understanding of basic concepts such as freedom, equality, the rule of law, and the distinction between a federal and a central government would reveal a total absence of the type of cultural foundations which could make a discussion of inter-cultural education realistic.

Enthusiasts for the introduction of "non-Western" cultures into the curriculum—and I have been one of them—sometimes forget that the "inter" in *inter-cultural* implies that the student understand his own culture. Today, with the disappearance of the study of the Bible as well as the inherited classical culture of Greece and Rome (and both of them represented *inter-*cultural education), it is probable that our total educational impact has become *more* parochial rather than less—and primarily because the present programs do not supply an adequate basis for understanding the student's own culture, which is a prerequisite for comparative study. The "take-off" of our new pilot projects should be based on a study of our best existing practice in faculty and student participation,[16] in the evaluation of the faculty's teaching, in functional decentralization, and in continuous evaluation of effectiveness in relation to a carefully stated rank order of objectives. It would also be rewarding if there could be some study of the rich British and German literature concerning new academic establishments as well as a systematic evaluation of many of our own recently established "colleges within colleges."[17]

My stipulation that there should be four to six such experimental baccalaureate projects is rooted in the assumption that we need a diversity of approach and that we should avoid the temptation to impose uniform patterns as a remedy to our problems, especially in view of the fact that those who are the most deeply committed to "freedom" in the area of student life —such as the American Association of University Professors and the American Civil Liberties Union—are the most deeply tinged with the heresy that "freedom" and "uniformity" are somehow synonymous. Diversity will also afford opportunity to experiment with problems of size and functional decentralization, and with a variety of methods of developing a faculty who will be committed to a career of teaching college students.

The need for diversity in the pattern of experimentation is also indicated by some of the positive aspects of our current experience, and they are more numerous than the selective publicity of the mass media might suggest. Whatever we may think of details in the succeeding chapters of the Berkeley drama, a great movement of creative and critical innovation has developed on all levels at the University of California, and any teacher would be impressed with the opportunity held out in the following paragraph of a Berkeley faculty report:

Studies already known to us show that a significant and growing minority of students are simply not propelled by what we have come to regard as conventional motivation. Rather than aiming to be successful men in an achievement-oriented society, they want to be moral men in a moral society. They want to lead lives less tied to financial return than to social awareness and responsibility. Our educational plans should recognize these values.[18]

I was awestruck at finding this lovely spiritual rose blooming in what is supposed to be the secular desert. It would not be good pedagogy to confront the new Believers with the relevant citations from the old Gospel until they have clarified their new identity, but there may be a harvest coming in that will be a new tribute to youth's perennial ability to reject false idols and to expose sham. I do not know whether a publicly supported college could respond to this challenge, but if we are looking for polarity, balance and, hopefully, equilibrium in the Great Society, "venture capital" in education might well be interested in this symptom of spiritual growth in the time of our troubles.

THE NEW CONDOTTIERI

The strengthening of Federal fiscal involvement in meeting the country's educational needs—strengthening in the size of budgets and in the quality of leadership—raises one other large question that will be pressed with increasing urgency as we examine our current experience. Clark Kerr in his perceptive Godkin lectures poses the question in his forthright and realistic chapter on "The Realities of the Federal Grant University." A generation ago strong resistance "in principle" against direct "Federal aid" channeled the process through contracts negotiated by mission-oriented Federal agencies. It is not necessary to agree with all the implications of the use some of the student-rebellion leaders are making of President Eisenhower's warning in his final speech as President of the United States against "the potential for the disastrous rise of misplaced power" in "the military-industrial complex," to become reflective when the current facts indicate that fifteen percent of all expenditures in United States institutions of higher learning and fully seventy-five percent of all research expenditures are now defrayed from those sources. The distinctions between private and public institutions are blurred, to put it mildly, when we note that Federal funds are responsible at the minimum for thirty-two percent of the total budget of one of our largest private universities and this percentage ranges to eighty-five percent of the total budgets elsewhere.

The impact of this fiscal dependence of our largest institutions on a project basis with grants rarely ranging beyond a two-year basis is, of course, emphatically clear throughout the country, including all the institutions that are not directly involved, and an entrepreneurial spirit is rampant wherever administration has become dependent on such sources. It is literally true that administrations as well as faculties have lost control over their own fate —only one institution in this category is able to report that it would be able to honor all its tenure commitments to permanent faculty members if Federal funds were to be cut off tomorrow. It may well be that Federal aid is indispensable if high-quality research operations are to be maintained, but the question is surely ripe to be faced openly and directly: If we are not to be destroyed by vulgar and entrepreneurial rivalry inappropriate to the preservation of the quality of higher education, should we not recognize the present grant system as a subterfuge for Federal aid and replace it with direct public subsidy allocated to the institutions at their professional discretion? How else can we restore academic control over our own operations?

Gerard Piel, the publisher of the *Scientific American,* a sympathetic and friendly observer, has surveyed this whole field in a paper prepared for the American Philosophical Society this spring under the title "The Treason of the Clerks." It is an astonishing and provocative challenge and merits prayerful consideration throughout our academic community. The Federal panel disbursements have not only "made the rich richer and the poor poorer," but the "poor" as well as the "rich" have suffered the consequences in the impact on the quality of motivation of every applicant or candidate for a faculty appointment. The senior member of the faculty is chronically engaged in negotiations for the renewal of his project contracts and grants, and he "comes to think of the granting agencies as his alma mater, his 'true source of nourishment,'" identifying himself ever "more closely with his colleagues and competitors around the country than with his fellow faculty members." He even regards contributions to the overhead of his own university as deductions from "his" grant and he bargains them away in negotiations for the "transfer" of his grant to a less scrupulous administration elsewhere. In this connection I cite the following colorful paragraph from page 30 of the mimeographed version of Piel's paper:

With funds abounding for projects in every field of learning, the university campus has come to harbor a new kind of *condottieri,* mercenaries of science and scholarship hooded with doctorates and ready for hire on studies done to contract specification. Studies of this kind have been solemnly entered in the records of Congressional hearings, released as reports to Federal executive agencies and published by university presses.[19]

The impact of the operations of the *condottieri* on the quality of faculty motivation and on the characteristics sought in candidates for high positions in academic administration is clear to any informed observer. It is also clear that the *condottieri* do not contribute to the clarification of academic educational objectives: their life interests and their personal values are manifestly subversive of the idea itself. The whole movement is clearly undermining the rich pluralism of the American academic establishment; impersonal competitive market forces are imposing a concrete-mixer uniformity, and in another decade the impact of the whole process on the quality of academic and faculty administration will make it almost impossible to reverse the trend. It is doubtful if the trend which has developed would have gone as far as it has if the successive stages proposed by individual members of the faculty had been submitted to collective faculty review and decision—"the professor is sometimes right."[20]

Higher education is rightly proud of its contribution to material productivity and national power, but the country's colleges and universities cannot serve the end of building a Great Society by allowing themselves to be confused with the research and development department of a modern industry. We have other and more demanding values to serve, and the preservation of the pluralist variety of our heritage is an essential *end* as well as *means* in this process.

Freedom is the presence of choice and liberty is a blessing that must be earned before it can be enjoyed. Its vitality depends upon the clarification of the moral priorities in the exercise of choice. These are just modern ways of expressing the Biblical conception that freedom is service. "Where there is no vision, the people perish." If we restore the grip on our mind and on our will of what the prophet called the "vision," there will be no difficulty in bringing order to the present conflict in priorities. If the priorities are recognized as real we shall have commitment, and where there is commitment there is voluntarily accepted discipline—the discipline of shared values which de Tocqueville and Lincoln have taught us to recognize as the healthy core of a free society.

The things we fear lose their power, if the things we really believe have clear priority. In this age in which the distinction between science fiction and national defense is becoming blurred, it will profit us nothing if we gain the moon and lose our own good earth. If we can recapture the "vision" for ourselves and for our youth, the rearrangement in individual and social priorities will see us through the hazardous journey, like John Bunyan's pilgrim, "against wind and tide."[21]

Michael Polanyi, in a seminal book written some years ago, dealt with the problem in terms of the values taken for granted in the sciences themselves:

We are living in the midst of a period requiring great readjustments. One of these is to learn once more to hold beliefs, our own beliefs. The task is formidable, for we have been taught for centuries to hold as a belief only the residue which no doubt can conceivably assail. There is no such residue left today, and that is why the ability to believe with open eyes must once more be systematically re-acquired.[22]

If we are to avoid what John Stuart Mill described as a conflict "between ignorant change on one hand and ignorant opposition to change on the other," the relation of science and society should not be studied in a panic of fear stimulated by recent dramatic examples in physics, or the even more radical social and political implications of the emerging molecular biology, but in the larger perspective of clarifying the moral presuppositions of free society, and of science as an aspect of free society.

THE COMPENSATORY CONCEPT OF EDUCATION

Education is more than just a matter of running a school or a college. It is a matter of channeling all the formative influences brought to bear on youth so that we shall develop men and women fit for the intellectual and moral responsibilities of free society, and this clearly calls for a program that will *offset* many of the cultural influences that are increasingly exercised by the society itself.

The call for a *compensatory* conception of education, in which our formative or educational agencies would deliberately develop an educational program designed to *offset* some of the lopsided educational consequences of the general drive for enhanced productivity, should be carefully distinguished from the present concern throughout the world about the relation between educational policy and economic growth. It is true that economic growth depends upon investment in man as well as in physical and technical equipment, and it is clear from recent research in the causes of economic productivity that investment in education has been a major cause of economic development in the past; in fact, recent research points to American education outlay in the past as probably the largest single component of *all* investment.[23] In a rapidly changing economic order, educational development directly related to accelerated productivity is—although desirable in itself—simply an accelerating force in the promotion of the cultural byproducts of productivity which I have traced here.

Compensatory education is the exact opposite of the trend to "consistency with the surrounding society," and if we are to achieve "equilibrium" and "balance," the compensatory idea may be a vital and constructive force in the educational future of free society.[24]

Intellectual and moral fitness for the responsibilities of free society will not be found in exclusive pursuit of material security. The maturity of a free man is anchored in his moral and intellectual capacity to cope with the insecurity that is unavoidably interwoven with the pursuit of values which are all in some measure and to some degree in conflict with one another. The ability to cope with tension and with polar values has been recognized as the criterion of a free man by social philosophers as widely divergent as Alexis de Tocqueville and Martin Buber, and in walking "the narrow ridge" education can play a positive rather than a passive role.

We live in a time of danger and also in a time of great hope. Whoever offers us complacency blinds us to the danger and denies us the hope. Let me summarize and repeat: Every society gets the kind of youth it deserves. Young people do not make the world in which they grow up. Adults make the world in which young people grow up. These are simple words. They describe a terrifying characteristic of our present society.

The mission-oriented approach to our fiscal support and to the commitment of our talent threatens to convert our institutions to the role of *means* with which we pursue conventional

ends defined by others, and, in a time in which the fruits of
affluence stimulated by the development of science are so abundantly available, nothing is more clearly urgent than the need for
imagination and perspective in the redefinition of the ends themselves. The American Academy of Arts and Sciences has recently
devoted a full issue of *Daedalus* to the study of "Utopia," which
affords a suggestive introduction to the study of the potentials
of the Great Society. In a brilliant essay in this volume[25] Bertrand de Jouvenel reminds us that Utopian writers of the past
paid scant attention to the material basis upon which the good
life was to be reared, and one of the inexplicable characteristics of our generation of liberals and intellectuals is that we
pay little or no attention to the nature of the Great Society and
the good life which we might seek to establish on our unparalleled material basis.

It is characteristic of the World's Fairs of the past century that
they were designed to display the *means* of material life; we
need to prod our imagination by exhibitions of alternative and
achievable *ends,* and these will be the expression of a progressive
process of clarification of alternative *values.* French television
programs, concerned with illustrating the basic problems of
long-term economic and national planning, are seeking to bring
this new philosophical approach to a mass audience. In our
world of rapid technical progress, philosophy in the broadest
possible sense of the term is the most practical subject in the
curriculum. It is also the subject which is most sadly missing in
our discussions of the problems of the multiversity. There is a
staleness in our basic assumptions which recalls Whitehead's
warning about "inert ideas."

The unchallenged primacy in the multiversity of the basic
assumption that all fruitful intellectual inquiry must proceed
in terms of precedents set in the study of inanimate nature has
given—as Michael Polanyi has recently reminded us—an archaic
flavor to the study of freedom and the responsible choices open to
man, to the concern with man's moral and esthetic values, as
well as to William James', Alfred North Whitehead's or Sir
Richard Livingstone's insistence on the need for education "in
the presence of greatness." Even the social sciences and the
humanities suffer from this self-inflicted weakness, and any sen-

sitive college administrator can contribute to the discussion of what I sometimes call the search for a "humanistic" professor of philosophy or of political economy. This is not new in the history of formal higher education, and in the past the essential correction in focus has sometimes come from responsible and creative *political* leadership in the community.

In one of John F. Kennedy's final speeches, delivered on October 26, 1963 at Amherst College, I find two paragraphs on "the great national purpose" and "the deepest sources of our national strength" as they are embodied in the study of the liberating arts. These statements are directly relevant to our concern here today. They were not the work of some script writer, and I am told the manuscript was covered with longhand insertions. They read as follows:

When power leads man toward arrogance, poetry reminds him of his limitations. When power narrows the areas of man's concern, poetry reminds him of the richness and diversity of his existence. When power corrupts, poetry cleanses. For art establishes the basic human truth which must serve as the touchstone of our judgment.

* * *

I look forward to restraint . . . a future in which our country will match its military strength with our moral restraint, its wealth with our wisdom, its power with our purpose. I look forward to an America which will not be afraid of grace and beauty . . . which commands respect throughout the world not only for its strength but for its civilization as well. And I look forward to a world which will be safe not only for democracy and diversity but also for personal distinction.[26]

At the White House Conference on Education in the summer of 1965, I was deeply interested in a paragraph of President Johnson's address. It was not featured in the newspaper publicity that accompanied the conference. It certainly did not reflect a desire to restrict American higher education to a program "consistent with the culture of our society." It was closer to the old homiletical principle that we should always preach to the culture but never preach the culture. I quote from the President's address to the White House Conference on July 21, 1965:

Most of all we need an education which will create the educated mind. This is a mind—not simply a repository of information and skills—but a source of creative skepticism, characterized by a willingness to challenge old assumptions, and to be challenged, a spaciousness of outlook, and convictions deeply held; but it is a mind which new facts can modify. For we are a society which has staked its survival on the rejection of dogma, on the refusal to bend experience to belief, and in the determination to shape action to reality as reality reveals itself to us. This is the hardest course of all to take. Without education it is an impossible course.

All of this means not merely more classrooms and more teachers. It means a fundamental improvement in the quality of American education. It means an educational system which does not simply equip the student to adjust to society, but which enables him to challenge and modify and at times reject the wisdom of his elders.[27]

Every word in that statement deserves further thought and meditation, but as a challenge in the definition of the purpose of higher education it sets the stage for the critical and dangerous decade that lies ahead of us—a decade in which the nation's academic community which was established to be the custodian of a critically maintained intellectual and moral tradition will either restore or lose its function as an autonomous source and an independent critic of the values of the Great Society.

Notes

THE HIGHER LEARNING IN A DEMOCRACY

1. For the search for harmony and order through the adoption of a collectivist "frame of reference," see *A Charter for the Social Sciences in the Schools* by Charles A. Beard, Part I of the Report of the Commission on the Social Studies of the American Historical Association, and the subsequent volumes of this report.

For the search for harmony and order through the selection of a "metaphysics," see Robert M. Hutchins, *No Friendly Voice* (Chicago: University of Chicago Press, 1936) and *The Higher Learning in America* (New Haven, Conn.: Yale University Press, 1936). For a critical discussion see T. V. Smith, "The Chicago School," *International Journal of Ethics*, XLVI (April 1936), 378-87; James Weber Linn, "Notes on a Textbook," *University of Chicago Magazine* XXVIII (December 1936), 18-19; Charles E. Clark, "The Higher Learning in a Democracy," and Charner Perry, "Education: Ideas or Knowledge," both in *International Journal of Ethics*, XLVII (April 1937), 317-35 and 346-59 respectively.

2. Abraham Flexner, *Universities: American, English, German* (New York: Oxford University Press, 1930), p. 213.

3. *The Higher Learning in America*, p. 119.

4. Ibid., p. 32.

5. Throughout the manuscript HL refers to *The Higher Learning in America;* NFV, to *No Friendly Voice.*

6. *Dialogue on the Great World Systems*, in the Salusbury translation, rev., annotated and with an introduction by Giorgio de Santillana (Chicago: University of Chicago Press, 1953), 123-24.

7. Reprinted from the 4th ed. (London: G. Bell & Sons, 1931), p. 401. Spelling is modernized.

8. Even in *The Higher Learning in America*, Mr. Hutchins disclaims the criticism that he is "arguing for any specific theological or metaphysical system" (HL, 105), but the remark is offset by evidence throughout the volume—and cited in this essay—that the Great Tradition is definitely envisaged. See also the qualification in Mr. Hutchins' position in his article "A Reply to Professor Whitehead," *Atlantic Monthly, CLVIII* (November 1936), 582-88 and in the series in the *Social Frontier*, III (1937), beginning with John Dewey's review "President Hutchins' Proposals to Remake Higher Education" in the January issue (pp. 103-4), continued with Mr. Hutchins' reply "Grammar, Rhetoric, and Mr. Dewey" in the February number (pp. 137-39), and concluded with John Dewey's rejoinder "The Higher Learning

in America" [Was President Hutchins Serious?] in the March issue (pp. 167-69). In a later article "What Is the Job of Our Colleges?" *New York Times Magazine*, March 7, 1937, pp. 1-2, 25, the earlier position is, however, substantially maintained.

9. After Mr. Hutchins' sharp and deserved criticism of the tendency of education to yield to every current fad and fashion, it is puzzling to read that "under present economic conditions" our education must be recast to provide for the young "up to approximately their twentieth year" (HL, 15, 61). Does the proposed plan follow the fluctuations of the business cycle under the guise of a vision of eternity?

10. It is certainly not true of the University of Chicago program—and it is probably not true of the program of any reputable American university or college—that its "study of history and the social sciences" begins with "the industrial revolution," or that its study of philosophy "begins with Descartes and Locke," or of psychology "with Wundt and William James." Mr. Hutchins makes this unsupported assertion in *The Higher Learning in America*, p. 79.

11. Flexner, pp. 17-18.

12. Ibid., pp. 23-24.

13. As to research institutes, which Mr. Hutchins separates from the university because they are fact-gathering institutions, see Mr. Flexner's strikingly different observations, ibid., pp. 31-35.

14. Hastings Rashdall, *The Universities of Europe in the Middle Ages* (New York: Oxford University Press, 1936), III, 453-54.

15. *Science and the Modern World* (New York: Macmillan Co., 1925), p. 230.

16. Schiller's picturesque characterization of science may be in point here: "To some she (science) is the sublime, heavenly Goddess; to others a diligent cow that provides them with butter."

17. *The Republic* VII. 539, trans. into English by B. Jowett (New York: Modern Library, 1941), p. 288.

18. The next few paragraphs follow my article on "Integration of the Social Sciences and the Quest for Certainty," *Social Studies*, XXVII (October 1936), 363-72.

19. *The Quest for Certainty* (New York: Minton, Balch & Co., 1929), p. 37 (Gifford Lectures).

INAUGURAL ADDRESS

1. Cf. "Quality of Teaching or Content of Education?" *Proceedings of the Institute for Administrative Officers of Higher Institutions*, X (1938), 65-75 and "The Present Chaos in Education," *Proceedings of the First Phase, 1938, of the Conference on the Problems of Higher Education* (Urbana, Ill.: University of Illinois Press, 1939), pp. 200-215.

2. Cf. *The Higher Learning in a Democracy*, pp. 3-31 in this volume.

THE DISCIPLINE OF FREEDOM

1. *New York Times*, Nov. 22, 1940, p. 25.

2. *Vital Speeches*, Jan. 15, 1941, pp. 200-203.

THE GOLDEN OPPORTUNITY FOR PUBLIC EDUCATION

1. Paul T. David, *Postwar Youth Employment: A Study of Long-Term Trends* (Washington, D.C.: American Council on Education, 1943), p. 156.
2. October 21, 1946, p. 27.
3. October 21, 1946, p. 76.

FREE SCIENCE AND THE SECURITY OF AN OPEN SOCIETY

1. Boston: Little, Brown & Co., 1946.

POLITICAL EDUCATION

1. New Haven, Conn.: Yale University Press, 1950.
2. *Atlantic Monthly*, CLXXX (December 1947), 40.
3. *Time and Tide* (London), August 25, 1951, pp. 801-2.
4. *Atlantic Monthly*, CLXXX, 40.
5. New York: Henry Holt & Co., 1950.
6. New York: Charles Scribner's Sons.
7. *Journal of Political Economy*, XLIII (December 1935), 778-99.
8. *The Treason of the Intellectuals* (New York: Wm. Morrow & Co., 1928).
9. *The Whig Interpretation of History* (London: G. Bell & Sons, 1931), p. 81.
10. Washington, D.C.: Educational Policies Commission of the National Educational Association, 1951.
11. New York: Charles Scribner's Sons, 1934.
12. Chicago: University of Chicago Press, 1948.
13. New York: Macmillan Co., 1948.
14. New York: McGraw-Hill Book Co., 1951.
15. Reinhold Niebuhr, "American Conservatism and the World Crisis," *Yale Review*, XL (March 1951), 391.
16. Ibid., p. 399.
17. New York: Prentice-Hall, 1951.
18. New York: Charles Scribner's Sons, 1944.
19. *Conservatism Revisited* (New York: Charles Scribner's Sons, 1949), p. 6.

ON RETHINKING LIBERAL EDUCATION

1. Clarence B. Randall, *Freedom's Faith* (Boston: Little, Brown & Co., 1953), pp. 90-91.
2. New York: McGraw-Hill Book Co., 1953.
3. Maxwell H. Goldberg, "Cooperation and Noblesse Oblige," *CEA Critic*, XIV (November 1952), 5.
4. For an excellent contemporary statement of the goals of liberal education, see *General Education in School and College* (Cambridge, Mass.: Harvard University Press, 1952), p. 20; and Theodore M. Greene, *Liberal Education Reconsidered* (Cambridge, Mass.: Harvard University Press, 1953). See also the report on liberal education by a committee of the Association of

American Colleges in the *Association of American Colleges Bulletin,* XXIX (May 1943), 269-99.

5. Many of the formal addresses delivered at the Corning Institute were reprinted in a special issue of the *Saturday Review,* Nov. 21, 1953.

6. Randall, p. 92.

7. *The Curse of Bigness, Miscellaneous Papers of Justice Brandeis,* ed. O. K. Fraenkel (New York: Viking Press, 1934), p. 270. Italics are added.

8. Ralph Waldo Emerson, "Civilization," *Society and Solitude* (Boston: Houghton, Mifflin & Co., 1892), p. 34.

9. Jacques Barzun, "English as She's Not Taught," *Atlantic Monthly,* CXCII (December 1953), 29.

10. For a more elaborate statement of the political and historical background, see the paper on "Political Education" pp. 88-107 in this volume.

11. "A 'Terminal' Course in Philosophy," *Journal of Higher Education,* XXIV (November 1953), 403 ff.

12. Grayson Kirk, "Knowledge: Most Potent of Weapons," *New York Times Magazine,* Jan. 3, 1954, p. 26.

13. Philadelphia: Jewish Publication Society of America, 1951.

14. Robert H. Knapp and Joseph J. Greenbaum, *The Younger American Scholar: His Collegiate Origins* (Chicago: University of Chicago Press, 1953).

15. *Saturday Review,* Nov. 21, 1953, p. 43.

16. Robert M. Hutchins, *The Higher Learning in America* (New Haven, Conn.: Yale University Press, 1936), p. 86.

17. Mark Van Doren, *Liberal Education* (New York: Henry Holt & Co., 1943), p. 60.

18. "General Education, an Analysis," Part I of the *Fifty-first Yearbook of the National Society for the Study of Education* (Chicago: University of Chicago Press, 1952), p. 3.

ACADEMIC FREEDOM: A DECADE OF CHALLENGE AND CLARIFICATION

1. Sidney Hook, *Heresy, Yes—Conspiracy, No* (New York: John Day Co., 1953), p. 13.

2. Russell Kirk, *Academic Freedom* (Chicago: Henry Regnery Co., 1955); cf. Chap. II (on President Stout) and Chap. III (on Chancellor Hutchins).

3. CC (November 1938), 102-18.

4. Cf. T. E. Coulton, *A City College in Action* (New York: Harper & Bros., 1955) for a detailed study of the impact upon a large public college.

5. Cf. *Communism and Academic Freedom: The Record of the Tenure Cases at the University of Washington* (Seattle, Wash.: University of Washington Press, 1949).

6. Reprinted in the *Bulletin of the American Association of University Professors,* XXXV (1949), 66-72.

7. For a detailed examination of the issues as they presented themselves after the University of Washington decision, cf. Harry D. Gideonse, "Changing Issues in Academic Freedom in the United States Today," *Proceedings of the American Philosophical Society,* XCIV (1950), 91-104.

8. Hook, p. 154.

9. Kirk, p. 1. Italics are added.

10. Ibid., p. 153.

11. These paragraphs are excerpts from the full statement as quoted in the *New York Times*, March 31, 1954, p. 12.

12. The effort to confuse the issue by comparing the disciplinary relation of the Communist party with its members to that of the Roman Catholic Church with its communicants is adequately analyzed by Hook, pp. 219-20. It is also discussed with great cogency in Ernest van den Haag's paper, "Academic Freedom and Its Defense," published in *Strengthening Education at All Levels*, Report of the Eighteenth Educational Conference sponsored by the Educational Records Bureau and the American Council on Education, Washington, D.C., 1954.

13. Hook, Chaps. I, III, IX. The argument that professional competence should be based upon evidence "from the classroom" is, of course, an invitation to initiate the type of educational policing that is itself—and rightly so—the subject of the most acute "liberal" attack. Teachers who perjure themselves or who engage in scurrilous and anonymous libel of their colleagues are unfit for membership in the teaching profession, irrespective of their performance in the classroom or as practitioners of their scholarly speciality. In any case, Communists who attempt to conceal their membership in accordance with party instructions are likely to use the classroom to "spot" possible candidates for recruiting purposes who are then "solicited" later (and outside the classroom) by student leaders. Also, faculty members have other-than-classroom contacts with students, in guidance and in service on faculty committees. Cf. Hook, pp. 186 ff.

14. "Freedom of the University," *Ethics*, LXI (January 1951), 97.

15. "Are Our Teachers Afraid to Teach?" *Look*, March 9, 1954, p. 28.

16. *The Conflict in Education in a Democratic Society* (New York: Harper & Bros., 1953), p. 17.

17. Cited by Hook, p. 59 and pp. 66-67.

18. Ibid., p. 61.

19. Cf. Gideonse, "A Congressional Committee's Investigation of the Foundations," *Journal of Higher Education*, XXV (December 1954), 457-63.

20. For typical evidence of legalistic straining at a gnat, and simultaneous willingness to swallow a camel of the appropriate ideological family, see Hook's discussion of the sworn evidence in the Rapp-Coudert investigation as it is explained away in Dean L. H. Chamberlain's volume, *Loyalty and Legislative Action*, published in 1951 in the Cornell University series (Hook, pp. 186-201).

21. For details, cf. Gideonse, "Are Congressional Investigations Helpful?" *Educational Record*, XXXV (April 1954), 104-7.

22. Professor Alexander Meiklejohn as quoted in Kirk, p. 32. Italics are added. See also Hook, pp. 233-38.

23. Professor Robert S. Lynd of Columbia University as quoted in the *New York Times*, April 8, 1953, p. 18.

24. *The Logic of Liberty* (London, Routledge & Kegan Paul, 1951), p. 194. See also the proceedings of the Congress for Cultural Freedom held in Hamburg on July 23-26, 1953, published under the title, *Science and Freedom* (London: Secker & Warburg, 1955), and containing papers by M. Polanyi, John R. Baker, Raymond Aron, and others.

25. *The Logic of Liberty*, p. 39.

26. Ibid., p. 29.

27. Cited by Kirk, p. 25. Italics are added.

COLONIAL EXPERIENCE AND THE SOCIAL CONTEXT
OF ECONOMIC DEVELOPMENT PROGRAMS

1. *International Technical Assistance* (Chicago: Public Administration Service, 1952).

2. *New York Times Magazine*, January 4, 1953, p. 10.

3. It is Professor W. Röpke's great contribution to the defense of free society to have kept a clear focus on the sociological penumbra of the free market. See especially his *Civitas Humana* and *Mass und Mitte*.

4. New York: McGraw-Hill Book Co., 1951.

5. S. Herbert Frankel, *The Economic Impact on Under-Developed Societies* (Cambridge, Mass.: Harvard University Press, 1953), pp. 93-96.

6. New York, 1951, p. 13.

7. "America's Aims and the Progress of Underdeveloped Countries," in *The Progress of Underdeveloped Areas*, ed. by B. F. Hoselitz (Chicago: University of Chicago Press, 1952), p. 201.

ON THE EDUCATIONAL STATESMANSHIP OF
A FREE SOCIETY

1. Helmut Becker, *Kulturpolitik und Schule* (Stuttgart: Deutsche Verlags-Anstalt, 1956), pp. 36, 44.

2. Alexander G. Korol, *Soviet Education for Science and Technology* (New York: John Wiley & Sons, 1957), pp. 76-77.

3. *Dialogues of Alfred North Whitehead*, ed. Lucien Price (Boston: Little, Brown & Co., 1954), p. 46.

4. Korol, p. 85.

5. January 25, 1959, p. 62.

6. Some of the detail of these comparisons with Western European and Russian education is based—with the permission of the American Council on Education—on my article on "European Education and American Self-Evaluation" in the *Educational Record*, XXXIX (July 1958), 213-21.

7. See, for example, Erich Hylla and William L. Wrinkle's *Die Schulen in Westeuropa* (Bad Nauheim, West Germany: Ian Christian Verlag, 1953).

8. On the vocational trend in German academic education, see Helmut Schelsky, *Die skeptische Generation* (Düsseldorf-Köln: Eugen Diederichs Verlag, 1957), especially Chap. IX.

9. Convened by the French Commission for UNESCO and held in Sèvres from April 8-19, 1958.

10. *Curriculum and Examinations in Secondary Schools*, Report of the Committee of the Secondary School Examinations Council (London: His Majesty's Stationery Office, 1943), p. 13.

11. *Colorado Quarterly*, VI (Spring 1958), 395-408.

12. Archibald MacLeish, "Loyalty and Freedom," *American Scholar*, XXII (Autumn 1953), 393-98.

13. "The Kentucky Resolutions" (November 1798), *The Complete Jefferson*, ed. Saul K. Padover (New York: Duell, Sloan & Pearce, 1943), p. 133.

PLATO AND EISENHOWER'S AMERICA

1. *Current Issues in Higher Education*, the Proceedings of the Fifteenth Annual National Conference on Higher Education, Chicago, March 6-9, 1960 (Washington, D.C.: Association for Higher Education [c1960]), p. 3.
2. Ibid., p. 8.
3. New York: Harper & Bros., 1958.
4. New York: Harper & Bros., 1959, p. 273. Italics are added.

THE LITERATURE OF FREEDOM AND LIBERAL EDUCATION

1. For a valuable selection of relevant literature, see Dorothy Fosdick, *What Is Liberty?* (New York: Harper & Bros., 1959).
2. F. Boas, "Liberty Among Primitive People," in Ruth Nanda Anshen (ed.), *Freedom: Its Meaning* (New York: Harcourt, Brace & Co., 1940), p. 376.
3. C. L. Becker, *New Liberties for Old* (New Haven, Conn.: Yale University Press, 1941), p. 4.
4. Robert M. MacIver, "The Meaning of Liberty and Its Perversions," in Anshen, p. 285.
5. R. W. Gerard, "Organic Freedom," ibid., p. 423.
6. Mortimer J. Adler, *The Idea of Freedom* (New York: Doubleday & Co., 1958).
7. Since an ounce of fact is worth a ton of abstraction, it may be useful to remind ourselves that in the great area of American unfinished business regarding freedom that is suggested by the word "Negro," the Church of England in the eighteenth century took the position that Negroes could be baptized only if they solemnly swore that they had no wish to be free. Said the Anglican Bishop Gibson in 1727: "The freedom which Christianity gives is a Freedom from the Bondage of Sin and Satan, and from the Dominion of Men's Lusts and Passions and inordinate Desires; but as to their outward condition, whatever that was before, whether bond or free; their being baptised and becoming Christians makes no manner of change in it." What relation did the Church of England's conception of "duty" or "wisdom" have to freedom? Compare this with the Quakers, who voted in 1772 to abolish slavery, and who were the first, at their annual meeting in 1758, to expel from membership all those who bought or sold slaves. (The quotations are from *The Times* (London) *Literary Supplement*, July 22, 1960, p. 457.)
8. Christian Bay, *The Structure of Freedom* (Stanford, Calif.: Stanford University Press, 1958), pp. 7, 116, 134, 145, 319, 321.
9. Cf. Frank H. Knight, "The Ideal of Freedom," Chap. IV in C. M. Perry (ed.), *The Philosophy of American Democracy* (Chicago: University of Chicago Press, 1943), especially pp. 108-13; Harry D. Gideonse, *Organized Scarcity and Public Policy* (Chicago: University of Chicago Press, 1939), and George D. Stigler, *Five Lectures on Economic Problems* (London: Longmans, Green & Co., 1949), Chap. V.
10. Chicago: University of Chicago Press, 1960.
11. Cf. Knight, *Freedom and Reform* (New York: Harper & Bros., 1947),

"The Meaning of Freedom" and "The Ideal of Freedom," respectively Chaps. III and IV in Perry; "The Meaning of Freedom" in *Ethics*, LII (1941), 86-109, and "Conflict of Values: Freedom and Justice" in A. D. Ward (ed.), *Goals of Economic Life* (New York: Harper & Bros., 1953).

12. Originally published in 1944 and reprinted in 1960 by the Indiana University Press, Bloomington, Ind.

13. New York: Harper & Bros., 1960.

14. V. I. Lenin, *The Proletarian Revolution and Kautsky, the Renegade* (1919), reprinted in E. Burns (ed.), *A Handbook of Marxism* (London: Victor Gollancz, 1935), p. 830.

15. *Time*, Aug. 23, 1954, p. 26.

16. Cf. Lord Acton, *Essays on Freedom and Power*, ed. G. Himmelfarb (Boston: Beacon Press, 1948), p. 154, especially the paragraph beginning with the sentence: "The deepest cause which made the French Revolution so disastrous to liberty was its theory of equality"; and the principal thesis of Alexis de Tocqueville's *Democracy in America* (New York: Alfred Knopf, 1945), which is summarized in his sociological law of despotism in these words: "The foremost, or indeed the sole condition which is required to succeed in centralizing the supreme power in a democratic community is to love equality, or to get men to believe you love it. Thus the science of despotism, which was once so complex, is simplified, and reduced as it were to a single principle." (II, 302.) This is identical with the viewpoint of Shigalev in Dostoyevsky's *The Devils*.

17. Alfred Rosenberg, *Der Mythus des 20. Jahrhunderts* (Munich: Hoheneichen Verlag, 1936), pp. iii and 531.

18. Alexis de Tocqueville, *The Old Regime and the French Revolution* (New York: Doubleday Anchor Books, 1955). p. 169.

19. Cf. Hayek, *The Constitution of Liberty*, Chap. IV and the first note on p. 431; also the significant books by J. L. Talmon, *The Origins of Totalitarian Democracy* and *Political Messianism* (London: Secker & Warburg, respectively 1952 and 1960).

20. Hayek, Chap. IV.

21. Ibid., pp. 19-20.

22. As an example, and as a summary of Niebuhr's rising influence during the past thirty years as a political philosopher, see Kenneth W. Thompson, *Political Realism and the Crisis of World Politics* (Princeton, N.J.: Princeton University Press, 1960), pp. 22-25. Niebuhr's writings on political philosophy have now been made available in an admirably edited volume entitled *Reinhold Niebuhr on Politics*, ed. Harry R. Davis and Robert G. Good (New York: Charles Scribner's Sons, 1960).

23. Ortega y Gasset, *The Revolt of the Masses* (New York: New American Library, 1951), pp. 99-100.

24. As in J. Bentham's *Theory of Legislation* where we find the statement that "every law is an evil for every law is an infraction of liberty." Cf. Hayek, pp. 60-61.

25. On the "rule of law," see Hayek, Parts I and II. Also John H. Hallowell, *The Decline of Liberalism as an Ideology* (Berkeley, Calif.: University of California Press, 1943), and Walter Lippmann, *The Public Philosophy* (Boston: Little, Brown & Co., 1955).

26. *Freedom and Civilization*, p. 68.

27. Cf. *Les Etudes philosophiques*, special issue on "La Liberté" (Paris: Presses Universitaires de France, January 1959), especially the article by Paul Chombart de Lauwe on "Vie sociale et liberté."

28. Vladimir Dudintsev, *Not by Bread Alone* (London: Hutchinson, 1957), p. 365.

29. My interpretation is based on a reading in both English and German translations. The poems of Yurii Zhivago are published as an appendix to any text of the book. The German text with significant variations can be found in Boris Pasternak, *Wenn es aufklärt—Gedichte 1956-1959* (Frankfurt a. M.: S. Fischer Verlag, 1960). The German edition includes poems that have never been published in Russia.

30. "The Future in Education," Part I of *On Education* (New York: Macmillan Co., 1944), p. 121.

31. The issue of two Masaryk commemorative stamps in its Champions of Liberty series by the United States Government, on the occasion of Masaryk's 110th anniversary, led to a refusal by the Communist Czechoslovakian Government to deliver letters carrying these stamps, an implicit testimonial to the vitality of the Masaryk tradition. See *New York Herald Tribune,* Aug. 26, 1960.

32. 2 Vols.; London: Allen & Unwin, 1919.

33. See B. D. Wolfe, "Operation Rewrite," *Foreign Affairs* XXXI (October 1952), 39-57. Hitler merely burned books; in Stalin's era they were rewritten to make the present safe in the light of the past.

34. The following pages on the Russian literature concerning freedom are partly based on a larger study of the political implications of Dostoyevsky's writings on which I am currently engaged. They were prepared with the generous assistance of my colleague at Brooklyn College, Professor Fan Parker, whose knowledge of Russian language and literature has offset some of my own deficiencies in this field. The responsibility for the use I have made of this material is, of course, my own.

35. Words are the currency of intellectual exchange, and they reflect the changing influences of history, geography, and human passion. Freedom as a word has a different connotation to Indians, as discussed later in this paper, and the Russian language has two words for liberty. The first, *svoboda,* is the dictionary equivalent of freedom; the second, *volya,* carries overtones of disregard of social and community constraint. It suggests escape from society and it cannot be used in contrast with tyranny, since a tyrant enjoys *volya* to the highest degree. See the extract from Georgii Fedotov in Hans Kohn's rich and suggestive *The Mind of Modern Russia* (New Brunswick, N.J.: Rutgers University Press, 1955), pp. 268-69.

36. *Dostoevski* (New York: Meridian Books, 1957), p. 11. See also his *Slavery and Freedom* (London: Geoffrey Bles, 1943).

37. New York: Oxford University Press, 1953. The heart of the sociological case was stated by Emile Durkheim in *Le Suicide* (Paris: Félix Alcan, 1930), p. 446: "What is in fact characteristic of our development is that it has successively destroyed all the established social contacts; one after another they have been banished either by the slow usury of time or by violent revolution, and in such fashion that nothing has been developed to replace them." Cf. the views of Bay, who wants to strengthen freedom through "a high level of anomie," p. 354.

38. Dostoyevsky preceded them, however, in his assertion that Belinsky's denial of moral responsibility was a denial of freedom, and in his anticipation that a scientific substitute of morality would end in scientific objectivity in the planning of murder. See Reinhard Lauth, *Die Philosophie Dostojewskis* (Munich: Piper & Co., 1950), pp. 200 and 207, for the appropriate citations.

39. See E. H. Carr, *Michael Bakunin* (London: Macmillan & Co., 1937),

and *Studies in Revolution* (London: Macmillan & Co., 1950), which contains an admirable chapter on "Some Nineteenth Century Russian Thinkers" (Chap. VI). *Daedalus* has published a special issue on "The Russian Intelligentsia," which makes a great deal of new information available for the first time in English (published by the American Academy of Arts and Sciences and the Wesleyan University Press, Summer 1960). See also Franco Venturi, *Roots of Revolution* (London: Weidenfeld & Nicolson, 1960), which is a thorough study of Russian "populism" based on years of study in Moscow. The study was originally published in Italy in 1952, and has been favorably received by Soviet scholars on the basis of the author's use of untapped Russian sources and his critical attitude towards nineteenth-century "liberals." A first-class study of Russian "liberalism" has become available in Victor Leontovitsch, *Geschichte des Liberalismus in Russland* (Frankfurt a. M.: Klostermann, 1957).

40. For the general philosophical significance of Dostoyevsky, see Lauth. I am greatly indebted to this magnificent and massive volume (568 pages, including a comprehensive bibliography). Dostoyevsky's chauvinism in his political journalism, his view of the Russian people as "the God-bearing nation" *(narod bogonosets),* his contemptuous references to Western Europe's social and political life, and to Roman Catholic as well as Protestant versions of Christianity, all helped to obscure the core of his philosophical rejection of the "incomplete" ideas of Western rationalism. In his mystical nationalism Dostoyevsky's choice of words almost exactly paralleled the development of similar "popular" movements in Germany during the preceding generation. Cf. Kohn, pp. 17, 18 ff.

41. Cf. Klaus Mehnert, *Der Soviet-Mensch* (Stuttgart: Deutsche Verlags-Anstalt, 1958), pp. 228-31.

42. E. J. Simmons, Introduction to the Laurel edition of *The House of the Dead* (New York: Dell Publishing Co., 1959), p. 19.

43. See Carr, *Michael Bakunin,* which has a carefully documented chapter on "The Affaire Nechaiev," which was the historic model for Dostoyevsky's *The Devils.*

44. Fyodor Dostoyevsky, *The Devils* (Penguin, 1953), p. 404.

45. The confusion of scientific progress in the study of nature with increasing knowledge of man in society and the pursuit of "scientific" social objectives with the rational intensity of a mathematician and the fanatical commitment of an inquisitor are, of course, characteristic also of Western developments. Cf. F. A. Hayek, *The Counter-revolution of Science* (Glencoe, Ill.: Free Press, 1952).

46. London: Faber & Faber, 1959, pp. 339-40.

47. For the appropriate references, see Lauth, pp. 138-39. On "alienation" in Dostoyevsky as well as in Western sociological thought, see Nisbet, pp. 12, 19, and 44.

48. R. W. Seton-Watson, *Masaryk in England* (New York: Macmillan Co., 1943), p. 12.

49. Official publication dates show the following figures: *Poor Folk* (1955 Leningrad edition, 100,000; 1956 Tblisi edition, 10,000; 1956 Alma Ata edition, 15,000; 1956 Frunze edition, 6,000; 1956 Riga edition, 20,000); *Notes from the House of the Dead* (1956 Omsk edition, 75,000); *The Idiot* (1955 Moscow edition, 225,000); *The Gambler* (1955 Moscow edition, 225,000; 1956 Vladivostok edition, 40,000; 1956 Tashkent edition, 90,000); *Crime and Punishment* (1955 Moscow edition, 225,000; 1956 Moscow edition, 30,000).

50. Mehnert, pp. 228-31. See also F. Parker, "The Revival of Dostoyevsky on the Soviet Stage," *Slavic and East European Journal,* XVI (1958), 33-41.

51. Ortega y Gasset, *The Revolt of the Masses* (New York: Mentor Books, 1950), p. 100.

52. Irving Kristol, "High, Low, and Modern," *Encounter,* XV (August 1960), 33-41.

53. *The Works of Edmund Burke* (London: P. & C. Rivington, 1801), VI, 64.

54. Kristol, pp. 38-39.

55. Walter P. Rogers, *Andrew D. White and the Modern University* (Ithaca, N.Y.: Cornell University Press, 1942), p. 42.

56. See my article on "Walter Lippman and Educational Reconstruction," *School and Society,* Sept. 5, 1942, 169-73.

57. London: Williams & Norgate, 1932, p. 106.

58. Part II: "Education for a World Adrift," especially pp. 50-89.

59. "Reflections on Mass Culture," *American Scholar,* XXIX (Spring 1960), 227-34.

60. See "An Unsentimental Look at India," *Harper's Magazine,* CCIX (June 1954), 78-84.

61. See Alexis de Tocqueville in a letter to Arthur de Gobineau: "You know what are my theories on this point [money worries]. There is in our day only one kind of strength which is lasting, it is that proceeding from *character.* Only in one way can one be certain of preserving one's character intact, and that is by never feeling the need of money. *Ergo,* my conclusion is that if one cannot augment one's income, one must learn to limit one's expenses." *Oeuvres complètes* (Paris: Gallimard, 1959), IX, 190.

62. For a useful collection of Thoreau's writings on liberty, see *Thoreau: Philosopher of Freedom,* ed. James MacKaye (New York: Vanguard Press, 1930).

63. Africa is now producing its quota of definitions of freedom. William H. Hessler of the *Cincinnati Enquirer* reports as follows: " *'Uhuru'* is the one Swahili word known in every corner of Africa. And it does mean 'freedom.' But the typical African's notion of *uhuru* has little or nothing to do with democratic self-government, or civil rights, or citizens' obligations—and certainly nothing to do with such distasteful things as taxes. For him, independence means catching up with the living standards of the white Western World—at once." "The Agenda for Africa," *Reporter,* June 23, 1960, p. 33.

64. For the dependence of the "rule of law" on shared values and "community," see Hayek, *The Constitution of Liberty,* pp. 181 and 206, and Hayek, "Individualism: True and False," in *Individualism and Economic Order* (Chicago: University of Chicago Press, 1948). It is one of the saddest byproducts of our intellectual specialization that the development of an awareness concerning the significance of the social context of a free society (and of a free market), which has been primarily the work of sociologists, has received very little attention from economists although it is concerned with the core of their subject.

65. John Scott, *Democracy Is Not Enough* (New York: Harcourt, Brace & Co., 1960), p. 110.

66. For a more detailed examination of the dependence of freedom upon the social context, see "Colonial Experience and the Social Context of Economic Development Programs," pp. 144-63 in this volume.

67. Pp. 108-29 in this book.

68. See "Academic Freedom: A Decade of Challenge and Clarification," pp. 130-43 in this volume.

69. New York: Harper & Bros., 1960.

70. See his *The Second World War*, Vol. VI: *Triumph and Tragedy* (Boston: Houghton Mifflin Co., 1953), pp. 126-27.

71. *A Dissertation on Liberty and Necessity, Pleasure and Pain* (New York: Facsimile Text Society, 1930), p. 32.

ECONOMIC GROWTH AND EDUCATIONAL DEVELOPMENT

1. New York: McGraw-Hill Book Co., 1953.

2. *Social Service Review*, XXXIII (June 1959), 109-17.

3. *Journal of Political Economy*, LXVIII (December 1960), 571-83.

4. *American Economic Review*, LI (March 1961), 1-17. See also his *The Economic Value of Education* (New York: Columbia University Press, 1963). Cf. S. Fabricant, *Basic Facts on Productivity Change* (New York: National Bureau of Economic Research, Occasional Papers, No. 63, 1959).

5. Selma J. Mushkin (ed.), *Economics of Higher Education* (Washington, D.C.: Office of Education, U.S. Department of Health, Education and Welfare, 1962). For a careful and critical examination of the sprawling literature in recent years, cf. Fritz Machlup, *The Production and Distribution of Knowledge in the United States* (Princeton, N.J.: Princeton University Press, 1962).

6. Mushkin, p. 99.

7. Ibid., p. 168.

8. Cf. Machlup, pp. 107-44.

9. Cf. A. K. Cairncross, *Factors in Economic Development* (London: Allen and Unwin, 1962), pp. 63, 228-29, 304. The presentation is entirely from the economic point of view. It is not concerned with the recent discussion of human investment, but it reflects throughout the viewpoint that "development is primarily an educational process." For a comprehensive survey of recent economic work on investment in "on-the-job training" and in "health," cf. the special supplement entitled "Investment in Human Beings," published by the *Journal of Political Economy* (Chicago: University of Chicago Press), October 1962.

10. For a comparison of the Marshall Plan and Indian development experience, cf. Cairncross, pp. 92-93.

11. Cf. H. G. Johnson, "The Political Economy of Opulence," *Canadian Journal of Economic and Political Science*, XXVI (November 1960), 562.

12. For a good sample of the type of educational ferment that has been released by the productivity studies conducted under the Marshall Plan, cf. *Policy Conference on Economic Growth and Investment in Education*, a report on the 1961 Conference in Washington, D.C. (5 vols. in 1; Paris: O.E.C.D., 1962). See also A. H. Halsey (ed.), *Ability and Educational Opportunity* (Paris: O.E.C.D., 1961).

13. Cf. Richard S. Eckhaus, "Education and Economic Growth" in Mushkin, especially pp. 108-9.

14. *Investment in Education* (Nigeria: Federal Ministry of Education, 1960). UNESCO has shown a remarkable capacity to adjust to the new tendency to think of education "as an investment in the future rather than as a consumer service to be enjoyed in the present." Cf. *Final Report of the Conference of African States on the Developmnt of Education in Africa,*

Addis Ababa, May 1961 (Paris: UNESCO, 1961). The volume contains valuable papers by W. Brand, F. H. Harbison, G. Leduc, W. Arthur Lewis, H. M. Phillips, and H. W. Singer.

15. Pp. 144-63 in this volume.

16. New York: Harcourt, Brace & World, 1963.

17. See also the pages on "goal-setting weaknesses" in Robert L. Heil-broner, *The Making of Economic Society* (Englewood Cliffs, N.J.: Prentice Hall, 1962), pp. 230-36, and his provocative and courageous *The Great Ascent* (New York: Harper and Row, 1963).

18. Cf. *On the Educational Statesmanship of a Free Society* and "The Literature of Freedom and Liberal Education," pp. 181-211 and 223-60 in this volume.

THE PURPOSE OF HIGHER EDUCATION

1. New York: Basic Books, 1962.

2. New York: W. W. Norton and Co., 1964, p. 93.

3. New York: Harper & Bros. [1941], p. 706.

4. New York: Dial Press, 1963, p. 90.

5. New York: Harcourt, Brace & Co., 1943.

6. *Recent Social Trends in the United States*, Report of the President's Research Committee on Social Trends (2 vols.; New York and London: McGraw-Hill Book Co., 1933). See also John Dewey's review in *International Journal of Ethics* XLIII (April 1933), 339-45.

7. Ibid., I, xv. Italics are added.

8. Ibid.

9. For a consideration of the problem of semantic confusion about free-dom, see "The Literature of Freedom and Liberal Education," pp. 223-60 in this volume.

10. "College to University—and After," *American Scholar*, XXXIII (Spring 1964), 212-19.

11. *Current Issues in Higher Education, 1963* (Washington, D.C.: Association for Higher Education, N.E.A., 1963), pp. 13-21.

12. New York: John Wiley and Sons, 1962, p. 24.

13. Ibid., pp. 19-20.

14. Henry C. Johnson, Jr., "Are Our Universities Schools?" *Harvard Educational Review*, XXXV (Spring 1965), 173.

15. In *The American College*, p. 21.

16. Cf. Sidney Hook's article on academic freedom and the rights of students (entitled "Freedom to Learn but Not to Riot") in *New York Times Magazine*, January 3, 1965, pp. 8-9, 16, 18. See also Dael Wolfle's editorial "The Great Teachers" in *Science*, December 11, 1964, p. 1421.

17. There is nothing specifically American about most of our problems, as will be clear from an evening spent with a collection of British articles edited by Marjorie Reeves and entitled *Eighteen Plus: Unity and Diversity in Higher Education* (London: Faber and Faber, 1965).

18. *Preliminary Report of the Select Committee on Education*, Academic Senate of the University of California (May 24, 1965).

19. Published in *Proceedings of the American Philosophical Society*, CIX (October 19, 1965), 259-66. The paragraph quoted is on p. 265.

20. Cf. the perceptive treatment of these issues in Don K. Price's lectures at New York University, published by the New York University Press in

1954 under the title *Government and Science.* For a lucid comparison of university and multiversity, or university and publicly supported center for research and development, see Johnson "Are Our Universities Schools?" See also Alvin M. Weinberg, "But Is the Teacher also a Citizen?" *Science,* August 6, 1965, pp. 601-6.

21. Cf. Logan Wilson, "Setting Institutional Priorities," *Current Issues in Higher Education, 1965* (Washington, D.C.: Association for Higher Education, N.E.A., 1965), pp. 33-39. When the latest eager beaver in pursuit of the scent of a possible grant argues his case for space, time, staff, and nervous energy, how many of us remember the old rule: "How do we rate the *priorities* of the educational needs we now serve and those we are at present unable to meet? Is the lowest need now met more urgent than the highest need not met?"

22. *The Logic of Liberty* (London: Routledge & Kegan Paul, 1951), p. 31.

23. Cf. "Economic Growth and Educational Development," pp. 261-72 in this book.

24. See also *On the Educational Statesmanship of a Free Society,* pp. 181-211 in this volume.

25. "Utopia for Practical Purposes," *Daedalus,* XCIV (Spring 1965), 437-53.

26. *Public Papers of the Presidents of the United States, John F. Kennedy, Containing the Public Messages, Speeches, and Statements of the President, January 1 to November 22, 1963.* 1963. (Washington, D.C.: U.S. Government Printing Office, 1964), p. 817.

27. *American Education,* I (July-August 1965), 28.

Selected Bibliography

Books and Articles by Harry D. Gideonse

A. ECONOMICS

America in a World Economy: Markets, Tariffs, Debts and International Conflict. Washington, D.C.: American Association of University Women, 1934.

"American Economic Policy in Recent Literature," *Weltwirtschaftliches Archiv,* XLII (November 1935), 227-32.

"L'Augmentation et la répartition des exportations de capitaux américains," *Revue économique internationale* (Brussels), XIX (1927), 426-40.

"Colonial Experience and the Social Context of Economic Development Programs," in *Economics and the Public Interest.* Robert A. Solo, Editor. New Brunswick, N.J.: Rutgers University Press, 1955, pp. 247-67.

"Comment on Reparation Payments," *American Economic Review,* XX (December 1930), 691-95.

The Commodity Dollar. Chicago: University of Chicago Press [1938] (Public Policy Pamphlets, No. 26).

"La Crise actuelle et la politique Hoover," *Revue économique internationale* (Brussels), XXIV (April 1932), 8-26.

The Economic Foreign Policy of the United States. Cairo, 1953.

"Economic Foundations of Pan-Europeanism," *Annals of the American Academy of Political and Social Science,* CXLIX (May 1930), 150-56.

"An Economist Looks at the Constitution," *University of Chicago Magazine,* XXVIII (March 1936), 3-5, 30.

"Étude générale du programme Roosevelt," *Revue économique internationale* (Brussels). XXVI (April 1934), 8-44.

"Évolution économique des États-Unis après la guerre," *Revue économique internationale* (Brussels), XXII (March 1930), 434-50.

"Franco-American Tariff Difficulties and Inter-Allied Debts," *Tariff Review*, LXXX (March 1929), 71-73, 91.

The International Bank. New Brunswick, N.J.: Rutgers University Press, 1930 (Bureau of Economic and Business Research, Rutgers University. Bulletin No. 1).

"Money and Finance," *American Journal of Sociology*, XXXIX (May 1934), 749-58.

"Monopolistic Tendencies and Their Consequences," *Proceedings of the Academy of Political Science*, XVIII (January 1939), 172-75.

"Nationalist Collectivism and Charles A. Beard," *Journal of Political Economy*, XLIII (December 1935), 778-99.

Organized Scarcity and Public Policy: Monopoly and Its Implications. Chicago: University of Chicago Press [c1939] (Public Policy Pamphlets, No. 30).

The Political Economy of American Foreign Policy: Its Concepts, Strategy, and Limits (with a Study Group sponsored by the Woodrow Wilson Foundation and the National Planning Association). New York: Henry Holt & Co. [1955].

"Quinze années de législation douanière aux États-Unis," *Revue économique internationale* (Brussels), XXIII (May 1931), 270-87.

"Relation of American Foreign-Trade Policy to New Deal of Domestic Policy," *American Economic Review*, XXX (March 1940), 87-97.

"La Stabilisation des prix de gros comme objectif monétaire. Essai sur le 'Commodity Dollar,' " *Revue économique internationale* (Brussels), XXVIII (1936), 66-99.

"Die Steuerung der Wirtschaft durch den Wettbewerb als Ziel der amerikanischen Wirtschaftspolitik," in *Wirtschaft ohne Wunder, Aufsätze* von Luigi Einaudi et al. Erlenbach-Zürich: E. Rentsch, 1953, pp. 158-86.

Transfert des réparations et le plan Dawes. Lausanne, Genève: Payot & Cie, 1928.

"The United States and the International Gold Standard," *Annals of the American Academy of Political and Social Science*, CLXXI (January 1934), 118-26.

War Debts. Chicago: University of Chicago Press [c1933] (Public Policy Pamphlets, No. 4).

World Depression. World Recovery. Chicago: American Library Association, 1933 (Exploring the Times [No. 1]).

B. EDUCATION

"Academic Freedom: A Decade of Challenge and Clarification," *Annals of the American Academy of Political and Social Science,* CCCI (September 1955), 75-85.

"Are the Basic Issues of Our Times Economic?" *Journal of Adult Education,* XII (October 1940), 365-68.

"Between Hysteria and Complacency," *Educational Record,* XL (October 1959), 312-18.

The Challenge of Soviet Education. New York, 1958 (A Freedom House Report).

"Changing Issues in Academic Freedom in the United States Today," *Proceedings of the American Philosophical Society,* XCIV (1950), 91-104.

"Economic Growth and Educational Development," *College and University,* XXXVIII (Summer 1963), 421-33.

"European Education and American Self-Evaluation," *Educational Record,* XXXIX (July 1958), 213-21.

"The Function of Higher Education in the Present War Crisis," *Journal of Negro Education,* XI (July 1942), 247-56.

"The Golden Opportunity for Public Education," *Mental Hygiene,* XXXI (January 1947), 14-28.

The Higher Learning in a Democracy: A Reply to President Hutchins' Critique of the American University. New York, Toronto: Farrar & Rinehart [c1937].

"Ideals and Goals of Citizenship Education," in *Citizenship Education, 1903-1953-2003,* Proceedings of the Middle States Council for the Social Studies, L (1953), 25-33.

"Inaugural Address," in Brooklyn College. *Inauguration of Harry D. Gideonse as the Second President.* [Brooklyn, N.Y., 1939], pp. 13-26.

"Integration of the Social Sciences and the Quest for Certainty," *Social Studies,* XXVII (October 1936), 363-72.

"The Literature of Freedom and Liberal Education," in *Measurement and Research in Today's Schools,* a Report of the Twenty-fifth Educational Conference, New York City, October 27 and 28, 1960. Washington, D.C.: American Council on Education [c1961], pp. 133-73.

"On Re-thinking Liberal Education," in *Strengthening Education at All Levels,* a Report of the Eighteenth Educational Conference, New York City, October 29-30, 1953. Washington, D.C.: American Council on Education [c1954], pp. 30-52.

On the Educational Statesmanship of a Free Society. New York: Woodrow Wilson Foundation [1959] (Education in the Nation's Service, No. 5).

Plato and Eisenhower's America [Syracuse, N.Y.: Syracuse University, 1960].

"Political Education: A Plea for Cultural Parochialism Properly Defined," in *Education in a Period of National Preparedness,* a Report of the Sixteenth Educational Conference, New York City, November 1 and 2, 1951. Washington, D.C.: American Council on Education [c1952], pp. 27-46 (American Council on Education Studies, Series I: Reports of Committees and Conferences, No. 53).

"The Present Chaos in Education," in *Proceedings of the First Phase, 1938, of the Conference on the Problems of Higher Education.* Urbana, Ill.: University of Illinois, 1939, pp. 200-215.

"The Purpose of Higher Education: A Re-examination," in *The College and the Student,* ed. by Lawrence E. Dennis and Joseph F. Kauffman. Washington, D.C.: American Council on Education [c1966], pp. 23-46.

"Quality of Teaching or Content of Education," in *The Preparation and In-Service Training of College Teachers,* Proceedings of the Institute for Administrative Officers of Higher Institutions, X (1938), 65-75.

"Walter Lippmann and Educational Reconstruction," *School and Society,* September 5, 1942, pp. 169-73.

C. POLITICAL AFFAIRS

American Policy in Indonesia [Brooklyn, N.Y., 1949].

"The Discipline of Freedom," *Christian Register,* CXX (September 1941), 275-77, 297 (The Ware Lecture, 1941).

"First Congress for a United States of Europe," *Current History,* XXV (December 1926), 365-68.

"Free Science and the Security of an Open Society," in *Education for the Preservation of Democracy,* a Report of the Thirteenth Educational Conference, New York City, October 28 and 29, 1948. Washington, D.C.: American Council on Education [c1949], pp. 23-29 (American Council on Education Studies, Series I: Reports of Committees and Conferences, No. 35).

"How to Survive an Election Year," *Saturday Review,* July 19, 1952, pp. 7-8.

"Is Citizenship Enough?" in *Do We Still Need Religion?* Three Addresses and Discussions by Charles P. Taft, Harry D. Gideonse, Kirtly F. Mather, held in Town Hall, New York, 1942. New York: Association Press, 1942, pp. 35-58.

"It Would Be a Mere Armistice," *Asia*, XL (June 1940), 294-95.

The London Naval Conference (with Willmott Lewis and Burton L. French). New York: Foreign Policy Association [1929] (Foreign Policy Association Pamphlet, No. 60. Series 1929-30).

"Non-Partisan Education for Political Intelligence," *Social Frontier*, I (January 1935), 15-18.

The Politics of Atomic Energy (with Raymond B. Fosdick, William F. Ogburn, and Frederick L. Schuman). New York: Woodrow Wilson Foundation [1946].

United States Foreign Policy: Its Organization and Control (with McGeorge Bundy, George F. Kennan, Don K. Price, Arthur M. Schlesinger, Jr., and William Yandell Elliott [Chairman] of the Woodrow Wilson Foundation Study Group, 1950-51). New York: Columbia University Press, 1952.

"An Unsentimental Look at India," *Harper's Magazine*, CCVIII (June 1954), 78-84.

De Vrijheid heeft vele Gestalten. Amsterdam: Civitas Humana [1955].